Holy Misogyny

Holy Misogyny

*Why the Sex and Gender Conflicts in the
Early Church Still Matter*

April D. DeConick

B L O O M S B U R Y
NEW YORK • LONDON • NEW DELHI • SYDNEY

Bloomsbury Academic
An imprint of Bloomsbury Publishing Inc

1385 Broadway	50 Bedford Square
New York	London
NY 10018	WC1B 3DP
USA	UK

www.bloomsbury.com

First published 2011 by Continuum
First published in paperback 2013

Library of Congress Cataloging-in-Publication Data
A catalog record for this book is available from the Library of Congress.

ISBN: HB: 978-0-82640-561-6
       PB: 978-1-62356-556-5
     ePub: 978-1-44112-402-9
     ePDF: 978-1-44119-602-6

Typeset by Fakenham Prepress Solutions, Fakenham, Norfolk NR21 8NN, UK
Printed and bound in the United States of America

To Alexander Wade DeGreiner

Contents

Preface to the Second Printing

It's just like ancient times. That is what I felt when I saw the now-famous picture of President Obama's national security team in the White House Situation Room monitoring the raid on Osama bin Laden's compound. The photo was published by the Orthodox Jewish paper from Brooklyn, *Di-Tzeitung*.

Photo courtesy of Shmarya Rosenberg, FailedMessiah.com.

"Now you see her, now you don't," wrote David Jackson of USA Today about the picture. The photo published by the Jewish newspaper pictured a room full of men, including President Obama intently watching the raid. But in the original photo posted by the White House on May 1, 2011, the Secretary of State, Hillary Rodham Clinton is seated at the table across from President Obama, and the Counterterrorism Director, Audrey Tomason is standing in the back of the room. Yet they appear nowhere in the photo that was published by *Di-Tzeitung*.

The first person to notice this was the blogger, Shmarya Rosenberg who publishes the blog "FailedMessiah.com." On May 5, 2011, he wrote that a Hasidic newspaper cut Hillary Clinton out of an iconic picture of government leaders watching the Osama hit. Where did the war room women go? They had been erased, literally airbrushed out of the picture, photoshopped out of history.

Rosenberg dug up the original photo that the White House had posted on May 1, along with its caption and disclaimer which allowed for its reprinting by news organizations under the condition that the photograph would not be manipulated in any way. What had happened with the Brooklyn paper? Why had they published this fake picture as authentic?

The newspaper responded by posting an apology on its website stating that, because of religious beliefs, the editors are not allowed to publish photos of women. Women, according to the Orthodox Jewish community, are strictly governed by Jewish laws of modesty called *Tzniut*. According to these rabbinic laws, their bodies cannot be exposed in any way that attracts attention, especially sexual. So the paper laid out a strong defense of its policy to remove all women from its photographs based on this modesty code. The editors wrote that "in accord with our religious beliefs, we do not publish photos of women, which in no way relegates them to a lower status... Because of laws of modesty, we are not allowed to publish pictures of women, and we regret if this gives an impression of disparaging women, which is certainly never our intention."

They went on in their defense stating that "women should be appreciated for who they are and what they do, not for what they look like, and the Jewish laws of modesty are an expression of respect for women, not the opposite." Their only wrongdoing, they claimed, was not reading the fine print, which disallowed them from publishing an altered photo, something they sincerely regretted having done.

This practice is not unique to this particular Orthodox Jewish newspaper. On April 1, 2009, a photo was taken of the newly elected Israeli government posing with Prime Minister Benjamin Netanyahu and President Shimon Peres. Two female cabinet members, Limor Livnat and Sofa Landver appear prominently front and center at the shoulders of Netanyahu and Peres. Except in the published versions of the photos in two Orthodox Jewish newspapers. The *Shaa Tova* blackened out the women in their published photo. *Yated Neeman* went a step further. The editors digitally replaced the women with men, by moving two male ministers into the women's spots. No clarifications or apologies were given by these papers, even when asked by the Associated Press for an explanation.

If the erasure of women from history and their marginalization as leaders even within the most prominent and powerful of government ranks is evident in the modern world, how much more so must it have been in the ancient world when there weren't watchdogs like Rosenberg or the secular editors of the Associated Press, when the media was controlled by ancient religious men whose interests were anything but egalitarian. The locus of women's erasure from history and leadership continues to be about our bodies, which continue to be hidden away, covered, controlled and removed.

Whatever the rationalization – and there are many throughout history and cultures – it boils down to the archaic perspective that women's bodies are inferior to the bodies of males. While the male body was considered by ancient people to be THE human body, the female body was considered something less, something deficient, something subhuman. Because of this natural deficient state, female bodies were believed to be shameful and deceitful and, consequently, were to be controlled and dominated by the human male. This misogyny is still with us, although we don't see it as such. Why? Because it comes to us via the Bible and other sacred texts from the ancient world which have made misogyny "holy". Because it is a sacred perspective, it fuels the modern mistreatment and abuse of women. Because misogyny is accepted as natural and sacred, it is insidious, which makes it all the more difficult to uproot and destroy even in secular contexts. But uproot and destroy it we must, one day at a time.

April D. DeConick
Holy Saturday 2013

INTRODUCTION

A lady god?

When my son turned 5 years old, he began to become interested in God. Even though he has been raised in a fairly secular environment, he had encountered God through his family, teachers, and friends. It was not long before he had become familiar with the traditional concept of God as the old man in the sky, living in a place called *heaven* where people went after they died.

From my many conversations with him, I knew that he had been giving this serious reflection. Yet still he caught me by surprise one afternoon when he asked me out of the blue, "Mom, where is Lady God?"

Not knowing what else to say at the moment, I asked him what he meant. He explained, "If God doesn't have a wife, how can he have babies? Wouldn't he be lonely? Did Lady God die?"

A bit shaken by the seriousness of his tone and the thoughtfulness of his questions, I asked him what he thought. He responded, "I know. God is half man and half woman."

It was a moment that brought all my years of study, reflection, teaching and writing to a screeching halt. Here was my 5-year-old child giving voice to what has been for hundreds of years *the* prickly thorn of Christian theology and ecclesiology, the absence of "Lady God" and its consequences. In his thoughtful response, I heard the echo of the centuries and the voices of people before him who had also tried desperately to answer this question, certain that the first chapter in the book of Genesis revealed to us an androgynous or hermaphrodite God who created male and female in his image: "God created man in *his* own image; male and female he created *them*."[1]

Since my first years of teaching, I have been studying issues of gender and sex in early Christianity. I came across gender studies by accident when I was being interviewed to teach a sabbatical-release course at a local college on the subject of gender and the Bible. At the time I was finishing my Ph.D. coursework on the history and literature of early Christianity, and I desperately needed the job to pay my bills. When I was asked whether or not I could teach the course, "Yes," flew out of my mouth before I had time to think about the fact that this was an area of study that I was not familiar with. Although I knew a great deal about early Christianity, I knew next to nothing about the study of gender. This meant that I had an immense amount of reading ahead of me if I were to get the class ready to go the following semester.

It turns out that I thrived on the challenge, immersing myself in the literature until I felt conversant enough to organize a course and teach it. Since then, my class on sex, gender, and the Bible has been a regular part of my university course rotation, and it is one of my most successful courses. Students have told me repeatedly how transformative the course has been to their lives, allowing them to explore and understand attitudes toward gender and sex that surround them and affect them in subtle and insidious ways.

The book that you are holding comprises 25 years of my own reflections and study of the Bible and its relationship to ways in which gender and sex operated in the ancient Mediterranean world, and how these attitudes continue to affect us in the western world today. In this book, I attempt to map out an honest answer to my son's question, "Where is Lady God?" While I try to explain her ephemeral presence in the traditions alongside her sustained absence, I do so with full awareness of the social and political dimensions of the question.[2] I am convinced that this is not a matter of theology and hermeneutics, which can be adjusted to retain the Mother God as several early Christian traditions did. Rather it is a matter of the female body and the violence that has been done to it over the centuries. In Christian tradition, this violence is justified in the story of paradise with sex and the serpent – when woman was cut from man's side and made his servant by God's command, as a consequence of her own sin.

In these pages, I explore the complex web of interactions that led to the erasure of the Mother God from conventional Christianity. After charting, in Chapters 1 and 2, how her erasure happened within the Jewish and Christian traditions, I wrestle with the *why* question. This is a particularly important question for early Christianity where the Mother Spirit was originally part of the Godhead, but erased by later theologians and replaced with a neuter or male Spirit as the third aspect of the Trinity. The *why* question is very complex and, in order to answer it, requires a thorough mapping of early Christian attitudes and practices when it comes to sex and gender. This mapping is what I undertake in the main chapters of the book.

In Chapters 3 and 4, I provide the foundational narratives on sex and gender from the New Testament gospels and Paul's letters, trying to represent as best as possible the earliest recorded memories of Jesus' and Paul's opinions on sex and gender issues. Both Jesus and Paul emerge as typical ancient Jewish men in terms of their attitudes about sex. They both regard it as suspect because, while it is a good impulse leading to the birth of children, it is also a wicked impulse leading to fornication and adultery. So both men advocated limiting sex. Jesus argued that men needed to become responsible for controlling their lustful thoughts, while Paul argued that women needed to veil themselves. Jesus appears to have been something of a woman's advocate during his era, and women were present in his mission as patrons and disciples. Although Paul had female compatriots in the mission field, we begin to see the first impulses to reframe the movement in patriarchal terms, and to justify it based on the creation of the female as secondary and for the "glory of man."[3]

Early in the Christian movement, Christians began to talk about the overriding need for self-control or *encrateia* when it came to sex. This discussion led to a lifestyle that various groups adopted and enacted. The centerpiece of their lifestyle was the utter rejection of marriage as a state of sin, a lifestyle we call *encratism*. They were Christians who devoted themselves to a life of singlehood and celibacy. In Chapter 5, I map out a number of groups that fall in this category, including the early Syrian Christians, the Marcionite Church, and the Church of New Prophecy. These groups tended to allow women into leadership roles within their churches and worked to develop an interpretation of scripture to support this.

There were early Christians who thought that the encratic lifestyle was a joke. These were limited to a couple of Gnostic Christian groups who taught that sex was a sacred and powerful act. In all cases, women appear to have been prominent in leadership positions within their churches or conventicles. For the Valentinian Gnostics, marriage was reframed in strict terms where the sex act between the Gnostic husband and wife was cast as a sacred ritual act of religious devotion and contemplation that would result in the conception of a pious child. Their marriages were perceived to be reflections of the marriages between the various aspects of the male–female God within the divine world. Other Gnostics discussed in this chapter thought that marriage laws were the silly idea of the despised creator god and should be shunned. The result? A sex life modeled from the natural order of the animals where wives are not given away as property. The final group I discuss is the scandalous group of Gnostics that Bishop Epiphanius personally knew in the fourth century. They performed a masturbatory ritual in order to gather the souls they believed were trapped in the cycle of life. They did this by collecting sexual fluids which they thought contained the souls of children yet-to-be-born and returning them to the divine world during their eucharist offering.

The Apostolic churches are explored in Chapter 7. In these churches, we find the deterioration of the female aspect of God most prominently, as well as the gradual exclusion of women from leadership roles within their churches. It is also within this environment that sex as a wicked impulse is fostered, while marriage is maintained. In this context, women and their activities are bridled and made subservient through marriage, either to physical men who are their "head" or to Christ who is their divine husband. The Genesis story is interpreted in the most damaging and damning way possible for women, so that woman's interactions with the serpent make her sex the Devil's gateway.

In the process of this intense study of sex and gender conflicts in the early church, the prominent Christian woman, Mary Magdalene, comes to the forefront. She has been the object of increased scholarship in recent years, and consequently a wide array of images of her has emerged in the popular mind. She is no longer only known to us as the repentant whore. She is also known as the Apostle to the Apostles, and even Jesus' lover or wife. We have been left in a quandary, wondering who the real Mary might have been. As I have examined the evidence from the early Christian sources, it has become clear to me that Mary Magdalene served as a cipher for the ideal woman according to each of the early Christian groups I explored. The fashioning and refashioning of her story and image represented various understandings of what the ideal woman should be, whether a disciple and apostle, a married woman, or a repentant whore. Her portrayal corresponds to the variety of Christian views on women, sex, and gender that I have mapped in this book. So I tell her story as a case study in Chapter 8.

Chapter 9 brings this book to a close. In this chapter, I argue that the locus of the erasure of women and the Mother within the Christian tradition was the female body itself, which was misogynously conceived by the ancients as a body deficient, as an imperfect male, even as subhuman. This was the epicenter from which the rest of the story falls out, spirals around, and weaves back into itself, creating a web that ensnared everything from gender roles and politics to the sex act itself. Little was left untouched by its menace, leaving its imprint on scripture, hermeneutics, and church institutions to this day.

There are so many who have helped me over the years as I have studied gender and women in early Christianity, not the least of whom are hundreds of students who enrolled in my course. I would like to single out a few students who went on in the field or the church: Sharon Stowe Cook, who is now a United Methodist minister; Christine Luckritz Marquis, finishing her Ph.D. in late antiquity at Duke; Katie Stump Holt, a Methodist youth director; and Jared Calaway, who graduated from Columbia University and is now teaching his own version of the sex and gender course. I am proud of you all. Thank you for the opportunity you gave me to share gender studies with you. Thank you for every one of those tough questions you posed. Thank you for the encouragement you gave me to continue to think and teach on this subject.

I would like to give special thanks to Jane Schaberg, Professor of Religious Studies and Women Studies at the University of Detroit Mercy. When I first began teaching my course, Jane provided me with initial reflections on my syllabus and has been a mentor to me in many ways over the years since then. Her own academic contributions to the study of women in early Christianity have been guiding lights.

I wish to thank Ann Graham Brock, Associate Professor of New Testament at Iliff School of Theology, for the encouragement that she gave to me after reading the first chapters of this book and hearing my presentation on Mary Magdalene at the Third Princeton Symposium on Judaism and Christian Origins held in Jerusalem in 2008. Her own work on Mary Magdalene as the first Apostle has been instrumental to my research.

I extend thanks to Betty Adam, Canon Theologian at Christ Church Cathedral in Houston and author of *The Magdalene Mystique: Living the Spirituality of Mary Today*. Betty was with me every step of the way as I wrote this book. She read a number of drafts of different chapters, and then the final manuscript, and gave me helpful suggestions for revision and encouragement to spread the knowledge. I am inspired by her desire to continually learn, and then bring that learning into her church.

There were several colleagues who read the finished manuscript and gave me valuable comments. Thank you for the time you spent with this book, and for your generosity of knowledge: Kelley Coblentz Bautch, Associate Professor of Religious Studies at St. Edward's University in Austin; Jorunn J. Buckley, Associate Professor of Religion, Bowdoin College; Jeffrey J. Kripal, J. Newton Rayzor Chair in Philosophy and Religious Thought, Rice University; Rebecca Lesses, Associate Professor of Jewish Studies, Ithaca College. I would like to acknowledge my research assistant, Michael Domeracki, who searched the stacks and expediently found the books I needed as I revised this manuscript for publication. A big thanks to my husband, Wade Greiner, for helping me build the index. A round of applause to my editor Haaris Naqvi who has proven he can move mountains.

A special thanks goes to the Humanities Research Center at Rice University, which awarded me a semester leave (2009–2010) to prepare the last chapters of this book. I benefited immensely from my monthly interactions that year with the other humanities research fellows, and their keen comments on drafts of several chapters I was writing: Melinda Fagan, Rebecca Goetz, Mi Gyung Kim, Jeffrey J. Kripal, Joseph Manca, Tatiana Schnur, and Maria Elena Versari.

This book is dedicated to my son, Alexander Wade DeGreiner, *when he is old enough to understand the answers to his questions.*

CHAPTER 1

Where did God the mother go?

Where did God the mother go? For some Christians, this is not even a question. The Mother God was never there. Or at least that is what conventional Christianity has taught for ages. The orthodox doctrine is presented as a Trinity, in which one God is revealed as three: the Father, the Son, and the Holy Spirit. The gender of the first two is clearly male. But what about the third? When the doctrine was framed in the fourth century by three orthodox theologians known as the Cappadocians, the Holy Spirit was understood to be a nebulous "male" or neuter charisma that proceeds from the Father and Son and inspires the Church. This "male" or neuter image of the Spirit is the image that has continued to be nurtured in contemporary conventional Christianity. But was the Holy Spirit always so?

The Jewish spirit

One of the great tragedies of Christianity has been the *loss* of the female aspect of God. I emphasize the word *loss* because in the beginning of Christianity, the female aspect of God was present in the form of the Holy Spirit. The Holy Spirit, when gendered, was perceived to be female, partially because the word "spirit," is a feminine noun in Hebrew (*ruah*) and Aramaic (*ruha*). The first Christians were not Christians by any modern day standard. They were Jews. They spoke Aramaic and, if they could read, they read Hebrew or one of its dialects. So the Spirit, for them, was feminine.

According to what the Jews and first Christians knew of her from their scriptures, the Spirit was the vital force, the "breath of life," that indwelled the human body.[1] When she enters the human being, she enlivens it.[2] When she leaves, the human being dies.[3] But this is not all. As the life force, she is also the power of God that assists with the creation of the universe and the human being. As this power, she features prominently in the biblical creation story. The book of Genesis opens with the Spirit of God moving over the primordial waters, when "the earth was without form and void, and darkness was upon the face of the deep." Her movement sparks the separation of light from darkness, and the heavenly firmament from the waters underneath.[4]

In the book of Job, these dual roles of the Spirit are brought together in a single verse. She is the cosmic creator who fashions our bodies as well as the invigorating breath which quickens us, bringing us to life. Reminiscent of the story in Genesis when God creates Adam from the dust and breaths into his nostrils the "breath of life," Job proclaims, "The Spirit of God has made me, and the breath of the Almighty gives me life."[5]

In addition to her instrumental role in the formation of the universe and its quickening, the Spirit is also the power by which God instructs and saves, and by which he judges and destroys. Vivid images of her as the Spirit of God's judgment are preserved in the literature. The Spirit is called God's breath of steam and fire that purges sin, sometimes even killing those who are particularly rebellious.[6] The rebellion of the nation of Israel was believed by the Israelite priests to deeply grieve the Spirit who must live in exile as long as God's people remain iniquitous.[7] Through her judgment, it was believed that God washed away the sins of Israel, cleansing the stains of impiety. In so doing, the Spirit was thought to recreate the nation into a holy people in which the presence of God could dwell.[8]

So the biblical stories recount that Israel will be desolate and forsaken until the Spirit from the height can be poured out anew upon the repentant nation. Only then can justice, righteousness, and peace be had.[9] In this way, the priests of Israel taught that God puts his salvific Spirit into the hearts of his people to make them upright, peaceful and just.[10] She tabernacles in Zion, anointing its inhabitants with good tidings, liberty, and comfort.[11] He sends his Spirit especially in times of distress, to teach and guide his people, as he did in the wilderness after they came out of Egypt, when the Hebrews needed instruction.[12]

Even more startling, the Spirit is said to be God's covenant with Israel. She is his sacred Law. As such, the Law is a spirit that rests in his people.[13] The priests taught that the Jewish Law and other teachings of the Lord were carried by his Spirit and given to the prophets, who, in turn, delivered them to the people of Israel.[14] Along these lines, Jesus expected the Spirit to speak through his disciples, and taught his disciples that they should not worry about what they would say when preaching.[15] Among those prophets and great leaders named in the Jewish scriptures, she lodges in Joseph, Micaiah, David, Ezekiel, Zechariah, and Balaam.[16]

The story of Balaam particularly caught the attention of later Jewish interpreters since the great Angel of the Lord, the angel who is Yahweh's earthly manifestation, bids Balaam to go out and not worry about his speech. The Angel of the Lord tells Balaam that he will only be able to say the words that the Angel will inspire him to speak.[17]

But later in the narrative, when Balaam speaks on behalf of God, it is the Spirit of God who comes upon him and delivers the discourse.[18] On this account, Philo of Alexandria, a Jew writing at the turn of the Common Era, understood that the Angel of the Lord and the Spirit were the same entity.[19] Josephus, a Jewish historian in the late first century CE, understands them to be synonymous too.[20]

This identification between Angel and Spirit appears much older than Philo and Josephus, perhaps dating back to the book of Ezekiel. The Spirit, in this writing from the sixth century BCE, functions as an angel, transporting Ezekiel from place to place. Ezekiel claims that an angel took him by "a lock" of his hair. But then he says that the Spirit lifted him up between earth and heaven, and carried him "in visions of God" from Babylon, where he was a priest in Exile, to Jerusalem.[21] Afterwards, in another vision, the Spirit of God brought him back to Babylon, returning him to the Jewish exiles.[22]

In the Jewish scriptures, the end of times is forecast as the moment when the Spirit's presence will be accentuated. As it is written in Joel:

> I will pour my Spirit on all flesh.
> Your sons and daughters shall prophesy,
> your old men shall dream dreams,
> and your young men shall see visions.
> Even upon the menservants and maidservants in those days,
> I will pour out my Spirit.[23]

These words from Joel were particularly favored by the early Christians, who believed that their charismatic church movement was the fulfillment of this prophecy of the Spirit in the last days. The apostle Peter, in fact, is said to have recited this poem from Joel as an explanation for the ecstatic experience of the Holy Spirit at Pentecost. The Jewish Feast of Weeks or Pentecost was the celebration of the giving of the covenant, the Law on Mount Sinai. The mountain, according to the Exodus narrative, was shrouded in a cloud of smoke "because the Lord descended upon it in fire."[24] According to the author of Acts, the Spirit appeared as tongues of fire rushing from the heavens like a mighty wind, settling on the multitude who had gathered together in celebration of the festival after Jesus' ascension.[25] Philo describes the same commemorative scene from Exodus 19 as one in which angels took what God had said to Moses on the top of the mountain and carried it down on tongues of fire to the people below on the plain.

The Angel Sophia

The Spirit of God was thought by the Jews to be God's voice which revealed his thoughts and wishes to his people through the prophets. Because of this, she was linked with another feminine aspect of God, his Wisdom. This link between Spirit and Wisdom eventually forged their identification, so that Wisdom not only became known as the "Spirit of Wisdom," but also was amalgamated with the Spirit in terms of shared characteristics, features, and functions.[26] In a beautiful Jewish poem composed in the first century BCE about Wisdom, this amalgamation is apparent. The author connects her with "a spirit that is intelligent, holy, unique, manifold, subtle, mobile, clear, unpolluted, distinct, invulnerable, loving the good, keen, irresistible, beneficent, humane, steadfast, sure, free from anxiety, all-powerful, overseeing all, and penetrating through all spirits that are intelligent and pure and most subtle." The author of this poem goes on to speak of Wisdom in language reminiscent of the Spirit of God, as "a breath of the power of God, and a pure emanation of the glory of the Almighty." She is "a reflection of eternal light, a spotless mirror of the working of God, and an image of his goodness." She is "more beautiful than the sun" and more excellent than "every constellation of the stars."[27]

Like the Spirit of God, "in every generation she passes into holy souls and makes them friends of God and prophets."[28] Because of her inspiration, the holy prophets were able to guide the people of Israel to prosperity and reward. The wise person knows that unless God sends Wisdom, his Holy Spirit, from heaven to earth, God's counsel cannot be learned and the people will be lost.[29] Indeed, according to Jesus in the Gospel of Luke, "Sophia is justified by her children."[30]

Like the Spirit, she dwells in Israel so that God's people will experience his presence.[31] She protected Adam, rescued Noah and Lot, strengthened Abraham and Jacob, safeguarded Joseph, and generally helped the righteous Israelites to prosper.[32] She is associated with the great angel in the pillar of cloud and smoke who brought the Hebrews across the Red Sea according to Exodus 14.[33] Through Moses she delivered the Law. Just as the Spirit, she is even said to be the covenant itself, "the Law that endures forever."[34]

Wisdom is called in the literature by her feminine name, *Hokhma* in Hebrew, or *Sophia* in Greek. There is an entire corpus of literature known as the Jewish wisdom literature in which she is prominently featured. The standard Hebrew wisdom texts, which are found in the Tanakh or Old Testament, include Proverbs, Job, and Ecclesiastes. The Greek writings of the Jews that feature wisdom materials are mainly from the first centuries BCE and CE. They are located in the biblical Apocrypha and include *Sirach*, the *Wisdom of Solomon*, and *Baruch*.

What is so fascinating about the traditions of Sophia in this literature is that she is not just a personification of a divine attribute of God. As far back as the third century BCE, she is portrayed in the Jewish wisdom literature as a *hypostasis* of God's wisdom. This means that she is a divine attribute that had its own subsistence or individuation. In fact, scholars have noted that her speech in Proverbs presents her as a Near Eastern goddess brought forth by the male deity before creation:[35]

> The Lord created me at the beginning of his work,
> the first of his acts of old.
> Ages ago I was set up,
> at the first, before the beginning of the earth.
> When there were no depths I was brought forth,
> when there were no springs abounding with water.
> Before the mountains had been shaped,
> before the hills, I was brought forth,
> before he had made the earth with its fields,
> or the first of the dust of the world.
>
> When he established the heavens,
> I was there.
> When he drew a circle on the face of the deep,
> when he made firm the skies above,
> when he established the fountains of the deep,
> when he assigned to the sea its limit,
> so that the waters might not transgress his command,
> when he marked out the foundations of the earth,
> then I was beside him, like a master workman.[36]

Like some of the goddesses of the ancient Near East, she exists before creation and is a creator herself. Sophia is envisioned at the side of Yahweh when the world was being created.[37] Like the Spirit of God in Genesis 1.2 who was hovering over the waters when God spoke, Wisdom "came forth from the mouth of the Most High, and covered the earth like a mist."[38] Sophia sings about her infinity in a hymn, "From eternity, in the beginning, he created me, and for eternity I shall not cease to exist."[39] Thus she is the co-creator of the universe, "the fashioner of all things."[40] She assists God with the creation of the world, even forming human beings.[41]

In Jewish mythological terms, she is described like one of God's angels. In fact, when she is in heaven, she lives with the angels in the clouds. Like an angel, she is an intermediary, a divine being who descends to earth to reveal God's will and purpose to righteous and pious people. Elements of her myth suggest that she was not always successful, her righteous message rejected by the impious. At times this leaves her with no place on earth to dwell. When Israel is rebellious, she may not stay, so the repentant are admonished to seek her in the Law.[42] Her story is summarized in a poem embedded in an old apocalyptic text known as the *Similitudes of Enoch* written in the first century BCE:

> Wisdom could not find a place in which she could dwell,
> but a place was found in the heavens.
> Then Wisdom went out to dwell with the children of the people,
> but she found no dwelling place.
> Wisdom returned to her place
> and she settled among the angels.[43]

Her place among these angels is extraordinary. She is a queen seated on her own throne "in a pillar of clouds" next to the throne of Yahweh, the male biblical God.[44] As a queen, she speaks in the heavenly court of Yahweh, addressing all the angels who surround them in council. [45] Her speech is exceedingly intelligent because she is "an initiate in the knowledge of God and an associate in his works."[46]

As Queen, she is also described as Yahweh's wife. "The Lord of all loves her," we are told in the *Wisdom of Solomon*, and so she brings glory to herself by "living with God."[47] The Greek phrase *symbiosin theou* is translated here and in most Bibles, *living with God*. This English translation, although standard, covers up the old original meaning of the phrase, because the people who have been responsible for translating this passage for centuries belong to later Jewish and Christian orthodoxies in which God does not – and *may not* – have a wife. But we easily can see in this expression the root of our English loanword "symbiosis," which we understand to mean a union of two entities. In the ancient world, when it is used in reference to male and female parties, it can denote "marriage," as it does in the case of Yahweh and Sophia here. That this tradition was not a simple metaphor is evident from the teaching of the Jewish theologian Philo who was living at the same time and in the same place as the author of the *Wisdom of Solomon*. Philo states that God is "the husband of Wisdom" who drops his "seed" into her ever virgin soil. He uses this example of sacred marriage to discuss the nature of human marriage which, by contrast, takes virginity away from women.[48]

A Hebrew goddess

Sophia as God's wife? The Queen enthroned next to God in heaven? True, these are not standard teachings in contemporary Jewish or Christian circles. In order to make sense of this, what must be realized is that Judaism and Christianity are products of centuries of religious developments. So what might have been considered "orthodox" at an early time, a few centuries later might be considered "heretical" because the tradition and practices had drastically changed by then. It was quite natural for later authors and communities to rethink and rewrite the earlier received stories on the basis of their current beliefs and practices precisely because their current beliefs and practices were substantially different from the former ones. Oftentimes, however, echoes of the earlier traditions can be heard beneath the new chorus.

What this means in terms of the biblical scriptures is that they were written over several centuries by different authors who had varying agendas. These authors would attempt to use old narratives to promote new agendas. This meant that the old history would be rewritten with an eye to explaining the present social needs of the community and theological views of its leaders. This is very evident in the Hebrew Bible whose core narratives were written into the form we have them largely during the period of the Babylonian Exile. In the sixth century BCE the nation of Judah was conquered by the Babylonians and the Temple, which Solomon had built in Jerusalem, was destroyed. In order to control the conquered lands, the Babylonians took the nation's rulers and priests into captivity, transporting them to Babylon.

While living in Babylon, the Jewish priests were faced with explaining why their nation had been conquered. Whether conscious or not, the result of their explanation averted the blame of the conquered people away from its leaders, including the priests themselves who were part of the ruling aristocracy. They framed their failure to avert a national disaster in theological terms – that their God had allowed his nation to be defeated and destroyed. In order to explain why Yahweh could do such a thing, the priests scribed down the old stories, but within a new theological context. This new theological framework served to explain why Yahweh had abandoned them and what needed to happen for Yahweh to allow them to have back their national land.

It has been said by many scholars that this priestly framework was a monotheistic one, one that advocates Yahweh as the only god in the heavens, such as the writer of second Isaiah envisioned.[49] But the framework that was put into place by the priests creating the Torah was more *monolatrous* in nature than monotheistic because most of these priests appear to have been advocates for the devoted worship of one deity, *while not denying the existence of other gods*. Thus one of the

Ten Commandments in Deuteronomy and Exodus states that graven images of other gods should not be worshiped, neither should these gods be served.[50] The monolatrous priests, who wrote the books that now make up the Tanakh or Old Testament, identified the worship of the goddess Asherah as one of the main reasons that Israel had been destroyed by the Babylonian army. These priests said that the Israelites had been polytheists when, in fact, they should have been worshiping *only* Yahweh. Now Yahweh was angry, and he was taking vengeance on the people of Israel.

The exclusive devotion to Yahweh that we see emerging in these biblical narratives does so over centuries of theological speculation, debate, and refinement. By the exilic period, these new religious sensibilities have overlaid the old, and are highly critical of the past polytheistic practices. This priestly rewriting suggests that there was a time in the history of the religion of ancient Israel when Yahweh was not worshiped alone. The Jewish mythology of Sophia as Queen from the first century BCE represents repressed echoes of the earlier traditions belonging to the ancient Israelites, traditions that show that the Israelites were not always – or even originally – monolatrous.

To begin with, the very name used for God in the Jewish scriptures is plural. The Hebrew, which we translate "God," is actually the plural form, "*Elohim*," meaning "gods." Although *El* is its singular form, it is the plural form that survives in the scriptures as one of God's names. Scholars have long noted this, but have been hard pressed to explain it, except as an echo from an earlier time when more than one god was being addressed and worshiped by the Israelites.

Additional evidence from the Jewish scriptures indicates that this polytheistic form of the Israelite religion included, alongside the warrior god Yahweh, the worship of a particular goddess, who was his Queen. It may be that the oldest references to her are to be located in the first chapter of Genesis when God speaks in the plural, "Let *us* make the human being in *our* image, and after *our* likeness."[51] What does God create? Both genders, as the biblical narrative goes on to clarify: "God created the human being in his own image. In the image of God he created him. Male and female he created them."[52] Such a literal reading of this text suggests an old Israelite tradition where Yahweh was not envisioned alone, but was a male god with a female aspect or partner. Both human genders were created simultaneously to reflect the image of the male and female Elohim.

Yahweh's consort appears to have gone by the name Asherah, which was also the name of the goddess worshiped in Canaan by the local inhabitants. It is quite likely that the Hebrews, when they initially settled in Canaan, either brought the local goddess Asherah into their pantheon, or assimilated her into a goddess whom they were already

Digging in

Box 1.1 Who is it?
This figurine is represent-
ative of a great number of
pillar figures manufactured
and used in Judea during the
seventh and eighth centuries
BCE. This clay figure comes
from ancient Lachish (modern
Tell ed-Duweir) which was a
major Judean city. These types
of figures are often dug up in
domestic or household contexts.
Whom do they represent? What
was their use? Scholars have
offered many suggestions.
Some think they were toys, an
interpretation that may reflect
more our modern culture and
its fascination with the Barbie
doll than anything else. Other
scholars have suggested that
these pillars are votives or
"stand-ins" for women devotees, symbolizing the prayers she was
offering to God. But this explanation does not take into account
the fact that there is plenty of evidence outside Judea in other
ancient Mediterranean cultures that similar figurines represented
the Mother Goddess, either Asherah, 'Anat, or Astarte. Why
should we be surprised that the worship of the Great Mother
was occurring in Judea too? Were these figurines talismans of
the Queen of Heaven to whom people in Judean households
were praying? What did the ancient Israelites think she could
do for them? Scholars say that this talisman likely was used for
fertility purposes. There is some literary support for this, since
the Jeremiah narrative suggests that the men and women prayed
to the Queen of Heaven and offered her ritual cakes in order to
ward off famine.

Reprinted as public domain image.
For deeper digging, read William G. Dever, *Did God Have a Wife?
Archaeology and Folk Religion in Ancient Israel* (Grand Rapids:
Eerdmans, 2005).

worshiping. At the end of the seventh century BCE the prophet Jeremiah tells us that in times of distress, the Israelite women living in Jerusalem would bake ritual cakes for the "Queen of Heaven," pour out libations to her, and burn incense for her because they believed that she had more power than Yahweh to avert disasters like famine.[53]

In fact, throughout their history, the Israelites set up carved wooden images or poles, called in the biblical literature "asherahs," at old local shrines and other sacred places. King Rehoboam, grandson of David, set up an Asherah image in Jerusalem where it stood until the time of King Hezekiah who tore it down. An altar and an Asherah image were erected during the reign of King Manasseh in the Jerusalem Temple itself, the official cult center where, according to the narrative, the worship of Yahweh was conducted by the priests.[54] Now one has to stop and consider seriously the placing of an altar and an Asherah image in the Jerusalem Temple. This is not the act of popular religion nor is it the rebellion of a few priests or a king. Rather, it is an act that requires the power and support of those in charge, as well as the consent and compliance of the populace. It requires the sponsorship of the priests who control what goes on in the Temple, as well as the patronage of the king along with the consent of the people.

The evidence from archaeological discoveries supports these findings.[55] We now possess several inscriptions as old as 800 BCE containing blessings "by Yahweh and his Asherah."[56] These inscriptions show that in the old Israelite religion, the great Near Eastern goddess Asherah was associated with Yahweh. They appear to have been a very popular divine couple worshiped for centuries prior to the religious changes introduced by King Josiah in 622 BCE.[57]

What prompted King Josiah to want to change the old religion? One day, after cleaning out the treasury rooms of the Temple, a previously unknown religious document was brought to him, or so the story goes. It appears that this document was some version of the book of Deuteronomy, written by a priest who was a radical monolatrist. How old the text was is not known. It may have been recently penned by a priest or scribe dissatisfied with the devotional practices of the Israelites. It may have been older, from the hand of someone who disagreed with the polytheistic practices of Israel, wanting Israel instead to devote itself exclusively to Yahweh, like the prophet Hosea or King Hezekiah. Whatever the document's origin, it was a text that described an exclusive covenant between Yahweh and Israel. After hearing about this document, King Josiah and the prophet Jeremiah attempt to purge Israel of the worship of Yahweh's Queen, deposing priests and outlawing the burning of incense to a plethora of deities.[58]

Their radical innovation of the religion of Israel is unsuccessful. The people of Israel continued in the old religion just as they had done previously when King Hezekiah had destroyed the bronze serpent and tried to outlaw traditional forms of worship immediately following the conquest and forced resettlement of the northern Kingdom in the eighth century BCE. The people, in fact, tell Jeremiah that they want no part of his new religion. The men of Jerusalem tell him that they will continue to do "everything that we have vowed," to "burn incense to the Queen of Heaven and pour out libations to her" just as they have always done, and as their fathers and kings and princes have always done, in Jerusalem and in all the cities across the nation. The women tell Jeremiah that they make cakes bearing her image, burn incense for her, and pour out libations to her, not on their own accord as the prophet seems to think. But they do it with the expressed blessing of their husbands who believe that the goddess helps them to prosper, keeping famine at bay.[59]

It is not long after King Josiah and Jeremiah's failed attempts at religious change, however, that the Babylonians conquer Judah. Priests who were devoted solely to the worship of Yahweh use this opportunity to radically innovate their religion by rewriting their history from the perspective of Yahweh, the angry and jealous god who was justified in allowing Israel's defeat as punishment. Because of the people's devotion to Asherah and other gods, the priests argued, Yahweh decided to punish them by allowing the Babylonians victory. So the priests said that the sin of the Israelites was idolatry. As they rewrote their ancient sources, creating the biblical narrative in the process, they pointed out that, throughout the past, the Israelites had been worshiping the Queen of Heaven, even erecting statues of her. This, they taught, had been considered all along by Yahweh to be adultery. Wasn't the Deuteronomic covenant he contracted with Israel like a marital contract? Wasn't Israel Yahweh's wife, and by implication, not Asherah?

Ezekiel, a priest in exile who is a radical supporter of the sole worship of Yahweh, is the one who tells us about a statue that was standing at the entrance of the inner court of the Jerusalem Temple immediately prior to the Babylonian invasion. He denounces it as the "image of jealousy" because he said that it provoked Yahweh's jealousy.[60] To what was he referring? This must have been the statue of the Queen of Heaven, the goddess whom the Jerusalemite women loved so much that they baked her special ritual cakes. Her worship by the Israelites, Ezekiel said, filled Yahweh with jealousy. Yahweh's withdrawal from Israel was the justified abuse of an enraged husband whose wife, Israel, had wronged him by loving someone else. Ezekiel attributes these brutal words to God:

> I will judge you as women who break wedlock and shed blood are
> judged, and bring upon you the blood of wrath and jealousy. And I

will give you into the hand of your lovers, and they shall throw down
your vaulted chamber and break down your lofty places. They shall
strip you of your clothes and take your fair jewels, and leave you
naked and bare. They shall bring up an army against you, and they
shall stone you and cut you to pieces with their swords. And they
shall burn your houses and execute judgments upon you in the sight
of many women. I will make you stop playing the harlot, and you
shall give hire no more. So will I satisfy my fury on you.[61]

These "words of God," and others like them in the Bible, have served
to sanctify violence, especially in domestic situations. They haunt our
relationships, as if such abuse and assault between husband and wife
were ever justifiable.

Nevertheless, it is in this brutal way that the Queen of Heaven
was vanquished from her throne, and Yahweh became the only
god of devotion in ancient Judaism. But her prior glory could not
be erased completely. As we have seen, she emerges in some of her
former glory as God's Spirit and as his Wisdom. Although she was no
longer worshiped apart from Yahweh, she was retained in the Jewish
consciousness as an independent angel, a *hypostasis* of a vital aspect of
God. She existed before the universe was created, and was a co-creator
beside Yahweh. She was enthroned next to her husband in the clouds
of heaven, and spoke out in the court of the angels. She communicated
Yahweh's will to the Israelites and later Jews as God's Spirit when
she descended upon the prophets. She was the voice of the prophets,
teaching God's people about his ways.

The recovery of God's wife

Strands of the story of the lost Hebrew goddess continue to be found
in the rabbinic period in the writings of the Talmud. The presence of
God on earth is called the *Shekhina*, and like the Spirit, it is a feminine
word. The Shekhina was believed to dwell in the Temple, in the inner
sanctum called the Holy of Holies. After the Temple was destroyed
for a second time by the Romans in 70 CE, it was not rebuilt. So the
Shekhina, according to these later sources, is left to dwell outside
its walls, wandering in exile with Israel, while doing what she can to
judge and redeem Israel. The rabbinic literature says that there are ten
moments in history at which the Shekhina descended to Israel. Five
of them are punitive: the times when she came to punish Adam, to
admonish Eve and the serpent after the fall, to confuse the builders of
the Tower of Babel, to destroy Sodom and Gomorrah, and to drown
the Egyptians in the Red Sea. In the future, she will come for the final
battle of Gog and Magog.[62]

Other memories of her float around the rabbinic sources, even of an intimate erotic relationship she had with God. When discussing the withdrawal of God's presence from the first Temple, as recorded in the book of Lamentations, one rabbi writes:

> When the Shekhina left the Sanctuary, she returned to caress and kiss its walls and columns, and cried and said, "Be in peace, O my Sanctuary, be in peace, O my royal palace, be in peace, O my precious house, be in peace from now on, be in peace!"[63]

Behind this rabbinic passage, I think there is the story of a woman who is being separated from her lover's boudoir. Was the inner sanctum of the Temple her bedroom? Was Yahweh her lover?

What the full story was, however, the rabbis do not reveal in their literature. Perhaps they did not know it or they did not wish to reveal it. But by the tenth century, in the mystical traditions of the Kabbalah, we learn that when the Shekhina is depicted as the female manifestation of God, she was his Queen.[64] She was separated from her lofty dwelling when Adam, by mistake, thought she was God. According to this story, when the Israelites built the Temple, she took up residence there and, on the night of the Sabbath, God the King and his Queen the Shekhina made love. Their erotic embrace, their unity, safeguarded the welfare of Israel and the world. But this relationship was not their own. Their relationship with each other was determined by the behaviors of Israel. Sins kept the divine couple apart and gave power to the forces of evil. Repentance and piety brought them together in a love affair that restored the primal unity.[65]

The restoration of this primal unity was particularly affected by the enactment of the marital commandment between human partners. Lovemaking between husbands and wives on earth persuaded God and the Shekhina to follow suit. This correlation between human lovemaking and the sacred was considered particularly vital now that the Temple had been destroyed and the Shekhina was living in exile with her children. She had been cut off from the divine world and her lover, leaving her grieving in solitude and suffering amidst the people of Israel whom she cares for. Even though it is only the coming of the Messiah that will enable the reunification of the divine lovers permanently, the Jewish mystics thought that the blessed union between human husband and wife arouses the Shekhina's husband to unite with her now. In this way the reconstitution of the primal wholeness of the godhead is brought about, which ensures the wellness of Israel and the world in the present.[66]

Although the Jewish story of the Queen of Heaven is not well known in Christian circles today, it can be recovered from the literature that has survived. When this is done, we discover that she and Yahweh were a popular divine couple, worshiped even in the Temple. But once the priests reshape the old traditional religion of Israel into a religion with monolatrous propensities, the Queen of Heaven is vanquished. The male priests, whether consciously or not, create a theological explanation of the destruction of the first Temple in Jerusalem in which the goddess becomes a scapegoat. Her centuries-old *orthodox* worship is reframed as *idolatry*. This reinterpretation of the past effectively deflects the blame for the nation's destruction away from its leaders, the priests included. In this way, the anger of the people is channeled away from their leaders who were unable to stop the national disaster. In the process of reschematizing their history, the blame for the disaster falls squarely on the shoulders of an idolatrous nation rather than on the shoulders of its leaders, and, in this way, the Hebrew goddess is sacrificed.

Although she is finally vanquished from the pantheon, she is not forgotten. Her story survives in a less threatening form, a form that does not compromise the program of the priests, which called for the exclusive worship of Yahweh. Her story echoes in the written memories that make up the Jewish wisdom literature, memories of a co-creator angel, a female Spirit, who comes to earth to rest in the prophets and redeem the people of Israel.

CHAPTER 2

Why was the spirit neutered?

The Jewish priests writing in the sixth century BCE were successful in suppressing the worship of the Hebrew goddess. They recreated the Hebrew epic in such a powerful and convincing way that the popular worship of the Queen of Heaven in the old religious cult of Israel was remembered by successive generations of Jews and Christians as idolatry and rebellion against the jealous god Yahweh.

Memories of her, however, could not be eradicated totally. Although she no longer is an object of worship and therefore does not compromise the monolatrous program of the new form of the Jewish religion that the exilic and post-exilic priests put into place, echoes of her former glory are preserved in the Jewish literature produced in the first centuries BCE and CE. In this literature, she resurfaces as a magnificent female angel, Sophia, and as the Holy Spirit. Eventually, she is even able to regain most of her former glory as a goddess when she reemerges in the early Christian tradition as the Holy Spirit, one of the three members of the Trinity in early Aramaic Christianity. But like the Hebrew goddess previously, her prominence in the newly conceived religion is not long lasting. How did she fall from grace again? This is her Christian story.

Introducing Jesus' true mother

Perhaps the Holy Spirit's most well-known act in Christian tradition is at the baptism of Jesus when, as the Greek Gospel of Mark reads, "the Spirit descended into him like a dove."[1] Immediately following the descent of the Spirit, the narrative recalls a voice heard from the heavens, "You are my beloved son, with you I am well pleased." Then the Spirit takes him out to the desert where he is tempted by Satan.[2]

I suspect that Christians who read this story today have understood the Spirit who descends into Jesus to be a genderless or quasi-male entity, a nebulous divine charisma that overtakes Jesus. They hear in their imaginations a male voice, the Father's, call out from the heavens, declaring Jesus his son. But was this how the first Aramaic Christians would have understood this story? Was the voice that they heard a male one?

Digging in

Box 2.1 Jesus' birth?
This is a beautiful fifth-century mosaic of Jesus' baptism. It covers the top of the dome in an old Arian cathedral, the Basilica of the Holy Spirit, in Ravenna, Italy. Not long after the orthodox baptistery in Ravenna was constructed, this basilica was built by Theodoric, a Goth who was himself an

Arian. The artwork in both cases is similar and suggests imitation. Jesus is depicted in the river flanked by John the Baptist and an old bearded man who is the personification of the River Jordan. One feature that is strikingly different is the Arian depiction of Jesus as a beardless youth. Was this depiction of Jesus as a youth intentionally invoking the Arian belief that Jesus was the *son* of God, *created* by God and therefore subordinate to him? What about the water pouring from the dove's mouth and the naked Jesus below it? These do not appear to me to be baptismal waters poured from John's hand. In fact, John's hand is on top of Jesus' head beneath the waters, as if John were pulling Jesus out of the waters above. Does this suggest that Jesus is being born from above out of the Spirit? Does the water above Jesus' head symbolize the waters of his birth? Is John the Baptist the midwife, delivering Jesus? It is intriguing to think that the tradition of the Mother Spirit might be surviving in this Arian artwork.

For deeper digging, read Deborah Mauskopf Deliyannis' treatment of this mosaic in *Ravenna in Late Antiquity* (Cambridge: Cambridge University, 2010) and Robin Margaret Jensen's in *Understanding Early Christian Art* (London: Routledge, 2000).

We are very fortunate to have another version of the baptism story preserved in an ancient gospel called the *Gospel of the Hebrews*. It is a version of the baptism of Jesus that may help to answer our question because it preserves old Aramaic Christian traditions that have been otherwise forgotten, but which predate the Greek traditions found in our New Testament gospels. References to the *Gospel of the Hebrews* are only available to us today because various theologians in the early Church quoted some passages from the *Gospel of the Hebrews* in their own writings. A full copy of this gospel does not survive. What we know about it we know only because some of the early Christians referenced it.

The famous western theologian and Bible translator, Jerome, mentions the *Gospel of the Hebrews* on several occasions. In 372 CE Jerome traveled to Antioch in western Syria. By 385 CE he had made an extensive pilgrimage of the Holy Land and in 386 CE he arrived in Bethlehem. He made frequent visits to Jerusalem and the library in Caesarea. It was during this time that he claims to have come across the "original" version of the Gospel of Matthew in Aramaic, which a Christian group called the Nazareans were using in Beroea, a Syrian city.[3] This version of the Gospel of Matthew Jerome also calls the *Gospel of the Hebrews*.[4]

Since the actual quotations we have of the *Gospel of the Hebrews* are in Greek and differ substantially from the known Gospel of Matthew, we are uncertain what Jerome had. He thought it was an earlier Aramaic version of our Gospel of Matthew, which may explain why other church theologians who were also under this impression, respected this gospel's contents too.

Eusebius of Casearea, writing in the fourth century, tells us about an early second-century church leader and Christian writer, Hegesippus. Hegesippus wrote a lost work known as the *Acts of the Church*, recording information that he had received about how Christianity began with the apostles. Eusebius states that Hegesippus' writings drew "on the *Gospel of the Hebrews*, on the Syriac Gospel, and particularly on works in Aramaic, showing that he was a believer of Hebrew origin, and he mentions other matters coming from Jewish oral tradition."[5] It is obvious from Eusebius' comment that Hegesippus was a witness to very old traditions about Jesus, which had survived in Aramaic and Syriac, the Semitic dialects spoken in Palestine and Syria. One of these sources was the *Gospel of the Hebrews*. It is equally interesting that Papias, Bishop of Hierapolis in Asia Minor, also writing in the early second century, says that he used an Aramaic source called "Matthew" which he describes as "sayings in Hebrew dialect" that everyone "translated as well as he could."[6]

In spite of these testimonies, most scholars who study this gospel today are convinced that the Greek version of the *Gospel of Hebrews* was its original, and that Jerome must have happened upon an Aramaic translation of it. Whatever the case, this gospel is not our New Testament Matthew or an early version of it. But the *Gospel of the Hebrews* is at least as old as the gospels in the New Testament, if not older. A Greek version of it was popular in Alexandria, Egypt, in the second century, and an Aramaic version of it existed in Beroea, Syria, in the fourth century. Regardless of its original language, the concepts and stories preserved in the *Gospel of Hebrews* appear to reflect those of the first Aramaic-speaking Christians from Jerusalem.

One of these old stories from Aramaic Christianity is a version of the baptism story. According to this story as it is recorded in the *Gospel of the Hebrews*, the Holy Spirit descends on Jesus and says directly to him, "My son, in all the prophets was I waiting for you, that you should come and I might rest in you. For you are my rest. You are my firstborn Son who reigns forever."[7] In the Greek New Testament gospels, after the baptism, the Spirit immediately drives Jesus into the desert to overcome Satan's temptations.[8] But in the *Gospel of the Hebrews* it is reported instead that Jesus is taken by the Spirit up the heights of Mount Tabor. Jesus says, "My mother the Holy Spirit took me by one of the hairs on my head and bore me off to the great mountain Tabor."[9]

We learn something very important about the Holy Spirit according to the *Gospel of the Hebrews*. In the earliest surviving Christian traditions, the Holy Spirit is not just a feminine word, but Jesus' mother! When she descends to him at his baptism, it is her voice that calls out to him, proclaiming him *her* son. The *Gospel of Thomas,* an early Christian text from eastern Syria also influenced by Aramaic Christianity, independently retains elements of this same tradition. In one of the sayings in this gospel, Jesus refers to his "true mother" who gave him "life," in contrast with his "birth mother" who gave him "death."[10]

Equally fascinating is passage from another independent source, the *Gospel of Philip*, a Valentinian Gnostic text from the mid-second century. Most scholars think that this gospel was written in Syria, since it gives the Syriac translation for the Greek word "Christos" and quotes part of the eucharist liturgy in Syriac.[11] At one point, the text preserves this poignant criticism of other Christians.

> Some say, "Mary conceived by the Holy Spirit." They are wrong. They do not know what they are saying. When did a woman ever become pregnant by a woman?"[12]

Like the *Gospel of Hebrews* and the *Gospel of Thomas*, this gospel is aware of the old Aramaic tradition that the Holy Spirit was Jesus' mother, not his father as many of the later Greek- and Latin-speaking Christians thought.

Carried up Mount Tabor

The second thing we learn from the *Gospel of Hebrews* is that the oldest version of Jesus' baptismal story was most likely connected with his ascent to Mount Tabor rather than his temptation in the wilderness. The reference to Jesus being carried by his mother, the Holy Spirit, to Mount Tabor is the type of image commonly used in Jewish and Christian apocalyptic literature to describe a hero's ascent into heaven. What is the importance of this? In terms of plot, the ancient audience would have expected his mother to have carried him to the top of Mount Tabor in order for Jesus to be exalted or glorified on high. So although we do not have the rest of the ascent story preserved in the *Gospel of the Hebrews*, it likely climaxed in Jesus' inauguration as God's son in the heights.

There is a remnant of this old inauguration story in the New Testament gospels. It is retained in the transfiguration story, when Jesus goes to the top of a high mountain, taking with him Peter, James and John. This mountain is traditionally known as Mount Tabor, the place in which Jesus is transfigured into a radiant being similar to an angel. The Mount represents heaven where Elijah and Moses live. As a glorified being, Jesus is able to converse with them. In the New Testament story, a cloud overshadows them all – the glorified Jesus, Elijah, Moses, Peter, James, and John – and a voice is heard exclaiming, "This is my beloved son. Listen to him."[13]

Does this pronouncement sound familiar? It is the same pronouncement that was heard at Jesus' baptism at the beginning of his mission in the New Testament gospels, when the voice says, "You are my beloved son, with you I am well pleased."[14] Since Jesus was already made God's son when he was baptized by John, this second pronouncement is repetitive in the gospel narrative and unnecessary in terms of plot.

How can this be explained? The oldest sequence of events likely connected the transfiguration of Jesus with his baptism, as it appears to have been in the *Gospel of the Hebrews*. As the transfiguration story passed from mouth to mouth in the early years of the Christian movement, it must have became separated from the baptism story. As the transfiguration story circulated as a story on its own, it was expanded to include the witnesses Peter, James and John. Then when it became part of the written cycle of stories, because its old connection with Jesus' baptism had been lost, it became sequentially confused in the written gospel narrative and ended up as an event toward the end of Jesus' ministry, rather than starting it.

As part of Jesus' baptismal story, the transfiguration is a highly significant moment. After his immersion in water, the mother Spirit takes Jesus to the height where he is glorified and proclaimed her son. His ascent to the heights and his bodily transformation into a being of light, represented for the early Christians the quintessence of their own redemption. Jesus' transfiguration marked for them the recovery of the lost "original" perfect body of Adam.

Generally, the early Christians thought that this lost body of Adam was a body of light, an angel-like radiant body that had been created in God's image. They noticed in Genesis 1.26–27, that God made the human being "in his own image." But then, after Adam and Eve sinned, they were found to be "naked" in the garden.[15] Following this, God gives Adam and Eve "garments of skins" to wear, and they are expelled from Eden.[16] The Christians wondered what was going on. Did God originally create the human being with a luminous garment that resembled God? Did Adam and Eve lose this luminous body when they sinned and became naked? Did God then give them bodies of flesh or "skins" as new garments as a punishment for their sin?

The early Christians reasoned in just this manner. They were convinced that God's original intent for humans when he created us "in his image" was to remain as luminous beings. But once Adam sinned, our luminosity was lost or degraded. We became embodied in the flesh. Jesus was part of God's plan to recover our lost luminous bodies, to restore us to our primal selves as beings of light made in the Image of God. This is the luminous body that the Christians believed had been restored by Jesus at his baptism, when he was exalted to the high places as God's son. The Christians thought that this body of light was not only the primordial body, but also the resurrection body. It was the body that we would receive at the end of time when we returned to Paradise.

This understanding of Jesus' baptism led the early Christians to develop their own initiatory rituals, which they patterned after Jesus' so that, like him, they would receive the Holy Spirit, recover their lost luminous bodies, be transported to Paradise, and named children of God. In order to actualize this drama, they used ritual invocations that called upon the Holy Spirit in combination with water immersion, anointing with sacred oil, and eating special foods. Although most references to baptism in the early Christian literature reveal some knowledge of this understanding of baptismal mimicry and its effects, it is in the early Syrian literature where the Mother Spirit and her instrumental role in the convert's baptism and transfiguration are well remembered. She, in fact, was invoked at baptism and the eucharist as one of the members of the Trinity.

In the name of the mother spirit

The early Syrian Church, which began to grow up along the Silk Road in the middle of the first century, retained traditions about the Mother Spirit and her instrumental role in baptism. The Aramaic-speaking Christians who started the church in Jerusalem after the death of Jesus were the Christians who proselytized the eastern zones along the Silk Road. James the brother of Jesus was their leader. Although James himself did not travel the mission roads, the community he established was mission oriented, and sister hubs were established immediately in Antioch, a major city in western Syria, and quickly in Edessa, a major city in eastern Syria.[17]

The Aramaic form of Christianity would hardly be recognizable to Christians today. It was a Jewish messianic movement with imminent millenarian expectations. Members self-identified as Jews. They observed all the Jewish laws in the Torah and attended Temple services in Jerusalem and synagogue gatherings in the diaspora. They read the Jewish scriptures as prophecies of Jesus' messiahship, and believed that he would return as fierce angel, the Judge on the last day. So soon would the world end that the members who lived in Jerusalem gave over all personal properties to the leaders of the Jerusalem church, and formed a millenarian commune. Then many of them hit the road as missionaries, zealous to convert as many people as possible since Jesus' return and the Judgment loomed on the horizon.

The dominant language along the Silk Road was an eastern dialect of Aramaic called Syriac. Many of the oldest Aramaic Christian traditions were forgotten by Greek- and Latin-speaking Christian communities. However, many were retained by the early Syrian Christians in the literature they produced in part because of the language similarities between Aramaic and Syriac. A case in point is the memory of the female Spirit. As in Aramaic, the word *ruha* or "spirit" in Syriac is feminine. Even as late as the fourth century, well-respected Syrian theologians and poets such as Ephrem, Macarius, and Aphraates still standardly conceive of the Holy Spirit as female.

What is most fascinating about references to the female Spirit in early Syrian literature is that she is not just a female, she is the Mother. Aphraates wrote 23 treatises between the years 337 and 345 CE. He was a Persian Jew who converted to Christianity and became an abbot of the Mar Mattai monastery near Mosul. In one of his treatises, Aphraates teaches that Genesis 2.24, "a man shall leave his father and mother," does not refer to ordinary parents, but to the heavenly Father and the Mother Spirit:

> Who leaves father and mother to take a wife? The meaning is as follows: as long as a man has not taken a wife, he loves and reveres God his Father and the Holy Spirit his Mother, and he has no other love. But when a man takes a wife, then he leaves his (true) Father and his Mother.[18]

Macarius, a monk who lived in northeast Syria in the middle of the fourth century, also is aware of the teaching that our true Father and Mother are the heavenly Father and the Holy Spirit. He says that once the "veil of darkness" came upon Adam's soul, humans have been unable to "see the true heavenly Father and the good kind Mother, the grace of the Spirit, and the sweet and desired Brother, the Lord."[19]

Although the retention of the female Spirit was due partially to linguistics, her memory as "mother" was the consequence of the fact that the Aramaic Christians from Jerusalem brought with them old stories about Jesus' baptism such as we saw preserved in the *Gospel of the Hebrews*. Since Jesus had received this Spirit at his own baptism, the Mother Spirit was understood to play a key role in the baptisms of new converts. In fact, she was invoked in early baptismal liturgies as one of the members of the Trinity.

In several prayers of praise preserved in the *Acts of Thomas*, a Syrian Christian text from the early third century, the Holy Spirit is called upon as the Mother. One of these fascinating prayers recited at baptism begins by invoking the "holy name of Christ that is above every name." Then the apostle Thomas says as he is about to baptize several young men, "Come, power of the Most High, and perfect compassion. Come, gift of the Most High. Come, compassionate Mother. Come, partner of the male. Come, revealer of secret mysteries…Take part with these young men! Come, Holy Spirit, and cleanse their loins and their hearts. And seal them in the name of the Father and the Son and the Holy Spirit."[20]

These titles given to the Holy Spirit appear to be standardized words of invocation since several of them are echoed in other prayers in the *Acts of Thomas*. When the eucharist is being consecrated, the apostle Thomas invokes the Holy Spirit with these words, "Come, perfect compassion. Come, partner of the male. Come, revealer of the mysteries…Come, hidden Mother…Come, and take part with us in this Eucharist…"[21] The power of the Spirit and her son is invoked to come to those who gather around the Eucharist table in another prayer, "We name the name of the Mother…We name the name of Jesus…"[22] Twice in the *Acts of Thomas*, we find a standard concluding prayer, praising the exalted Father and the Holy Spirit, the Mother of all creation, who is Sophia or Wisdom.[23]

Knowledge of the Mother as the second person of the Trinity can be tracked as far east as Arabia where the Quran was composed. In a Quranic passage, Jesus is interrogated by God about the origins of the doctrine of the Trinity. God wants to know if Jesus started it. In a striking testimony to the Mother aspect of the Trinity, God asks him, "Jesus, son of Mary, did you tell mankind, 'Take me and my mother as two gods beside God?'"[24]

Born from the womb of water

I cannot emphasize enough how important liturgy is. Ritual words and actions tend to be treated conservatively. They remain stable over generations, even centuries. To change them takes a concerted effort on the part of those in power who usually face great resistance. The reason for this is that rituals, according to the ancient people, are not merely symbolic words and actions. The ancient people performed rituals because they believed that the ritual really truly did something. The ritual words and actions were powerful, *magical* even. The words and actions had to be repeated precisely, with no variation, in order to influence and harness the sacred powers and achieve the desired outcome.

In the case of baptism, water was used to cleanse the initiates of their former sins. Sometimes consecrated oil was smeared on their bodies to exorcise lurking demons. Also, oil was used to convey the Holy Spirit, so that she would rest in the new Christians like she had in Jesus. In some Syrian traditions, anointing occurred before the descent into the water, while in the west, it was usually performed following immersion. In Syria, they believed that anointing the converts with holy oil began the process of altering the initiates' bodies. By smearing their bodies with the oil, they were exalting and transfiguring them, restoring the luminous image of God that had been Adam's prior to his fall. They were being resurrected, they said, and now could sit down at the heavenly banquet table. Thus, the eucharist meal was the pinnacle of the Syrian baptismal ceremony, the climactic moment when the initiates, wearing their new resurrection bodies, joined the banquet in Paradise as children of God. It was the mother Spirit hovering over the waters who brought about their transfiguration. And so it was she whom the Syrian Christians invoked in their liturgical prayers during their baptism and eucharist ceremonies.

Jesus' baptism and transfiguration story as it is preserved in the *Gospel of the Hebrews* provided the footprint for their own baptisms and transfigurations. A beautiful example of this is captured in a famous old hymn that is embedded within the narrative of the *Acts of Thomas*. It is called the "Hymn of the Pearl."[25] The hymn is an allegory that tells the story of the languishing of the embodied soul on earth and its redemption. The language of the poem is rich with images. A prince (=Jesus) lives in the east (=heaven) with his father and mother (=the Father and the Mother Spirit). In order to become heir to their kingdom, he is given a commission to descend into Egypt (=the earth) and bring back a pearl that is in the mouth of a sea serpent (=the embodied soul). Before he leaves on his journey, he is stripped of his glittering robe (=the image of God), but is promised to receive another (=the restored image of God) when he returns.

When the prince gets to Egypt, he is distracted and falls asleep (=embodied and weighed down by the flesh) until he receives a letter from his parents reminding him of his commission. So he remembers the pearl (=embodied soul) and goes to the sea (=baptism) where he charms the sea serpent by pronouncing the name of his father (=the Father God) and the name of the "second" in power, his mother the queen (=the Holy Spirit). He snatches the pearl (=the soul), strips off his dirty clothes (=his body of flesh), and leaves Egypt.

The prince is led by the light (=the Holy Spirit) through various cities (=planetary spheres) as he makes his way home (=ascends to heaven). Once there, the prince (=Jesus) receives a glorious garment embroidered with the image of the King of Kings (=the restored image of God). The prince's stature grew as he wrapped himself in the robe (=Jesus' transfiguration) and was allowed to re-enter the gates of his Father's kingdom (=the Kingdom of Heaven) and present the pearl (=redeemed soul) to the King (=the Father God). This archaic hymn presents the story of Jesus' incarnation, baptism and transfiguration as an allegory of a prince, an allegory complete with the Mother Spirit, the second person of the Trinity.

A century later, when Aphraates describes baptism in his own church, he shows that he is aware of the same story about Jesus' baptism and his reception of the Mother Spirit as it is preserved in the *Gospel of the Hebrews*. He writes, "From baptism we receive the Spirit of Christ, and in the same hour that the priests invoke the Spirit, *she* opens the heavens and descends, and hovers over the waters, and those who are baptized put *her* on. From all who are born of a body, the Spirit is absent until they come to birth by water, and then receive the Holy Spirit."[26] Ephrem, another fourth-century father of the Syrian church, wrote about his understanding of the Spirit's "hovering" over the baptismal waters in one of his Epiphany hymns, "The Spirit descended from on high and *she* sanctified the water by *her* hovering."[27] Clearly the version of Jesus' baptism found in the *Gospel of the Hebrews* was still the template for the Syrian baptismal liturgy even as late as the fourth century.

Memories of the Mother Spirit's primary role in baptism survived for centuries in Syria and can be tracked in two later writers. Around 600 CE the Bishop of Mahoze, Martyrius, depicts the Christian convert as one "who has been held worthy of the hovering of the all-holy Spirit, who, like a mother, hovers over us as she gives sanctification, and through her hovering over us, we are made worthy of sonship."[28] Three hundred years later, in a homily by the Bishop of Bet Raman, Moshe bar Kepha, the Spirit is remembered as the "compassionate mother" who hovered over the waters of John the Baptist.[29]

Reverberations of the old teaching about the Mother Spirit's central role in baptism continued to be developed in Syria, where the early Orthodox theologians focused on John 3.3–5 as the true meaning of baptism. In the west, the Catholic theologians followed Paul's opinion, that in baptism we die with Christ and are raised with him.[30] But in the east, John's view prevailed, that in baptism we are reborn through the water and the Spirit. So in Syria, the baptismal waters are depicted as a womb from which we are reborn. And the Spirit is the mother who gives birth to us. This interpretation of baptism is known in the fourth century to Ephrem, who is the first theologian to mention the "womb of water."[31]

It becomes commonplace in later orthodox Syrian Christianity to call the baptismal font, the "womb of the font."[32] This theme is carried into the sixth-century orthodox liturgies. In a common Syriac prayer, the baptismal invocation is made, "Blessed are you, Lord God, through whose great and indescribable gift this water has been sanctified by the coming of the Holy Spirit so that it has become the womb of the Spirit that gives birth to the new man out of the old."[33] In the service from eastern Syria, when the water is consecrated, it becomes "a new womb and gives birth spiritually."[34] In the sixth-century baptismal hymn written by Severus of Antioch, a western city of Syria, this teaching is also visible. The hymn begins, "Stretch out your wings, O Holy Church, and receive the perfect sheep to whom the Holy Spirit has given birth in the baptismal water."[35] Although the Mother Spirit is no longer the second person in the Trinity, her memory resounds in the contemporary Syriac church liturgy where baptism remains today a new birth from the womb of the font.

Digging in

Box 2.2 Entering a womb?

The early Christians built baptismal fonts in a variety of shapes. The earliest known font is in the house- church of Dura Europos. It is rectangular and some scholars have suggested that its shape may symbolize a tomb. Other shapes include octagonal, hexagonal, polylobed, round and cruciform. Perhaps the most interesting shaped font is the one pictured here, a fifth-century font in the ancient north African town, Sufetula (modern day Sbeitla in Tunisia). But the pattern for it was a century older. This model was carefully restored in the fifth century, copied from the fourth-century original. Professor Robin Jensen has studied this Catholic font and has suggested that the font looks like a woman's vulva. She writes: "Candidates would enter from one direction and stand in the well of the font to be baptized. Emerging, then, from the Mother Church's vagina, they would climb out on the opposite side and present themselves, wet and naked, as new-born babies, ready to join their new siblings and perhaps receive a symbolic swallow of sweetened milk along with wine and bread at the altar rail" (2008: 153). Were these Christians performing the words of Nicodemus in John 3.4: "How can a man be born when he is old? Can he enter a second time into his mother's womb and be born?"

Photo courtesy of Robin M. Jensen.
For deeper digging, read Robin M. Jensen, "*Mater Ecclesia* and *Fons Aeterna*: The Church and her womb in ancient Christian tradition," in Amy-Jill Levine (ed.), *A Feminist Companion to Patristic Literature* (London: T&T Clark, 2008: 137–155).

Milking the breasts of God

We have a set of beautiful old hymns from the Syrian churches called the *Odes of Solomon*. There are 42 hymns in total, and several contain references to the female Holy Spirit. There are certain features of the hymns that suggest that they were originally written in Aramaic or Syriac, although all that remains today are Greek and Coptic translations of them. They were written down sometime in the late second or early third century, although their original composition and use in liturgy must have been earlier than this and more widespread than eastern Syria since Ignatius of Antioch, around 125 CE, appears to know some of them.[36] Most likely, these hymns were recorded by the Syrian Christians around 100–125 CE in Edessa.[37]

They are so Jewish in tone that they were mistaken for Jewish writings by some scholars in the past.[38] Rather than being Jewish, however, they represent the beliefs and practices of old Aramaic Christianity from Jerusalem which had a mission in Edessa by the mid-first century, and also one in Antioch. Even though this is the case, we must remember that, like all of our early Christian texts, they have a long history of transmission before the written text became stable in its wording. Older hymns inherited by a community were sometimes rewritten in order to update them because the community's theology had changed. So the *Odes* contain archaic features from the first Aramaic Christians alongside newer features from the younger Syrian congregations.

Many of these hymns were performed during baptismal ceremonies, sung or chanted as the converts were baptized in water, anointed with oil, and ate at the table of the eucharist following their baptism. One of the hymns even includes instructions to the "singers" to sing "the grace of the Lord Most High" with "gentle voices," in unison, "hallelujah!"[39] Ode 24 begins with an allusion to the version of Jesus' baptismal story that we found recorded in the *Gospel of the Hebrews*:

> The dove fluttered over the head of our Lord Messiah,
> because he was her head.
> And she cooed over him,
> and her voice was heard.[40]

This stanza celebrates the joy of the Mother Spirit when she declares Jesus her son, when "her voice was heard."

In one startling *Ode*, a transgendered image of the Father emerges alongside the traditional image of the Mother as a nurse:

> A cup of milk was offered to me,

And I drank it in the sweetness of the Lord's kindness.
The Son is the cup,
And the Father is he who was milked,
And the Holy Spirit is she who milked him,
Because his breasts were full,
And it was undesirable that his milk should be released without
purpose.
The Holy Spirit opened her womb,
And mixed the milk of the two breasts of the Father.
Then she gave the mixture to the world without their knowledge,
And those who have received (it) are in the perfection of the right
hand.[41]

The transgendered Father, who has breasts, is curious since there
are no scriptural passages to support this image, although there are
scriptural passages where he is described as a midwife and a mother in
labor.[42] Scholars have been hard pressed to explain the transgendered
Father, calling the image "altogether grotesque."[43] I wonder, however,
might this odd image have been created by the Christians when they
first began to downplay the Mother's role, giving her breasts to the
Father? Did the hymn originally recall a flight to heaven where the
initiate was fed milk from the Mother's breasts? As we will see later in
this chapter, the hymn shows clear signs of being overwritten to lessen
the Spirit's mothering role by assimilating her to the Virgin Mary with
the addition of several extra stanzas. So it would not be unreasonable
to suggest that the Mother Spirit's nursing role was transferred to
Father as well in order to downplay it.

In this transgendered hymn, the interaction of the divine Trinity
– the Father, the Mother, and the Son – is paramount. The Holy Spirit
as Mother has opened her womb. She has given birth in baptism to the
initiate, the child she now feeds with the cup. The convert sings that he
has just drunk the milk of the Lord expressed from the double breasts
of the Father by the Holy Spirit. The initiate is fed from the cup of the
Son. The word casa' or "cup" is used in later Syriac texts when writers
refer to the eucharist chalice, so this is likely a reference to the post-
baptismal eucharist.[44]

In Ode 35, the initiate is "overshadowed" with the "sprinkling of
the Lord." Reminiscent of Jesus' baptism, following the "sprinkling" a
"cloud of peace" stands over his head. Then, just like Jesus tells us in
the Gospel of the Hebrews, the believer says, "I was carried like a child
by its mother," ascending to the Most High. In the presence of God,
the believer was given "milk" to drink, "the dew of the Lord."

The following hymn, Ode 36, continues the initiate's story. The
initiate describes being carried into heaven. He echoes Jesus' story as it

was spun in the *Gospel of the Hebrews*, saying, "I rested on the Spirit of the Lord, and she raised me up to heaven and caused me to stand on my feet in the Lord's high place." Standing before the God's Glory, the initiate improvises hymns to praise God at that moment. The hymn that he composes and sings is a retelling of the story of Jesus who was brought at his baptism by the Spirit to stand before God's face, receive the name "Son of God," and be transformed as "the greatest among the great ones." So the initiate says that she, the Spirit, created Jesus, while he, the Most High renewed him. Jesus has been "anointed" with perfection, and has become one of the holy angels who stand in God's presence. "Hallelujah!" In Ode 4, the singer tells us that after he has been sprinkled with the waters of baptism, God will open his "bountiful springs" and supply him with milk and honey to drink.

Clearly, these hymns are describing baptismal and anointing ceremonies that are very different from those performed today in Christian churches. Not only is the Holy Spirit the Mother Spirit, but the initiation ceremony included more than consecrated bath water and holy oil. The ancient ceremonies described in the Odes of Solomon also involved a cup ritual where the new convert was offered milk to drink. This cup ceremony is an old and special form of the eucharist, one that was performed only as the finale of baptismal initiations when the newly born "children" were fed.

Its oldest allusion may be in Paul's letter to the Corinthians where he mentions that he fed the "babes in Christ" with milk by giving them initial instructions, likely when they were baptized.[45] In the first letter of Peter found in the New Testament, the author says that newly baptized converts, those who have been "born anew," are like "newborn babes" who "long for the pure spiritual milk so that by it you may grow up to salvation, for you have tasted the kindness of the Lord."[46] The author mentions that the baptized were formerly ignorant, but have been instructed by their leaders about the teachings that the Holy Spirit sent down from heaven, "things into which angels long to look."[47] The performance of this milk ritual in Syria must have originally represented the delivery of the Christian catechism taught by the Mother Spirit who was the revealer of the heavenly mysteries.

Sometime in the late first century, honey begins to be mixed with the milk in the ritual, a small but meaningful change that begins to downplay the Mother's revelatory role. The milk and honey mixture rekeyed the action with the twin images from the Jewish scriptures where milk and honey represent the gifts of the promised land given to God's chosen people. According to the early Christians, the Promised Land was heavenly Paradise, the place where they would go after death. So the performance of this rekeyed ritual demonstrated to the new convert that he or she was already eating the foods of the Promised Land, having received God's gift of resurrection and immortality through baptism and anointing. The Mother's revelatory role has been marginalized. She no longer nurses her children, nurturing them with the secrets of the kingdom. Her breast milk has been replaced with a mixture of milk and honey, simple gifts that fulfill God's promises in the scriptures.

References to this rekeyed ceremony emerge in a number of early authors who lived in various parts of the Mediterranean world. In many cases, echoes of the older story of the nursing Mother Spirit can be heard resonating within the parameters of the newer story about the land of milk and honey. Around 135 CE, the author of the *Letter of Barnabas* mentions that the newborn baby is given milk and honey, just as Christians were when they "entered into life." His exposition on this subject appears to have been a short homily on initiation, that Christians have been remade into God's image, and have entered the land flowing with milk and honey.[48] The church theologian, Tertullian, who lived in Carthage, North Africa, in the late second century, knows some Christians, the Marcionites, who gave initiates, the "children," milk and honey.[49] Hippolytus, a presbyter of Rome in the early third century, also knows of this, but says that it was the practice of the Gnostic Naassenes. According to them, Christians who have tasted milk and honey are perfected. Through this ceremony, they have been liberated so that they can live in the divine world.[50]

Hippolytus' testimony against the Naassenes appears to be a swipe at the Naassenes' interpretation of the rite, not their performance of it. Hippolytus wrote a fascinating handbook of liturgies around 215 CE in Rome. He wrote the *Apostolic Tradition* because he was furious that the old church practices were being innovated by Pope Zephyrinus and Pope Callistus. Hippolytus wanted to preserve the old ways, the old rituals. And what he tells us in the Apostolic Tradition about the baptism initiations in the old Roman churches is fascinating. After full nude immersion and anointing, the new converts congregrated in the church where they were given to drink three cups. One of wine to represent the blood of Jesus shed for them. Another of water as a sign of their baptism. And another of milk and honey in fulfillment of God's promise to give them "a land flowing with milk and honey." The bishop was supposed to explain to them that they were being nourished "like little children" by the "sweetness of his Word."[51] Clement of Alexandria, a contemporary of Hippolytus, also mentions that new Christians, "babes," drink wine, water, and milk with honey at baptism in a full exposé on the meaning of each of the liquids.[52]

For this baptismal cup ceremony to be this widespread geographically among such diverse and independent forms of Christianity suggests that it is very old. It is extremely important to our investigation of the Mother Spirit because, as we saw in the *Odes*, the presentation of milk reminded the converts that they had been reborn as God's children through baptism, and that the Spirit was their true mother who would nurture them from God's breasts. She had taken them to the heights where they had been transfigured and had received hidden knowledge from her in the form of a cup of milk.

The mother's erasure

It is not easy to explain why the Mother Spirit was neutered and masculinized in the Christian tradition because none of the writings that have survived offers an explicit explanation. Rather, what we see in the literature is slippage, a gradual loss of her from Christian memory. The loss is quicker among Greek-speaking and Latin-speaking Christians where "spirit" is neuter in Greek (*pneuma*) and masculine in Latin (*spiritus*). In Greek and Latin Christianity, by the end of the second century, the Holy Spirit is understood in neuter or male terms almost uniformly, although her dying femininity bleeds through occasionally in the literature, even in Latin literature as late as the fourth century.[53]

One place in which the female Holy Spirit visibly thrives in the Greek and Latin west is within Gnostic traditions that were imported to Rome from Alexandria, Egypt. It is uniformly agreed among the various Gnostic groups that the Godhead consists of the Father, the Mother, and the Son, and, whenever the Holy Spirit is mentioned, she is female. This is a discussion that deserves a fuller treatment, so I take it up in Chapter 6.

There are a few remnants of her former femininity found in other Greek and Latin texts from the second century, such as Irenaeus of Lyons' formulation of the Trinity as Father, Son and Sophia.[54] But this remnant may only have survived because Irenaeus was a student in Syrian Antioch before moving to Lyons where he became a bishop. Theophilus of Antioch, from the generation proceeding Irenaeus, also knows the same Trinitarian formula.[55]

Irenaeus appears to be very aware of the Syrian traditions about the Mother Spirit, although he marginalizes them by saying that the Holy Spirit is the Church flowing from the body of Christ. Whoever refuses to join the church and receive the Spirit, will not be "nourished into life from the mother's breasts" and, "rejecting the Spirit," they will not be instructed in truth.[56] He says that "we need to flee to the church, to drink milk at her breast, to be nourished by the scriptures of the Lord."[57]

What has happened to the old liturgical tradition about the Mother Spirit feeding the new Christian milk after baptism? According to Irenaeus, she is the Mother Church. When the Christian has been baptized, he or she enters the Church. The Church is the Mother who provides the new Christian nourishment in the form of teaching. By equating the Mother Spirit with the Mother Church, her former glory as the mother aspect of the Trinity is diminished to the point of erasure.

Irenaeus makes reference to the milk nourishment of the new Christian elsewhere, and we witness the same sort of marginalization of the Mother Spirit. In this case, he says that Jesus offered himself to us as milk when we were infants. The new Christian is nourished from the breast of Christ's flesh with the milk of the Word or *logos*. The bread of immortality, which is eaten ceremoniously later once the Christian matures, is the Spirit of the Father.[58] In this discussion, which hints at the fact that Irenaeus is well aware of the special baptismal eucharist and the Mother's part in it, the female Mother Spirit is nowhere to be found. Her role in the baptismal eucharist has been given over completely to the Son and the Father. Her Spirit becomes his Spirit. By shifting the traditions ever so slightly to the males in the Trinity, her eventual erasure is cinched.

Clement of Alexandria, writing in Greek at the turn of the third century, presents his knowledge of the special baptismal eucharist traditions and the Mother Spirit's role in a similar fashion to Irenaeus. Clement too calls spiritual teaching "milk swelling out from breasts of love." He also assimilates the Holy Spirit with the Mother Church, the virgin who nurses her new children with holy milk. This holy milk is the Word or *logos*, given as drink to initiates along with honey. The Father's breast nourishes the new convert with "the milk of love." Only those who have suckled his breast are truly blessed. They have eaten sacred food and have been carried to the heavens. Because they have drunk this milk, they have been reared as "citizens of heaven and members of the angelic choirs."[59] Clement knows the old liturgical tradition, but the Mother Spirit is no longer prominent. The Church has become the nurse and the Father has grown breasts.

In another text, Clement demonstrates that he knows that the "compassionate Mother" is one of the members of the Trinity, but he diminishes her status. She is presented as an attribute of the Father who "begot of himself" the Son:

> You shall look into the bosom of the Father, whom God the only-begotten Son alone has declared. God himself is love. And out of love for us became feminine. In his ineffable essence he is Father. In his compassion to us he became Mother. The Father by loving became feminine, and the great proof of this is he whom he begot of himself. And the fruit brought forth by love is love.[60]

These subtle shifts that connect the Mother Spirit with the Church or hand her role over to male entities in the Trinity become so entrenched in the Christian tradition that they are commonplace by the time the famous western theologian Augustine writes. Augustine comments that "our milk is Christ" fed to us from the "Mother Church" whose "breasts are the two testaments of the divine Scriptures."[61] What is the "milk of our infancy?" According to Augustine it is the "Word made flesh," which is God's Wisdom, by which he created everything.[62] He understands himself to be nourished by Jesus' body in the Eucharist, "a creature suckled on your milk and feeding on you, the food that never perishes."[63]

In Syria, we notice the same type of slippage. Although the slippage can be seen in some of the third-century Syrian literature, it does not begin to occur with the same intensity as it did in the Greek and Latin west until the fifth and sixth centuries. As we already saw, one of the earliest examples is found in the *Odes of Solomon*, where the Father and the Son are transgendered.[64] Both of these male figures are envisioned as mothers with breasts. The archaic role of the Holy Spirit as the nursing Mother is beginning to be usurped by the males in the Trinity. Her old story is beginning to be rewritten. Male figures are superimposed over her.

In fact, in the case of *Ode* 19, which I previously discussed, the older baptismal hymn about the birthing and nursing Mother Spirit has been rewritten so completely that she is assimilated with the Virgin Mary. An entire set of new stanzas are added to an older hymn. These stanzas appear disjointed from the original hymn. They are intrusive, altering suddenly the subject of the hymn. They work to reinterpret the meaning of the old hymn whose language about the Mother Spirit must have been becoming a liability. By association, the womb of the Holy Spirit becomes the womb of Mary, who conceives and gives birth to the Son.

In fourth-century Syrian literature, slippage becomes more common, creating a situation in which the feminine Spirit remains prominent, but her role is becoming more and more confused with other entities. Ephrem, who retains the feminine Spirit, is uncomfortable with her mother role. So in his writings, her mother role is given to the Son who is the "breast of life" and the Father whose "womb" birthed the Word. The male God is the "wet nurse" who knows when his children should be nourished with milk and when they should be fed with solid food.[65] In the *Liber Graduum*, a late fourth-century Syriac manual of the spiritual life, the church "with its altar and baptism" is praised rather than the Mother Spirit, as that which "gives birth to people as infants, who suckle milk until they are weaned."[66] The old tradition of the Mother Spirit, the second person of the Trinity, is gradually diminishing.

The situation becomes a crisis in the fifth and sixth centuries when there is a systematic attempt to neuter the Holy Spirit altogether. It happens on the level of Syriac grammar. In complete defiance of the rules of the Syriac language, theologians begin treating the feminine word *ruḥa* or "spirit" as a masculine word whenever it refers to the Holy Spirit. However, when the same word is used to refer to "wind" or "spirit," the feminine grammar is maintained. Even though this grammar shift violates the very fabric of the Syriac language, it becomes routine by the sixth century. The feminine Holy Spirit only

Digging in

Box 2.3 Is this the Trinity?
This is a fresco painted between the years 1378 and 1395 CE. It was uncovered in the last century in the church of St. Jakobus in Urschalling, Upper Bavaria. The old fresco had been painted over in the 1600s when the church was remodeled. It was not until the new paint started to peel in the 1920s that the old fresco came to light. Does this fresco represent the Trinity as critics and church historians have suggested? The inscription on the fresco reads: "*Abraham tres vidit unum adoravit*: Abraham sees three; he worships one." The imagery is very suggestive too, since the three persons are joined below the waist as if they were one figure. Their unity is further demonstrated by the fact that the three torsos share one set of arms and the cross beams on their halos are only complete if the three halos are viewed as one. The gray-bearded Father is on the right, Jesus the golden-haired Son is on the left, and the Holy Spirit is in the center, as if proceeding from the Father and Son. The Spirit is depicted by the artist as a female. What does this mean? Medievalist Barbara Newman points out that Mary the Mother of Jesus was identified with the maternal Holy Spirit in the Middle Ages.

Marian Trinities were not uncommon in late medieval Catholic art, although they usually depict Mary's coronation with the Holy Spirit crowning her. In the thirteenth century, there even was a sectarian movement that reintroduced the idea that the Holy Spirit is a female, and announced her incarnation as the female Saint Guglielma of Milan. The Guglielites taught that she would return in order to found a new church under the leadership of a woman pope. The Urschalling fresco is unique in that it does not

portray Mary's coronation nor was it created by the Guglielites.
Yet it belongs to the repressed but insurgent tradition of the
Trinity that we have been tracing, where the identity of the Holy
Spirit is represented as female and maternal. Commenting on this
fresco, Professor Rosemary Radford Ruether asks the question,
"What would it have meant for Christianity if the Trinity had been
taught in this form?" (1985, 20).

For deeper digging, read Barbara Newman, *From Virile Woman
to WomanChrist: Studies in Medieval Religion and Literature*
(Philadelphia: University of Pennsylvania, 1995) and *God and
the Goddesses: Vision, Poetry, and Belief in the Middle Ages*
(Philadelphia: University of Pennsylvania, 2003); Rosemary
Radford Ruether, *Womanguides: Readings Toward a Feminist
Theology* (Boston: Beacon, 1985).

remains in a few Syriac liturgical texts and in poetry, the sorts of traditional literature most resistant to change.[67]

The most violent act against the Mother Spirit is found in the ancient handwritten manuscript copies of the *Acts of Thomas*. The *Acts of Thomas* was originally written in Syriac, although we do not possess that old original. We do have later Greek, Latin, Arabic, Armenian, Coptic, Ethiopic, and Syriac copies of it and comparison of these manuscript versions has led scholars to conclude that the Greek version goes back to a stage closest to the lost original Syriac, while the Syriac version we possess represents a later stage than the Greek.[68] Why is this important to our discussion of the Mother Spirit? Because in all the places we discussed previously where the Mother Spirit is invoked in the *Acts of Thomas* as the second person in the Trinity, her invocation is found in the early Greek version. In the later Syriac version, in these same places, the invocation to the Mother Spirit is gone: intentionally, the references to her have been erased. This erasure was managed at a later date when the scribe made a Syriac copy of the *Acts*. He chose not to copy references to the Mother Spirit so that the text would conform to later Syrian orthodoxy when the Mother Spirit no longer exists in the Trinity.

God's gender crisis

The gradual erosion of the feminine Holy Spirit and her erasure from the Trinity, led to a gender crisis in the Godhead. This crisis has left behind subtle footprints in the literature and theology of late antique and medieval Christianity. Gregory of Nazianzus, who writes in the fourth century, was the Archbishop of Constantinople and one of the three Cappadocian theologians who formulated the orthodox doctrine of the Trinity. Whenever he speaks of the Holy Spirit, she is a "he." Gregory addresses the consequences of this gender slippage in his *Fifth Theological Oration*. He says that some Christians he knows consider God to be male because God is called by the masculine name "Father." Some other Christians he knows think that the Spirit is a neuter entity because *pneuma* is neuter in Greek or because the Spirit has nothing to do with generating things. According to the Trinitarian doctrine that he had helped develop, the Spirit does not generate, but "proceeds" from the Father or Son. Gregory claims that he knows other Christians who are silly enough to think that God actually birthed his Son out of a marriage, a concept he considers the reintroduction of heresy.[69]

How confused the traditions had become in the Greek and Latin west by the fourth century with faded memories of the female Mother Spirit lingering as they were usurped by male and neuter images. God was in a real gender crisis. Gregory of Nyssa, another fourth-century theologian who helped formulate the catholic doctrine of the Trinity suggests a way out of God's gender crisis. In a famous passage from the seventh Homily of his commentary on the Song of Songs, he writes that both words "father" and "mother" must be understood to mean the same thing when referencing God. Why? "Because the divine is neither male nor female."[70]

Jerome, the famous Latin theologian in the fourth century, tries to untangle God's gender along similar lines. He says that the Spirit's femininity should not be scandalous. It is feminine, he says, only because the gender of the word in Hebrew makes it feminine. He reminds us that the word "Spirit" in Latin is masculine and in Greek is neuter. Why all these options? They are meant to teach us that "the deity has no sex."[71]

Although this may have provided solace for some, it did not do the trick generally. A genderless God never became the norm, perhaps because humans find genderless entities difficult to relate to. Rather, in the medieval cloisters, it became commonplace to talk about the transgendered God, where Jesus is the mother who has breasts to suckle his sons.[72] In a famous medieval prayer to Saint Paul written by Anselm, the invocation references Christ in startling transgendered language, "So you, Lord God, are the great mother."[73] How did the Holy Spirit fare in the medieval mind? The Holy Spirit is reduced to a "foster-father."[74]

It is, of course, not coincidence that at the time of the formulation of the masculine and neutered Trinity by the Cappadocians in the fourth century, the cult of the Virgin Mary blossoms in popularity. It offered one of the only acceptable options for the Mother traditions to continue to survive within a religion that had been stripped of the Mother God. Over time, Mary was given the titles Virgin, Bride, Mother of God, and Queen of Heaven.[75]

Mary also became known as the Nursing Virgin, *Maria Lactans.* She was given this title not only because she suckles the infant Jesus, but also because her milk nourishes believers. In this way, she takes over the archaic role of the Mother Spirit. In fact, this is a favorite image of the medieval Christian mystics who often meditated on the incarnation and birth of Jesus. They understood the image of the nursing Mary to represent an eternal mystery where the Christian's soul is nourished and sustained by God's grace. Legend recounts that the Cistercian mystic Bernard of Clairvaux in the early twelfth century was one day reciting the *Ave Maris Stella* while standing before the statue of the Virgin in the church of St. Vorles. When he recited the words, "Show yourself a mother," the Virgin suddenly appeared to him and, pinching her breast, let three drops of milk fall into his mouth.[76]

The distancing and then erasure of the Mother Spirit from the Godhead in early Christian literature has been cast by ancient and modern scholars as a consequence of fighting heretical doctrines of the Father–Mother God taught by the Gnostics. But is this correct? Is the Mother Spirit erased from the Trinity because this theology was heretical in early Christianity? Or is this understanding anachronistic and constructed, assuring the degradation of the Mother Spirit by making her a god of heretics? When we consider seriously all the evidence that the early Christians have left us, the doctrine of the Mother Spirit as the second person of the Trinity was not heretical to begin with. It only became heretical in the Greek and Latin west in the second century and in the Syriac East 200 years after that.

It is easier to trace how the Mother Spirit was neutered than it is to explain *why*. The *why* is more complicated than the *how*. The motivating impulse to neuter the Spirit or to recast her as a male cannot be reduced to any one thing. Her erasure is part of a broad conflict that gripped the early church, a conflict over women at the altar and in the bed. While theology and scripture are involved, they did not operate alone. In fact, they appear to me to be secondary factors in the erasure of the Mother, rather than primary ones. While the social mores governing the relationships of men and women in antiquity provided an amenable environment for her deterioration, they were not its chief cause. The locus was the female body and the sex act itself – how they were conceived and framed by the ancient people.

CHAPTER 3

Did Jesus think sex is a sin?

Is sex a sin? This may seem like an odd question. Doesn't God bless humans in the book of Genesis with the commandment, "Be fruitful and multiply"?[1] Indeed. But this does not mean that this commandment was straightforward to the ancient Jews and Christians. Consider its implications. Does it mean unlimited sex with any number of partners? Does it refer to procreative sex, at the exclusion of recreational sex? Does it require matrimonial parameters? Does it justify coerced or forced sex? Is any manner of sex permissible as long as it results in pregnancy? These and similar questions led to ambivalent attitudes toward sex among the ancient Jews and early Christians, especially given other divine commandments that restricted sex severely. Consider two of the commandments from the Decalogue. God says, "You shall not commit adultery" and "You shall not covet your neighbor's wife."[2]

So the question "Is sex a sin?" was very much on the minds of the ancient Jews and Christians, including Jesus and, as we will see in the next chapter, Paul. The answers that Jesus, and later Paul, provided to this question are not straightforward yeahs and nays. Their opinions about sex are ambivalent, and this ambivalence complicated further an already ambiguous subject, leaving a web of incongruities and inconsistencies for later Christians to struggle with, explain and try to implement in their lives. To sort it out, we must first attempt to understand their often unstated assumptions about sex, some of which we can recover from the Jewish literature written during the time of Jesus and Paul.

A double message

During the Hellenistic era, Jewish writings tell us that the ancient Jews were of opposite minds when it came to sex. On the one hand, the sexual impulse was considered to be a "good" drive. The sexual urge is beneficial because it makes possible the fulfillment of God's commandment, "Be fruitful and multiply."[3] It is the procreative impulse that leads to birth and babies and populating the earth.

Yet, on the other, this did not lead to a strictly positive attitude toward sexuality and the body among first-century Jews. It was quite clear from their practical experience that, without restraint, the sexual impulse could lead to all kinds of unwanted consequences and other behaviors that they had defined as sinful. Sexual immorality had been identified by the Jews as one of the three sins that brought guilt upon the earth and, if unchecked, could lead to our destruction. In fact, some Jews believed that sexual desire was derived from the *yeser hara'*, the soul's evil impulse. As such, it was the primary threat to our ability to control ourselves and live moral and pious lives.

In the *Testament of the Twelve Patriarchs*, a Jewish text of fatherly wisdom containing traditions as old as the second century BCE, it is explained that the soul has two mindsets or dispositions or spirits – good and evil – and the person must choose between them. If the soul chooses to follow the "good way" or "spirit," then its deeds are done rightly, wickedness is rejected, and any sins committed are repented immediately. But if the "evil way" or "spirit" is followed instead, the soul is disposed to sin. It allows the demon Beliar to become its ruler and the good is driven out. Even when such a soul attempts to do a good action it will lead to evil since "the Devil's storehouse is filled with the venom of the evil spirit."[4]

How sex fits into this picture is complicated. It is said in these Jewish testaments that freedom from sexual desire is a characteristic found among souls that are unpolluted and indwelt with God's spirit. For instance, the author of the *Testament of Benjamin* writes this fatherly advice, "My children, run from evil, corruptions, and hatred. Cling to goodness and love. Whoever has a mind that is pure with love does not look on a woman for the purpose of having sex with her. He has no pollution in his heart, because upon him is resting the spirit of God."[5] Men must beware of the beauty of the female body which is a distraction for them that can lead to the corruption of their souls and Beliar's sovereignty.[6] The female body was identified as the major threat to men and their honor. So according to the author of *Sirach*, men ought to avert their eyes from a beautiful woman lest passion be kindled like a fire.[7] According to another testament, if you try to perform a good act such as punctuating your diet with fasts, while committing adultery and being sexually promiscuous, you have chosen to follow the evil disposition in your soul. You are like a hare – halfway clean, but in truth unclean, enslaved to evil desires pleasing only to Beliar.[8]

A similar teaching turns up in the Dead Sea Scrolls. In their community rulebook, the Dead Sea Jews explain that God, when he created the human being, placed within us two spirits – the spirit of truth and the spirit of deceit. In a catalog of vices attributed to the evil inclination of the soul are found "lustful passion" and "filthy paths for indecent purposes."[9] The appeal to the creation story – as the time when the two inclinations were given to the soul – is part of a larger discussion that was taking place in the ancient world about origin of the human being. According to several Greek philosophers, the psyche or soul – our rational and emotive self – fell from the highest cosmic spheres at the moment of embodiment. As it fell into a physical body, it traveled through the seven planetary realms, receiving its inclinations during its downward rush. Certain planets gave to the soul its appetites and powers such as its abilities to speak, think, and perceive, as well as its desires to eat, respond emotionally, and have sex.

This philosophical teaching appears to have been common knowledge in the ancient world. It turns up in the *Testament of Reuben*, where it is said that the human being was given seven spirits at creation. The seventh inclination is the desire for "procreation and intercourse," which bring to the soul sins through fondness and pleasure. Because of this, the impulse to procreate and have sex were the last inclinations given at creation and the first of the inclinations that we experience in our youth. It is an inclination filled with ignorance. It leads young people like a blind man into a ditch and like an animal over a cliff.[10]

If I were to summarize the opinion that a large portion of first-century Jews had about sex, it would have a double message. As long as the sex act were performed between a man and a woman who were wedded to one another and the intercourse had a procreative purpose, sexual desire and lovemaking were considered "good." But sex for recreational pleasure was highly suspect because it could easily lead to sinful behavior and the loss of self-control. This double message meant that the sex act, and the drive that went along with it, had to be severely limited. So the Jews put into place a number of preventive restrictions and rules to control for this dangerous impulse.

Sex limits

The ancient Jews encouraged early marriage in order to prevent the fires of youthful passion from being stoked. Young men were expected to marry around puberty, and no later than 20.[11] Why? Rav Huna says, "A man of twenty who has not married spends all his days in sin." This was interpreted by some rabbis to mean, "in thinking about sin."[12] Rav Hisda thought that men should marry at 16. "Had I married at fourteen," he said, "I could have said to Satan, 'An arrow in your eye!'"[13] The actual *minimum* legal age at which a man could marry was 9. For women it was 3![14] Although this minimum age limit does not inform us about what the ancient Jews were doing in reality, it is known from the literature that the father of a young girl was legally able to betroth his daughter while she was still a minor and at least some rabbis thought that female minors could be married.[15] Early marriage was an acceptable way to channel sexual desire and behavior.

Regular lovemaking between married partners was encouraged to prevent lustful thoughts and immoral behavior. According to Rabbi Eliezer, sexual intercourse between spouses should occur every day among those who were independently wealthy (since they have no work to occupy their minds) and twice a week for laborers (whose minds are occupied with work). For those holding jobs that require them to be away from home for more extended periods, the rabbi recommends once a week for ass drivers, every 30 days for camel drivers, and every six months for sailors.[16]

Certain sacred festivals, such as the New Year's celebration – the Day of Atonement – and particular fast days required temporary abstinence.[17] But vows of sexual abstinence were usually not allowed for a period beyond two weeks, preferably no more than one. Day laborers were allowed one week of abstinence while married pupils studying the sacred Torah could go without sex for 30 days.

Some Jews were making the argument based on their reading of Exodus 19.10–15 that vows of permanent abstinence were permissible, especially for devotees who were trying to cultivate mystical experiences. According to this tradition, God gave very specific instructions to Moses about how the Israelites should consecrate themselves in order to endure the sight of the Lord when he came down onto Mt. Sinai. The final instructions for them: "Do not go near a woman." With reference to this passage, some ancient interpreters said that Moses was justified against his wife's wishes to live as a permanent celibate because God spoke with him frequently in unscheduled visits. Since Moses did not know when he would be visiting with God, he had to live as a permanently consecrated man, even avoiding sexual contact with his wife.[18]

There is a group of mystically oriented Jews who lived near Alexandria, Egypt, in the first century who embodied the ideal of permanent celibacy. They are described in detail by Philo of Alexandria, a Jew who spent some time visiting them and writing a book about them called *On the Contemplative Life*. Philo knows them as the "Therapeutae," a designation meaning "those who serve the gods." His book is fascinating, describing a commune of Jewish men and women who created an environment that allowed them to devote themselves to a life of contemplation. Their goal was to free their souls to journey through the heavens and soar above the sun seeking a vision of God. In order to join the group, all properties had to be abandoned to their relatives and friends, and the devotees moved out to the commune positioned on Lake Mareotic. They lived separated by gender in small houses with sleeping quarters consisting of wooden plank beds covered with papyrus, an austerity Philo considers appropriate for their ascetic lifestyle. The men and women who lived there worked to be "self-controlled," by rededicating their lives to perpetual virginity. Why perpetual virginity? Philo tells us that they had dedicated themselves to this lifestyle "following the truly sacred instructions of the prophet Moses."[19] So it appears that a group of first-century Jews was mobilized to create a commune in Egypt to enact their interpretation of Exodus 19.10–15. In other words, there were Jews who were not only talking about the possibility of permanent celibacy, but practicing it too.

This same passage from Exodus came into play when the Jews speculated what life would be like in the age to come after this world passed away. Some argued that sexual intercourse would be utterly forbidden. If God prohibited intercourse for three days prior to his appearance on Mt. Sinai, they argued, in the time-to-come, when Israel will dwell continuously in God's presence, will not intercourse be entirely forbidden?[20] Because of this, we find that first-century Jews who were extremely apocalyptic in their orientation also allowed for permanent celibacy. This may partially explain the celibate discipline known in the community writings from the Dead Sea.

Did the Jews think that sex was a vice or a virtue? According to the ancient Jews, the continuation of our world depended on avoiding murder, sexual sin, and idolatry, the big three pollutions that they thought brought guilt upon the earth. Since the Jews had identified sexual morality as one of the pillars upholding the world, without sexual restrictions and accommodations, the very existence of creation was thought to be threatened by uncontrolled sexual desire. Even though God had commanded them to procreate, because sexual desire could lead to sinful thoughts and behaviors, sex, although not a sin unto itself, had to be controlled. This ambiguity led to the establishment of specific restrictions and limitations in order to thwart potential trouble. These restrictions included early marriage with routine intercourse, as well as allowance for very short temporary times of abstinence. For those groups that were mystically and apocalyptically inclined such as the Egyptian Therapeutae or the Dead Sea Jews more permanent degrees of sexual restraint and celibacy were permitted.

Sex according to Jesus

The recovery of Jesus' own view about sex is not without its complications.[21] The gospel narratives were written at least 40 years after Jesus had been executed and, when examined carefully, they show signs of editing and revision. They are not firsthand reports written by Jesus, or even necessarily Jesus' disciples or the first generation of Christians, although they may have incorporated within them versions of some earlier documents. The perspective of the gospel authors is retrospective. Their view is interpretative. They seek to remember and report about Jesus in very specific, sometimes even contradictory ways.

Most of what is written in the gospels is written based on memories of Jesus and interpretations of those memories, which had been passed along orally from person to person for decades. So at best, what we can recover about Jesus' opinion on sex is some of the earliest Christian memories of his teachings about it, memories that had already been filtered and interpreted by the very people who were passing on the memories verbally and, eventually, in writing. Nothing we remember is "raw" data. It is all refracted. That is to say, everything we remember must pass through our minds and receive from us meaning before we speak it or write it. So the best we can recover from the gospels about "sex according to Jesus" are early memory refractions about Jesus' teaching on the subject from those who wrote the gospels.

The earliest sources recall a Jesus, who like his fellow Jews, treated sexual desire with suspicion. Why? Because he believed that it could lead you to lust and sin. So, in the Gospel of Matthew, he makes a very strong case for self-control, even threatening those who fail to control their lust with terrible images of judgment.[22] He reinterprets the commandment from Torah, "You shall not commit adultery," to mean that men should not even lust after a woman because if you lust after her, you have already committed adultery with her in your heart. So what should you do? Jesus says, "If your right eye causes you to sin, pluck it out and throw it away. It is better that you lose one of the parts of your body than for your whole body to be thrown into Gehenna." The same is true of your hand. If it causes you to sin, cut it off, or suffer your whole body to the torments of hell.

Like many other Jews in the first century, Jesus was concerned to prevent breaking God's prohibition against adultery. So he identified sexual desire outside marriage as the culprit, and then demanded a stricter code of conduct among men to prevent lust from developing in the first place. So, he said, *men* had the responsibility to avert their eyes and keep their hands to themselves. Even though Jesus' admonition is similar to the proverb already cited from the Jewish Testament of Benjamin – "Whoever has a mind that is pure with love does not look upon on woman for the purpose of having sex with her" – it is still startling, especially given the more general ancient worldview that the locus of lust was the female body, which was the sexual downfall of men. Because of this she needed to veil herself, ensuring that she would not be the object of the gaze of a man other than her spouse, something we will explore further in the coming chapters when we take up the subject of Paul's position on women and veils and other related issues.

Given Jesus' concern to stop adultery even before it starts, it should not be surprising that Jesus was a strong advocate for marriage, and staying married. In the earliest version of the story found in the gospel of Mark where the Pharisees ask him his opinion about divorce, Jesus does not support divorce, considering it to be a human concession that Moses *permitted* rather than a divine prescription.[23] According to the story we find in Mark, the Pharisees ask Jesus if it is lawful for a man to divorce his wife. He asks them what Moses says. They reply that Moses allowed the man to write a divorce certificate which would legally separate him from his wife, referring to Deuteronomy 24.1 which states, "When a man takes a wife and marries her, if then she finds no favor in his eyes because he has found some indecency in her, and he writes her a bill of divorce and puts it in her hand and sends her out of his house, she departs from his house."

During Jesus' own time the discussion among the rabbis does not appear to have been whether or not divorce was allowed. Divorce was part of God's Law. Rather, the rabbis were arguing about what grounds a man could or could not use to divorce his wife. What constituted indecency? Rabbi Shammai was the most restrictive, saying that only a wife's infidelity was a serious enough cause for a man to justify divorcing her.[24] Rabbi Hillel felt differently, arguing that a man can divorce his wife for any cause, even if she burns his meal.[25] Rabbi Akiba added, "and even if he finds another woman more beautiful than she."[26] Philo of Alexandria and Josephus the first-century Jewish historian agree.[27]

So it must have come as something of a surprise to the Pharisees when Jesus replied that Moses wrote this commandment only to accommodate *men's* stubbornness. This particular law was understood by Jesus to be a late concession made by Moses to comply with men's desires. It did not reflect God's original intent for the married. Jesus appeals to the creation story (which occurred chronologically before the establishment of the Mosaic Law), suggesting that God's original intent for men and women was a form of marriage that made the two inseparably one. He quotes Genesis 2.24, "For this reason a man shall leave his father and mother and be joined to his wife, and the two shall become one flesh." Then he adds, "So they are no longer two but one flesh. What therefore God has coupled, let no man separate." He went on to teach that if a man or woman divorces and marries another, the new couple are engaging in adultery.

This teaching does not appear to have been modified to allow for a man to divorce his wife for infidelity until sometime after Paul wrote his first letter to the Corinthians where Paul refers to the Lord's teaching against divorce and Jesus' insistence that if it should happen, remarriage should not be undertaken unless it were to the original spouse.[28] It is the author of Matthew who passes on a modified version of this earlier teaching of Jesus, so that it is more complementary to Shammai's opinion. Thus Jesus says in Matthew's gospel, "Whoever divorces his wife, *except for infidelity*, and marries another, commits adultery."[29]

A women's advocate

Was Jesus aware of how easily the divorce law could be abused by husbands, leaving women particularly vulnerable to coercion within the marital relationship, and little in terms of good options for their future survival once divorced? If so, Jesus' rejection of divorce may have reflected an effort to improve the quality of women's lives during his time. Unquestionably, Jesus identified the cause of adultery with unchecked male lust and believed that divorce was a concession Moses had made to accommodate male stubbornness. It certainly is the case, too, that women were an active and powerful part of his mission. According to Luke, women like Mary Magdalene, Joanna the wife of Chuza who was Herod's steward, and Susanna were the patrons of Jesus' movement, financing the entire operation.[30] The authors of the gospels of Matthew and Mark agree, naming Mary Magdalene, Mary the mother of James and Joseph, Salome, and the mother of the sons of Zebedee among them.[31] In fact, women ranked among his learned disciples, some even leaving behind their traditional roles in the kitchen to listen to his teachings. To this end, there is a story in the gospel of Luke in which Jesus defends Mary of Bethany's right to study with him rather than serve the meal and do the dishes. He says to Martha, "Martha, Martha, you are anxious and troubled about a number of things. There is one thing, however, that must be. Mary has chosen the right share, a share which will not be robbed from her."[32]

Many stories preserved in the New Testament reveal that Jesus was remembered as a man genuinely concerned for women's issues.[33] For instance, in the gospel of Mark, Jesus is remembered as the one who was able to heal a woman who had been bleeding continually for 12 years.[34] During that time, she had been attended by many physicians, but had found no relief, only more suffering. These medical treatments had left her penniless. So she was now destitute and ill. What is more, she would have been living a nightmare in terms of human companionship. According to Jewish Law, a menstruating woman is in a state of cultic impurity.[35] Whoever she touches is made unclean. Everything she sits on or lies on is made unclean. Whoever touches her, or her chair, or her bedding is made unclean. Sexual intercourse with her was strictly forbidden and could – at least theoretically – result in the execution of the woman and her partner.[36] As described by Mark, her situation would have left her practically untouchable.

To make matters worse, in this unclean state, her relationship with Yahweh, the God of Israel, was in jeopardy. Since she was in a continual state of bleeding, she could not follow the Torah prescriptions to make herself clean each month, sacrificing the proper birds on the eighth day after the flow stopped in order to atone for her discharge and worship Yahweh at the Temple. She would have been utterly isolated from her family, her friends, and her God.

This destitute and isolated woman heard reports that Jesus was a healer so great that if she were to touch the hem of his garment, her menstruation would stop. So she seeks Jesus out in a crowd, and touches him. Here the story has a twist. Instead of making Jesus unclean as we might expect, the story reports that Jesus perceived a power going out of him when he was touched. When he wants to know who touched him, the woman falls down in front of him, fearing that she will be harshly dealt with for contaminating him. But instead Jesus responds by praising her for her faith and telling her to go on her way healed of her illness.

Jesus' concern for mercy and his call for repentance and a change of behavior is well known in the traditional literature. The prominent women's story in this regard is the story of the adulteress who was brought before Jesus for judgment. In our Bibles, we find this story in the gospel of John sandwiched between the end of Chapter 7 and the beginning of Chapter 8. The passage is problematic in that it has a difficult manuscript history, appearing in different locations in the old manuscripts of the gospels of Luke and John, or omitted altogether. It is a roaming story whose origin and context is dubious. Yet it is significant, I think, because it shows continuity in Jesus' characterization. Even as later traditions about Jesus developed, he was still being remembered as a women's advocate. According to this roaming story, when "a woman who had been caught in adultery" was brought before Jesus to be condemned and stoned according to Jewish Law, Jesus refuses to stone her. Instead, he acts mercifully toward her while maintaining the issue of fairness and equity that the law was intended to enforce, by telling the crowd present, "Let the man who is without sin from among you be the first to cast a stone at her." When they all leave without picking up a stone, Jesus speaks to the adulteress. He refuses to condemn her either. He simply advises her to go out and stop sinning, to live her life better aligned with God and his regulations.

In light of this moving story, I am reminded of another preserved in Matthew's gospel. Jesus asks the male priests and elders who is better: a son who refuses to work in the vineyard but changes his mind eventually and takes the pruners in hand, or a son who says he will do it but does not follow through. The male leaders reply, "The first son." Then Jesus responds with an unconventional saying that flips upside-down the traditional hierarchies in terms of gender, social rank, and cultic status: "Truly, I say to you, the tax collectors and *the prostitutes* enter the kingdom of God ahead of you."[37]

Mark relates a story in which Jesus highlights the plight of widows who must have been like many widows in his world – legally defenseless, emotionally exhausted, financially at risk. He publicly criticizes the scribes for their unethical handling of widows' properties. Pious men should not oversee the affairs of widows in order to use the estates for their personal profit. They should not "devour widows' houses," Jesus states.[38] Jesus further implies that these widows should be protected and treated with reverence and respect, calling attention to the destitute widow who tithed her penny to the Temple treasury. He uses her as an exemplar of God's faithful, for giving more than all the wealthy people who put in large sums. Why? "For rich all contributed out of their abundance," Jesus says, "while she out of her poverty has put in everything she had, her entire living."[39]

In another story highlighting the plight of widows, the Temple priests associated with the Sadducees assume that Jesus is a proponent of levirate marriage. They question him about a widow's fate as a resurrected woman if she has had a series of brothers as husbands. Whose wife would she be in heaven? The priests are setting Jesus up since they themselves did not believe in the resurrection of the body. In their questioning, they are hoping to show Jesus how absurd the concept of the resurrection actually is since it is illegal for a woman to be married to more than one husband at a time. They hope to trick him into agreeing with them. Since levirate marriage is permitted while multiple husbands are not, then there can be no resurrection, they reason. Their argument would only have a chance to work if they knew that Jesus were a proponent of levirate marriage.

Why would Jesus support a tradition that treats women as the property of particular families to be passed from one brother to the next in serial marriages until a son was born? The practice of levirate marriage among the Jews was based on their interpretation of Deuteronomy 25.5, which states that if a man dies without an heir, his widow is to marry one of his brothers. If they conceive, the child born is to be counted as the dead man's son. But Josephus, the Jewish historian who lived in the first century CE, tells us that one of the main reasons levirate marriage was practiced during his time was to alleviate the misfortunes of widows.[40] Yet, even though this practice safeguarded the widow financially by keeping her part of the family unit, it was not popularly practiced because it meant that the dead man's brother would lose part of his inheritance to the son he had engendered for his dead brother. This appears to be the issue underlying the scandalous fate of Tamar, widowed following the death of her husband Er, according to Genesis 38. For Jesus to support the practice shows him to be an advocate for the widow rather than the man who served to lose property in the transaction.

How did Jesus make out in the discussion with the Temple priests about levirate marriage? He won, not by arguing against levirate marriage, but by reasoning that marriage is a human institution not suitable for the age-to-come. In fact, Jesus thought that marriage would be dissolved at that time.[41] His reasoning had to do with the type of creatures he thought we would become. Since we would be resurrected glorified creatures, we would have immortal bodies like the angels that have no need to propagate. So, while we marry in the present age, in the age to come when we are resurrected, there would be no need for it. We will be immortal, equal to the angels. Marriage and sexual relations will be abandoned because procreation will no longer be requisite. This teaching hints at the fact that Jesus was not unlike his Jewish contemporaries who had restricted the sex act to marriage for the purposes of procreation.

Given his opinion on marriage, why would we also find among Jesus' sayings, a teaching which blesses barren women instead of fertile? This teaching is preserved in apocalyptic contexts in which Jesus is addressing the advanced state of the world. Since Jesus thought that the age of the world was very advanced, and the end so near that God's kingdom was already inbreaking, stories about him suggest that he questioned whether or not it was necessary to continue to procreate in the short interim before the new world fully appeared and sexual behavior was abandoned altogether. Thus we find, in these apocalyptic contexts, Jesus agreeing with the beatitude, "Blessed are the barren, and the wombs that never bore, and the breasts that never gave milk," and the woe, "Damned are those who are pregnant and who are nursing babies in those days!"[42] Marriage, sex and procreation were human propensities that sustained life in this world. When the world ended – either through death or apocalyptically – marriage, sex, and procreation would end too. We would join God's entourage of angels and sex would be no more.

The gospel writers remember Jesus as a teacher sensitive to the domestic and social problems that faced Jewish women in his world, problems including adultery, divorce, remarriage, and widowhood. He even was remembered as interacting with non-Jewish or Gentile women, healing the daughter of a Phoenician woman after initially refusing to do so. The woman cried out to him to have mercy on her

Digging in

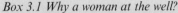

Box 3.1 Why a woman at the well?

The Via Latina catacomb was discovered in 1955 when construction work on a house in Rome uncovered a catacomb previously unknown to us. The catacomb had been looted in an earlier period, but beautiful paintings covering the interior walls remained. In a half-moon-shaped niche approximately six feet long and four feet high, one of the oldest visual representations of the Samaritan woman from the Gospel of John is painted. It was painted between the years 340–350 CE. A young beardless Jesus – a youthful Hermes – is shown in conversation with the Samaritan woman while she draws water from the well. This scene was popular, regularly found on early Christian funerary objects such as second- and third-century catacomb walls and fourth-century sarcophagi. Versions of this scene are found in the Chapel of the Sacraments at the catacomb of St. Calixtus, in the catacombs of Praetextatus and Domatilla. A version is found also in the Christian house-church of Dura Europos, which had an ancient baptistery with funerary motifs on its walls. The scene may have been popular in the funerary context because it reminded the viewer of Jesus' promise of eternal life for all who were baptized, regardless of gender or race.

For deeper digging, read Janeth Norfleete Day, *The Woman at the Well: Interpretation of John 4:1–42 in Retrospect and Prospect*, Biblical Interpretation Series 61 (Leiden: Brill 2002).

and her ill daughter. Jesus responded that he had only been sent to "the lost sheep of the house of Israel," that it would not be fair to "take the children's bread and throw it to the dogs." She persists with her request for mercy over equity, convincing him with her witty response to change his mind, "Yes, Lord, but even the dogs eat the crumbs that fall from their master's table." This interchange reveals a Jesus who is willing to alter his opinion based on the reasoning of a woman (and a non-Jewish woman at that!) who reminded him that mercy should sometimes trump equity.[43]

His interaction with non-Jewish women is also a highlight of the Johannine tradition. In the gospel of John, Jesus teaches a Samaritan woman who was drawing water at a well.[44] The case of the Samaritan woman is particularly noteworthy since Jesus speaks to her directly in public according, to the Johannine author, breaking with ancient etiquette standards that forbade a Jewish rabbi from talking publicly to a Jewish woman, let alone a Samaritan. She herself notes this as unusual behavior while the disciples regard it as scandalous.[45] Moreover, Jesus is not merely greeting her cordially. He is engaging her in a serious theological conversation and offers her the "water of life." Through this conversation, she comes to perceive Jesus as the messianic prophet expected to come at the end of days by the Samaritans. She returns to the village and teaches others what she has learned, and many of the villagers are converted because of her testimonial.[46] The cumulative evidence points to the fact that Jesus was being remembered as a man concerned for women's issues during his own time and place. His concern was not a fringe or marginal aspect of his mission. On the contrary, it was *central*.

CHAPTER 4

Did Paul silence women?

In Paul's correspondence to the Corinthian Christians, we find a rather startling passage in which women are admonished to keep quiet in the churches. Why? The passage reasons that they are not permitted to speak in the open assembly because they are subordinate to men, just as it is taught in the Jewish Law. They are told to ask their husbands their questions at home since it is shameful for women to speak in church.[1]

These words are misogynistic, yet they are considered to be divine prescriptions by many who read the Bible. Because of this, they have been used for centuries by church leaders to deny, and to continue to deny, women equal access to the pulpit. Yet, what happens if we read behind these words and pose the question, "What was going on in the early church that Paul (or someone else?) felt it necessary to write these words?" We might wonder, "Were they written by someone who wished to abolish the female leadership that existed in his own church? Were they penned by someone who did not approve of a practice at that time of women speaking to men as peers in the Christian assembly to which he belonged?"

In order to answer these questions, it is necessary to get a handle on Paul's view of gender and women's issues. His letters represent our earliest knowledge of the Christian community, and so they provide an invaluable window into the world of the mid-first century, revealing to us what some of the first Christians were thinking about sex and women.

The burgeoning of chastity

In 1 Corinthians, Paul responds to a letter he had received from the Corinthian community. From Paul's response, it is certain that the Corinthians in that letter had discussed their opinions about sex with him.[2] In fact, they appear to have thought that it was better not to have sex. This put the question of marriage – whether or not it was a sin – to the test.[3] Paul concedes to them that refraining from sex is good, writing, "Concerning the matters you wrote about – it is good for a man not to touch a woman."[4] Although we do not hear in Paul's response *why* the Corinthians thought they were better off if they refrained from sex, we do discover later in the letter that sexual abstinence was being practiced on the leadership level. The apostles and Jesus' brothers from Jerusalem who have visited the Corinthian community travel around with their "sister-wives."[5] The Greek is very explicit, using the word "sister" to qualify "wife." It appears to be used as a technical term for these women, likely indicating that the marriages of the apostolic leaders were chaste.[6] Paul himself declares to the Corinthian community the high regard he has for his own chastity, although he is a single man rather than married.[7]

Given this, you might think that Paul would have continued in his letter by insisting that all the Corinthians become chaste. But that is not what he says. Instead he writes:

> Because of sexual immorality, each man ought to have his own wife and each woman ought to have her own husband. The husband ought to give to the wife what is due, and likewise the wife ought to give to the husband what is due. The wife does not rule over her own body, rather the husband does. Likewise, the husband does not rule over his own body, rather the wife does. Do not refuse each other unless temporally by mutual agreement to spend time in prayer. But then come together again lest Satan tempt you through self-indulgence. I say this as an allowance, not as a commandment. I wish that all people were as I am.[8]

It is obvious that Paul's response is marked with the same ambivalence toward sex that Jesus and other Jews in the first century shared. Taking very seriously Jesus' cautions about the dangers of the roving eye, the first Christians (who were Jews) taught that the faithful must guard against sexual desire to avoid sinning.[9] The perfect person was defined as someone who could "bridle" the body, reining in the passions that were at war in the body.[10] When the body was bridled, the flesh would no longer be ruled by the passions, but the will of God instead.[11] The faithful are warned that God will punish "especially those who indulge in the lust of defiling passion."[12] They are admonished to "beware of lust for lust leads to fornication." Likewise they are told to "refrain from dirty language and the wandering eye, for these too can breed adultery."[13]

Similarly, Paul is concerned that uncontrolled sexual desire might lead to sin, so he limits sex and domesticates it. He encourages marriage in order to curb immoral thoughts and activities, to extinguish the burning fires of lust. Regular mutual lovemaking is suggested so that Satan will not tempt either of the partners to immorality because neither partner will have occasion to become indulgent through lack of self-control. Temporary abstinence is permitted for prayer. Paul, like Jesus, supports human marriage and marital sex as an acceptable way to curb sexual desire and, consequently, immoral behavior when the wandering eye would otherwise lead to adultery and sexual sins. He encourages the unmarried to marry since "it is better to marry than to burn with passion."[14] To the betrothed, he says, "if his passions are strong, and it has to be, let him do as he wishes – let them marry. It is not a sin."[15]

Yet, all this language is couched in another message, an opposite message, that it is better to be single and chaste, to choose permanent celibacy. Paul, however, makes it clear that this choice is only to be made if self-control can be exercised. If not, marriage should be undertaken.[16] Paul regards his recommendations about marriage to be "allowances" not "commandments." His real desire if for everyone to be able to be single as he is, if their bodies and passions are in check. Marriage is permitted, but refraining from marriage is better, as long as sexual desire has been firmly mastered.[17]

Why this double message? As in the teachings of Jesus, what creates this double bind is apocalyptic thinking. Paul, like Jesus, believed that the world was taking its last breath and the next inhale would be its final one. Since marriage and sex were human propensities that sustained the world, when the world ended, so would marriage and procreation. The angelic life was dawning. So Paul saw no reason for those faithful who were self-controlled to continue marriage in the meantime. In fact, he saw it as a nuisance that took away from the importance of God's mission during this urgent season.[18] The reason Paul gives for permanent chastity is apocalyptic, "in view of the present distress" as the world suffers its death throes.[19] The "appointed time has grown short," he argues. So "let those who have wives live as though they had none ... for the form of this world is passing away."[20]

What Paul is arguing appears to be in line with what we hear in other early Christian sources. If the believer truly has mastered the body and its sexual drive, and has no fear of falling into temptation, permanent chastity was encouraged even within marriage. This was done in anticipation of the end of the world when procreation would cease and the angelic life be enjoined. This "preferred" option seems to have been fostered particularly at the leadership levels of early Christianity since Paul claims this lifestyle for himself and mentions that the apostles, particularly Jesus' brothers and Peter, had "sister" relationships with their wives.[21]

Along this line of development, we find in Matthew a very notable secondary addition to Jesus' discussion with the Pharisees about divorce. The author of Matthew revised the version of the divorce story he received from Mark's gospel by adding to its end a dialogue between Jesus and his disciples. According to Matthew's revised story, when the disciples hear that divorce (except for infidelity) will not be permitted, they decide among themselves that "it is not to our advantage to marry." Matthew's version has Jesus agreeing with them, telling them that not everyone understands this situation. He goes on to say that among eunuchs are those who "have made themselves eunuchs for the sake of the kingdom of heaven."[22]

The eunuch, a castrated male, is used here to represent the ideal chaste man whose sexual desires have been severed from his body. In this version, Jesus encourages the disciples, "Whoever is able to practice this, ought to practice it."[23] It is clear that by the time Matthew was writing, permanent celibacy was an ideal that at least the leaders of the movement strove to embrace. And as far as practice is concerned, just over a century later, the great theologian and teacher Origen of Alexandria allegedly castrated himself in order to comply.

It is in this spirit of burgeoning chastity that the author of the gospel of Luke added "wife" to the list of relatives the faithful must leave behind to follow Jesus and "hate" to be his disciple. Neither Mark's nor Matthew's version of these saying has this qualification; and neither does *Thomas*'s.[24] "Wife" must be a recent Lukan addition to older sayings attributed to Jesus which did not include severing the spousal relationship as a condition for discipleship.

Luke 18.29: Honestly I am telling you, there is no man who has left house or *wife* or brothers or parents or children for the sake of the kingdom of God who will not receive manifold more in this time, and eternal life in the age to come.

Mark 10.29–30: Honestly I am telling you, there is no one who has left house or brothers or sisters or mother or father or children or lands for my sake and for the gospel who will not receive a hundredfold no in this time, houses and brothers and sisters and mothers and children and lands with persecutions, and eternal life in the age to come.

Matthew 19.29: And everyone who has left houses or brothers or sisters or father or mother or children or lands, for my name's sake, will receive a hundredfold, and inherit eternal life.

Luke 14.26–27: If anyone comes to me and does not hate his own father and mother and *wife* and children and brothers and sisters, yes, and even his own life, he cannot be my disciple.

Matthew 10.37–38: He who loves father or mother more than me is not worthy of me. And he who loves son or daughter more than me is not worthy of me. And he who does not take his cross and follow me is not worthy of me.

Gospel of Thomas 55: Whoever does not hate his father and mother cannot become a disciple of mine. And whoever does not hate is brothers and sisters and carry his cross as I do will not be worthy of me.

Gospel of Thomas 101: Whoever does not hate his [father] and his mother in the same manner as I do, he cannot be a [disciple] of mine. Also whoever does [not] love his [father and] his mother in the same manner as I do, he cannot be a [disciple] of mine. For my [birth] mother [gave death], while my true [mother] gave life to me.

The traditions preserved by Paul, Matthew, and Luke on the subject of sex and marriage have pushed the Jewish discussion about celibacy in an important developmental direction. Although a chaste lifestyle is still considered "optional," we see the literature begin to privilege it and give it more and more permanency. At the same time, marriage is being discussed not so much as a commandment from God to populate the earth, but as an allowance to keep lust from spawning sin.

Because Paul allows for marriage, he faces a series of related issues, which he tries to sort out. He knows Jesus' opinion that divorce should not be permitted and he upholds this as the ideal: "To the married I command – not me but the Lord – the wife ought not separate from her husband ... and the husband ought not divorce his wife."[25] However, he is practical and, knowing that separation and divorce occur, he qualifies Jesus' opinion with his own advice that a woman who separates from her husband should either remain single or return to the husband she left.[26] He continues to qualify Jesus' opinion with more practical advice. If a believer has a spouse who has not converted, the marriage should remain intact unless the unbeliever desires to separate. Then the believer is no longer bound to the marriage. He reasons that God's call to peace takes precedent over the Jesus' opinion not to divorce.[27] The only time he allows for second marriage is for women who are widowed, and then only to another Christian. But he prefers that she not marry again, but remain single.[28] He highly recommends that the unmarried stay that way.[29]

To veil or not to veil

Questions about the relationship between men and women are taken up again in Chapter 11 of 1 Corinthians. According to this chapter, there appears to have been a dispute in Corinth about women's headgear.

It had come to Paul's attention that women in the Corinthian church were praying without veils, while the men were wearing the requisite head covering. From Paul's reaction to this, it is clear that the issue for him was of major significance. It was not about decorum and fashion. It was about the relationship between genders, and how that relationship played out in terms of authority in Paul's churches.

Before we explore Paul's vigorous reaction to this situation, it is important for us to understand why the Corinthian women were praying without veils and what was at stake for them. Veiling adult women was a universal practice in the ancient Mediterranean world. It was part and parcel of Roman public life, and it was practiced by the Jews as well. Veils were worn by adult Jewish women in public to show their shame and modesty, as was believed to be proper for women who were good wives and not adulteresses.[30] To unveil was to invite sexual impropriety and even violence according to the ancient people. To unveil publically was a dishonor and a disgrace for women.[31]

Both Philo and Josephus tell us that a woman suspected of adultery would be unveiled at the temple during her trial, which consisted of forcing her to drink a draught containing the residue of a piece of papyrus with the name of God inscribed upon it. If she birthed a boy child within 10 months, she was exonerated. Otherwise, her belly swelled and she died convicted of her crime. The veil was removed by the priest during this trial, Philo reveals, because the woman's innocence was in question. She may be an adulteress and therefore should not be covered with the veil of modesty.[32]

It is noteworthy that the Greek term for "veil" is *krêdemnon*, a multivalent word that was also used to describe the "closed" uterus of a virgin. To "loosen" the *krêdemnon* connoted the deflowering of a virgin.[33] The veil provided a culturally acceptable way to curb sexual desire by establishing a physical barrier between the woman and the men she would meet in public. Tertullian of Carthage in the late second century described the veil as "a helmet" and "a shield" that protect the woman against "the blows of temptations, against the darts of scandals, against the suspicions and whispers and emulation, against envy itself."[34] Public exposure without a veil was comparable to the woman "suffering rape."[35] Tertullian admonishes women to "put on the panoply of modesty, surround yourself with the stockade of bashfulness, rear a rampart for your sex, which must neither allow your own eyes egress nor ingress to other people's."[36]

The female body had been identified by the men in power as the vulnerable link in the chain that sustained harmony in their society. Wearing the veil was demonstrative of the woman's modesty and her unwillingness to tempt men into licentious behavior and sexual sin. It was reasoned that the veil covered the woman so that when she went out in public, she would reduce the risk of becoming the object of the wandering male eye. While it was believed that the veil helped to protect her from adulterous liaisons and sexual assault, at the same time, it represented the woman's submission to male authority and to her "place" in the hierarchy of power. It displayed graphically that she was underneath the authority of her husband. This is why Paul himself calls the veil a woman's covering of "authority." This "authority on her head" is the authority of the man who, Paul reminds her, *is* her head just as Christ is the head of the man.

Women need to wear a veil on their heads, openly acknowledging their husbands' authority over them, Paul says, "because of the angels."[37] Paul's puzzling explanation here appears to have been such common knowledge to his readers that he did not need to explain himself further. More than likely, the angels that the veil protected the woman from were the fallen angels who raped women at the beginning of time according to Genesis 6. This story is retold in the literature, most prominently in *1 Enoch* 7, where women are taken by the fallen angels as their wives. They are raped by the fallen angels, become pregnant and bear giants. The fallen angels also teach the women magic, medicine, herbology, and cosmetics.

This story, among others, became the fodder for the very popular opinion among the ancient people that the fallen angels – that is, the demons – were quite capable and willing to commit sexual crimes with those who were not properly protected. Marriage was one of the ways in which that protection was afforded, as Paul suggests in his discussion of the veil, and as the author of the *Gospel of Philip* makes explicit in his discussion of the benefits of matrimony. In the *Gospel of Philip*, the author explains, "When the wanton women (demons) see a man sitting alone, they leap down on him and play with him and defile him. So also the lecherous male (demons), when they see a beautiful woman sitting alone, they persuade her and compel her, wishing to defile her. But if they see the man and his wife sitting beside one another, the female (demons) cannot come to the man, nor can the male (demons) come to the woman."[38] Paul effectively threatens the women of Corinth into submission by suggesting that they have left themselves open to angelic invasion and rape by male demons.

So the situation at Corinth was this: women in Corinth were not wearing their veils, at least while they were in church, a space which Paul understands to be a public place. Why? Paul tells us indirectly in his argument. He orders the women of Corinth to put their veils back on their heads because their veils represent the authority of their husbands. This is appropriate, he says, because "the head of every man is Christ" while "the head of every woman is man" and "the head of

Christ is God."[39] Paul turns to the Genesis story of creation in order to explain and justify this hierarchy. He states that man did not derive from woman according to scripture, but woman came out of man. The reference he is making is to the Adam and Eve story, when Eve was taken from Adam's side. He further justifies the male hierarchy as divinely sanctioned by explaining that the scripture says Eve was created for Adam, not Adam for Eve.[40] He pushes his interpretation by claiming that the derivation of woman from man and her creation for man means that man is the image and glory of God, while woman is the glory of man.[41]

Digging in

Box 4.1 A woman leader?

In the Priscilla catacomb in Rome, a funerary niche is decorated with a third-century fresco depicting three portraits. On the right, a woman is seated with a baby in her arms. On the left, a woman is standing in between two male figures. She is holding a scroll in her hands. The man seated on her left has a curly gray beard. He rests his hand lightly on her shoulder. The young man behind her right shoulder holds a piece of fabric. The focus of the fresco is the central portrait of the veiled woman, arms outstretched in a prayer position, with her eyes turned heavenward. One common interpretation of the right fresco demands us to see the mother figure as the Virgin with her Child. This symbolizes virginity. This allows the left scene to be interpreted as the deceased woman's ceremony to become a consecrated virgin when she was veiled and entered the church's order of virgins. The central image shows her as a consecrated virgin in prayer. But I wonder about this. Is it not more logical to read all the portraits as vignettes in the life of the deceased woman so that it is she that is being shown seated with the baby in her lap, not the Virgin? There is a striking resemblance between the three women in the vignettes. Another common reading of the portraits understands the left scene to represent the woman's wedding. The seated bishop gives his blessing and the youth presents her with the veil. She holds in her hand the document, which details her matrimonial duties. To the right, she is seated as a mother with her child. The trouble with this interpretation is that it would make for an odd wedding scene. Where is the groom? This has led some critics to posit that the scene on the left depicts the deceased's catechismal instruction before her baptism. If this be the case, then the deceased is being shown holding the scripture she is learning in preparation for baptism. This means that she wanted to be remembered as a person who could read and was trained in the scriptures. Does the central portrait then show this learned woman praying in the church, while the right as a mother as Denzey contemplates (2007: 85)? Or perhaps the vignette on the left shows an ordination ceremony and the center, her vocation as a church leader as Irvin argues?

For deeper digging, read Nicola Denzey, *The Bone Gatherers: The Lost Worlds of Early Christian Women* (Boston: Beacon, 2007); Dorothy Irvin, "Archeology supports women's ordination," *The Witness* 63 (1980): 4–8.

This suggests that Paul was reading Genesis 1.27 as a two-part sequence, that God created man in his own image first and then he created the female not in God's image:

> God created man in his own image, in the image of God he created him; male and female he created them.[42]

This interpretation tells us something very significant about Paul's view of women. He embraces a radically patriarchal interpretation of this verse, an interpretation he uses to subordinate the women in Corinth. As I will describe in detail in the next two chapters, this patriarchal interpretation was not the only way in which the early Christians were understanding Genesis 1.27. Neither was Paul's patriarchal interpretation the oldest Christian interpretation of Genesis 1.27. The other competing interpretations depended on reading Genesis 1.27 as a reference to the original "man" as an androgynous (neither male nor female) or a hermaphrodite (both male and female) creature formed in God's image. It can make a big difference in a church community if you understand Genesis 1.27 to say that the male is God's image while the female is derivative or if you think it means that God's image is neither male nor female but some kind of androgynous or hermaphrodite creature that encompasses both genders. The patriarchal interpretation is exclusive and can be used, as Paul does here, to give males the divine prerogative to dominate females. The androgynous interpretation is inclusive, leveling the male hierarchy.

Paul is not ignorant of these other competing interpretations. In fact, he makes a bold reference to the androgynous interpretation in his letter to the Galatians when he quotes the early Christian baptismal prayer used in his churches, "There is neither male nor female; for you are all one in Christ Jesus."[43] He even concedes to the women at Corinth that "in the Lord" men and women are interdependent. But what he means by this appears to be very different from what the Corinthian women thought it meant. Paul understands this gender interdependence to mean that male superiority yields to gender interdependence *only in the spiritual experience* of the converted Christians, not in the social reality of the church. It is revealing that Paul makes this argument in the case of gender in order to preserve the male social hierarchy, while making the opposite argument otherwise in his letters, admonishing his followers to live the gospel and allow the spirit of Christ to transform them so that they no longer belong or conform to the world but live their lives as those indwelt with the Christ spirit.[44]

From Paul's argument about veiling, we can gather that the women in Corinth had removed their veils (at least while worshiping) in order to align their social lives with their spiritual experience. They had mobilized their church by making their spiritual experience a social reality. Following the logic of Galatians 3.28 – "There is neither male nor female; for you are all one in Christ Jesus." – they believed that they had been recreated in the androgynous image of God as the result of their baptism with his Spirit. As such, the strict gender hierarchy of their immediate world had been abolished for them. Freed from its constraints, they tore off their veils, toppling the male hierarchy and dismissing the now illegitimate authority of their husbands. This is an astonishing action for them to have undertaken, since it would have marked them to other Jews and Romans as licentious women, even adulteresses, a point which Paul takes great strides to press home. In the end, Paul admonishes them to reveil and resubmit themselves to the social hierarchy of the ancient world, which he said complied with the natural hierarchy of God's created order.

Did the Corinthian women comply? Another letter written at the end of the first century by Bishop Clement of Rome to the Corinthian community contains some clues. The occasion for his letter was a revolt in the Corinthian community against its elders and leaders, some of which they had fired. At the time, leadership positions appear to have been appointed by a person of prominence in the church with the consent of the church. If the church became unhappy with the leader, the leader could be ousted, as was done at Corinth. Clement complains bitterly about this procedure (was he worried about his own job security in Rome?), arguing that a church should not be able to fire a leader. Why? Because the appointment had been made by an accredited person whose own authority, Clement claims, could be traced back to the Apostles themselves.

In his opening remarks, Clement applauds the management of the Corinthian church under the ousted leaders whom he calls the "presbyters." Under their leadership, the young men were counseled to be respectful and moderate, and the women "were given strict orders to do all things with a blameless, respectful and pure conscience, dutifully showing all the proper affection to their husbands; they were taught to live under the rule of submission, to manage their households respect-fully, being discrete in every way."[45] Later he remarks that, under the new leadership, husbands and wives have become estranged from one another, chastity is being bragged about, and the women have gotten out of hand.[46] "Let us set our wives," Clement writes, "on the straight path that leads to the good." They must be taught to be pure and worthy of love. They need to be willing to display genuine sincerity in their submissiveness. And they need to prove their moderation in speech. He uses Rahab (the harlot!) as an example of a woman who could be both a prophet and a faithful hospitable servant.

So was Paul successful suppressing the unveiled women at Corinth? Not if Clement is telling us the truth.

Vanishing women

Who were these brave women praying in the church, and why did they act with such assuredness and authority to have removed their veils? There are a number of references to women in Paul's letters and other early Christian literature, which suggest to us that women were not silent subordinate creatures in the first churches, but part of the active leadership of the nascent communities. For instance, Paul mentions (single?) women who worked as missionaries with him, acknowledging

Euodia and Syntyche as women co-workers, who labored side by side with Paul and Clement teaching others about the gospel.[47] In his letter to the Roman congregation, he greets Tryphaena and Tryphosa as women who have "labored hard in the Lord."[48]

I have already mentioned that the apostles and brothers of Jesus traveled around with their wives as missionary couples according to Paul. This must have provided a model for married couples who wished to serve as missionaries. We hear about one such missionary couple, Priscilla and Aquila, who traveled from Rome to Greece and Asia Minor, also working with Paul. Paul tells us that they also maintained a church in their home.[49]

In his letters to the Romans, Paul mentions as well Andronicus and Junia, a missionary couple described by Paul as "distinguished among the apostles," having converted to the faith prior to him.[50] It is very unfortunate that the name Junia has a history of being misidentified in our Bibles as Junias, a male, even though the manuscript evidence suggests that the earliest traditions knew this apostle as a woman, and that the male form of the name did not exist in antiquity. In other words, the masculine form, Junias was not used as a name. It does not show up anywhere in ancient Greek literature.[51] So the text from Romans reads incorrectly in most Bible translations something like this:

> Greet Andronicus and Junias, my kinsmen and my fellow prisoners. They are men of note among the apostles, and they were in Christ before me.

The manuscript tradition, however, suggests that it should be translated along these lines:

> Greet Andronicus and Junia, my compatriots and fellow prisoners. They are distinguished among the apostles, and they were in Christ before me.

The problem with the name Junia(s) is that the gender is only known by the way in which the name was accented in Greek. This means that manuscripts that are written in capital letters and unaccented are ambiguous. When manuscripts began to be copied in small letters and accented during the Middle Ages, the feminine form of the name is found in almost all of the first Greek critical editions of the New Testament starting with Erasmus' edition in 1516. This is true until 1928 when Nestle chose to print the masculine form in his critical edition without explanation. Since his edition of the Greek New Testament forms the basis for nearly all modern English translations of the Bible, the masculine reference has dominated the contemporary Christian tradition. This was changed in 1998, when the Nestle-Aland critical edition of the New Testament printed the female form of the name, removing the male version due to the overwhelming weight of the manuscript evidence favoring the feminine form. It appears that Junia and Andronicus, like Priscilla and Aquila mentioned a few verses earlier in Romans, formed a missionary team among the apostles, a team who came to know Paul in their journeys from church to church.

Paul's correspondences preserve direct firsthand evidence that women were functioning as frontline leaders – as apostles and missionaries – not only during Paul's time, but also at a time before Paul even showed up on the scene.[52] The role of "apostle," which is Paul's own self-identification as a missionary, was a prescribed title and position in the early church.[53] Paul considers it to be the highest level of authority in the church.[54] And it is a position that women in the early movement like Junia occupied.

Paul greets another female co-worker by the name of Phoebe in his letter to the Romans. He calls her the *prostatis* and a *diakonos* of the church at Cenchreae. What is the meaning of *prostatis*, the feminine form of the Greek word *prostatês*? *Prostatês* has a long history in Greek literature, meaning literally, "the one who stands before." Its most general use is to indicate the president, ruler, chief, leader or patron of a group. It appears that this is the way in which the word was being understood among the early Christians, as a title for the leader of the church community. In the earliest piece of Christian literature we possess, Paul uses the verbal cognate *proistamenous*, "those who are leading," in the first letter to the Thessalonians in which he admonishes the congregation to respect their leaders, the *proistamenous*, who are "over" them.[55] The same verbal cognate is used in 1 Timothy, written around 135 CE, to describe the church leadership roles of the elders or presbyters.[56]

There is no historical reason, or linguistic or archaeological evidence, for us to think that the word has any meaning other than this when applied to a woman in the early Christian literature. Unfortunately, English translations have not usually rendered her title properly, and have instead chosen to translate *prostatis* as "helper." Where does this come from? It is difficult to say for certain, but we can trace the problem back as far as the Latin translation of the Bible. When Jerome translated the Greek manuscripts into Latin, creating the Vulgate Bible, he chose to translate *prostatis*, "to stand before" with the Latin *adstitit*, "to stand near." Was Jerome uncomfortable with the leadership implications of the word since, in his time, women had been removed from the leadership level of churches? Did he intentionally fudge his translation to shift the meaning from "leader" to "helper" or did he make an honest mistake? Jerome's adjustment does not appear to be singular. In two late ninth-century Greek manuscripts of the Bible, the scribes who copied this verse made their own slight adjustments to *prostatis*, writing in its place *parastatis*, "to stand beside" as a comrade in arms would stand in his ranks.[57] Were these men influenced by their knowledge of Jerome's Latin translation, which they would have known by heart? Or were they making minor adjustments independently, since they would have been certain that women would not have been leaders in the early church given the fact that they were not leaders during their own time?

According to Paul's letters, many women led the first Christian congregrations. Chloe leads a group of early Christians in Corinth and sends reports to Paul about church activities in Corinth.[58] In Philemon 2, Paul begins his letter by greeting the three leaders of the church that was meeting in Philemon's home. One of the three church leaders named is the woman Apphia. Similarly Paul greets the woman Nympha who led the church congregation that met in her home.[59] From other New Testament literature, we hear about church meetings held in the house of Mary the mother of John Mark and the conversion of Lydia and her entire household in Philippi.[60]

Phoebe is also called by Paul a minister or deacon (*diakonos*).[61] It is important to note that *diakonos* is often translated "deaconess" in Bibles, but the word has not been feminized in the Greek. In Greek, the masculine *diakonos* is preserved, suggesting that "deacon" was an important and specific church title given to her, although we are unclear about what her function would have been since the duties of deacons in this period are not well understood.[62] There is evidence from other literature that women were appointed as deacons in the early churches. Pliny the Roman governor of the provenance Bithynia wrote a letter to the emperor Trajan who reigned from 98 to 117 CE. He specifically tells Trajan that there were two female slaves who were called "ministers" in the Bithynia congregation.[63] Since the Latin expression *ministrae* is synonymous with deacon, it is likely that these women were functioning in a capacity similar to Phoebe. Clearly these two women played a significant role in the life of the congregation, since Pliny felt them important enough to arrest and torture for information about the congregation, and makes note of their title in his letter to the emperor. He wanted Trajan to know that he arrested the leaders of the group, who in this case were two women, and had successfully suppressed the movement in his province.

The other pieces of evidence are archaeological. One is an inscription on a fourth- century stele found on the Mount of Olives in Jerusalem. It reads, "Sophia, Deacon, the second Phoebe."[64] What is most fascinating is that the word "deacon" is not feminized in the Greek. The masculine *diakonos* is preserved and applied to a woman, just as it is in Romans 16.2, where it is used to describe Phoebe. The woman Sophia is being recognized as a deacon of her congregation, so respected that she is memorialized in stone as the "second Phoebe." Another fourth-century inscription on a tombstone recognizes Maria as a deacon, also using the masculine *diakonos* as her title.[65]

These roles may have been original to the Jesus movement itself, since Luke reports that Mary Magdalene, Joanna wife of Chuza Herod's steward, Susanna, and "many other women" provided for the movement *out of their financial resources*, a subtle point lost in English translation but conveyed by the choice of the Greek word *hyparchô*, which means that they provided for Jesus and his mission out of their own possessions or belongings. Their roles are further described as "ministering" (*diakoneô*) to the community. The word *diakoneô* becomes *diakonos* or "deacon" when it forms a noun. Mark and Matthew provide us with the same evidence, describing the women at the cross (among whom were Mary Magdalene, Mary the mother of James and Joseph, and the mother of the sons of Zebedee) as faithful "followers" who "ministered" (*diakoneô*) to Jesus.[66] It is likely that these women were leaders and "deacons" in the original Jesus movement, roles which appear to have been associated with a patronage that financed Jesus' entire operation. Given this evidence, it may be accurately reported in Acts that women community "leaders" and those of "high standing" in Greek society were converting and supporting the churches.[67]

Although it is likely that some of the Corinthian women were filling roles of apostle, patron, and deacon, what we hear from Paul about the specific activities of the unveiled women of Corinth is very significant. He tells us that like the men, the women were praying and prophesying in church.[68] "Prophet" was a designation for another type of church leader, one that Paul ranks as second in the hierarchal structure of the churches, just below that of the apostle.[69] In Acts, we hear about a house-church in Caesarea led by Philip the gospel preacher and his four unmarried daughters who were early Christian prophets.[70] While Paul visited them, Agabus, a male prophet, journeyed from the Jerusalem church to Philip's. There he gave Paul a prophecy.[71] This same prophet earlier had journeyed from Jerusalem to Antioch where he prophesied about a worldwide famine, which the author of Acts claims occurred in the reign of Claudius.[72] The names of other prophets are also preserved in Acts.[73]

The charismatic role appears to have been warranted by the Christians and open to women on the basis of their reference to Joel

Digging in

Box 4.2 A female bishop?

In the Church of St Praxedis in Rome, there is a controversial mosaic of a ninth-century *Episcopa* (the feminine form of the word *bishop*). The portrait depicts a woman *Theodo(ra)*, with a square halo, indicating that the woman who was being honored was alive when the mosaic was created. Even though the Pope's mother died the year this chapel was dedicated, some scholars think that the inscription refers to Theodora, Pope Paschal's mother. There is a second inscription that mentions *Theodora episcopa* on the dedicatory column outside the Chapel. According to this inscription, Pope Paschal I built the chapel to house the relics of his mother Theodora. So, these critics think that it is her image and name that adorn the wall to the left of the women saints Praxedes and Pudentiana and Jesus' mother Mary. Was *Episcopa* on honorific title given to her because her son was the Bishop of Rome as Goodson thinks? There is evidence that wives of clergy were allowed to use the feminine form of their husbands' titles. Is this mosaic evidence of a mother doing so too? Or did the inscription refer to a different earlier Theodo(ra) who was a female leader associated with the original Church of Praxedis as other critics argue? There is external evidence that a certain Theodora of Alexandria brought relics of the saints with her when she traveled to Rome. She was devoted to Saint Praxedis and the relics eventually ended up in the Church during the time of Pope Innocent I, 402–417 CE (Morris 1973: 5–6). Irvin does not think that the mosaic is a depiction of the Pope's mother since the decorative coif she wears is indicative of the dress of unmarried women. Did the mosaic represent a female bishop, Theodora, who is depicted alongside the Virgin Mary and two women patrons who had build the original church structure? Whatever her historical identity, there is something disturbing about this mosaic. First, examinations of the mosaic have shown that there are a few modern mosaic cubes put under "Theodo" where the –ra had been eliminated earlier (Morris 1973: 5). According to Torjesen, across the glass tiles that form the letter "-a" on the end of "Episcopa," there are significant scratches. She has concluded from this that "attempts were made to deface the feminine ending" (1993: 10). If this is the case, the feminine form of the words must have evoked in onlookers enough angst to cause them to attempt to deface the inscription perhaps on more than one occasion.

For deeper digging, read Caroline J. Goodson, *The Rome of Pope Paschal I* (Cambridge: Cambridge University, 2010); Dorothy Irvin, "The ministry of women in the early Church: archaeological evidence," *Duke Divinity School Review* 45 (1980): 76–86; Joan Morris, *The Lady was Bishop* (New York: Macmillan, 1973); Karen Jo Torjesen, *When Women Were Priests: Women's Leadership in the Early Church and the Scandal of their Subordination in the Rise of Christianity* (San Francisco: Harper, 1993).

2.28–32. Consequentially, they expected ecstatic utterances from the "sons *and daughters*" in the last days:[74]

> And in the last days it shall be, God declares,
> that I will pour my spirit upon all flesh,
> and your sons and daughters shall prophesy,
> and your young men shall see visions,
> and your old men shall dream dreams.
> Yes! On my men and women servants in those days,
> I will pour out my spirit and they shall prophesy.
>
> And I will show wonders in heaven above
> and signs on earth beneath,
> blood, and fire, and smoke vapors.
> The sun shall be turned into darkness,
> and the moon into blood,
> before the day of the Lord comes,
> the great and manifest day.
> And it shall be that whoever calls on the NAME of the Lord shall
> be saved.

Since the charismatic role was possessory – a spirit possessed them and foretold the future through them – one could never be completely sure that a good spirit would inhabit the possessed. Paul may have thought that unveiled women prophets in the church were particularly vulnerable to demonic invasion and sexual assault by the fallen angels. By unveiling, they had left themselves in a vulnerable position and, he thought, the evil spirits would take advantage of this. At any rate, Paul does not insist that the women cease praying and prophesying, only that they do so veiled.

Later in Chapter 14 of his letter, Paul highly praises the gift of the prophet, even more so than the ecstatic tongue-speaker whose words must be interpreted by someone else for the members of the church to be able to understand the message.[75] Paul delivers specific instructions for the tongue-speakers and prophets in this chapter. It is in this context that we read the thundering words found in 14.33b–36:

> As (is customary) in all the churches of the saints, the women should keep silence in the churches. For they are not permitted to speak, but should be subordinate, as even the law says. If there is anything they desire to know, let them ask their husbands at home. For it is shameful for a woman to speak in church. Or was it from you that the word of God first went forth, or to you alone that it came?

Digging in

Box 4.3 A female-led eucharist?

In the Priscilla catacomb in Rome, we find an extremely controversial third-century fresco of seven figures seated at a meal. The one on the left is serving or officiating. What kind of meal are they celebrating? It is a heavenly banquet or a eucharist meal shared  among Christians? There are seven baskets of bread to the right and left of the table (not pictured here), which is reminiscent of the miracle of the loaves and fishes, a eucharistic symbol in the early church. Additionally a full meal is not being observed because there is no other food on the table. This had led most critics to think that a eucharist meal is being served. Are the seated figures men or women? It was interpreted by the original excavators as a eucharist meal celebrated by six men and one woman (the veiled figure third from the right). Some later interpreters have not been so convinced. Torjesen says that "the clothing and hairstyles worn by the participants suggests that most of them are women" including the officiating figure breaking the bread on the left (1993: 52). Irvin agrees, noting that one has a veil, while all are characterized by upswept hair, slender necks with sloping shoulders, and hints of earrings. The figure on the far left is clearly a woman since the length of her robe is that of a woman's long hemline common in this period (1980: 81–84). Denzey notes that the figures are not reclining as males did on special benches, but are seated upright as women did (2007: 98). The question of the gender of the diners remains fiercely debated today because there is so much dependent on our expectations and our conclusions.

For deeper digging, read Dorothy Irvin, "The ministry of women in the early Church: archaeological evidence," *Duke Divinity School Review* 45 (1980): 76–86; Karen Jo Torjesen, *When Women Were Priests: Women's Leadership in the Early Church and the Scandal of their Subordination in the Rise of Christianity* (San Francisco: Harper, 1993); Nicola Denzey, *The Bone Gatherers: The Lost Worlds of Early Christian Women* (Boston: Beacon, 2007).

Although it is clear from Paul's writings that he was one to maintain the patriarchal hierarchy as divine prerogative, there are serious questions about whether or not this passage was actually penned by Paul. In the first place, this passage blatantly contradicts Chapter 11 where the vocal participation of women in the churches as prophets is assumed and allowed to continue by Paul. Although the women are charged by Paul to veil, they are not charged to cease prophesying in church or stop praying aloud.

Second, in terms of literary flow and content, this passage reads as an interpolation, violently disrupting Paul's reasoning and argument. In other words, the verses immediately preceding 14.33b link to 14.37–40, not the thundering passage silencing women. When we remove verses 37–40, the original narrative flow of the passage is restored:

> Let two or three prophets speak, and let the others weigh what is said. If a revelation is made to another sitting by, let the first be quiet. For you can all prophesy one by one, so that all may learn and be encouraged. The spirits of the prophets are subject to the prophets. For God is not a God of confusion but of peace. [Verses 37-40 removed.] If anyone thinks that he is a prophet, or spiritual, he should acknowledge that what I am writing to you is a command of the Lord. If any one does not recognize this, he is not recognized. So, my brethren, earnestly desire to prophesy, and do not forbid speaking in tongues. But let all these things be done decently and orderly.

Third, the manuscript evidence suggests that the placement of this passage was uncertain in the early tradition. There are a number of old manuscripts that include these verses after verse 40 rather than between verses 33a and 37 as our Bible translations read today. In one manuscript that has the passage following verse 40, the passage is also copied in the margin of the manuscript at verse 33, thus preserving it twice, as if once were not enough![76] The scribal tendency to copy this passage in different textual locations suggests that the scribes were uncertain about its placement. Why were they uncertain about its placement? It is not uncommon in the New Testament manuscript tradition to find comments of the scribes and later readers written in the margins of the manuscripts as their own ruminations about whatever it was they were copying. It was the general practice of later scribes, when copying the manuscript that contained the marginal comment, to incorporate the comment into the main text of whatever they were copying, especially if they were uncertain about the origin of the gloss. In this way, glosses were incorporated into different spots in the copied texts, one scribe incorporating it in one place while another scribe in another place as each copied the glossed manuscript or manuscripts related to the glossed one.

It is very likely that the passage in question silencing women in the churches originated from the pen of a scribe commenting on Paul, rather from Paul himself. The words, in fact, appear to support the type of Christianity that grew up in the Apostolic churches in the second century as evidenced by the later Pastoral letters – 1 and 2 Timothy, and Titus – which, as we will see later in this book, severely censored and subordinated women in the church, removing them from their positions as apostles, prophets and deacons. Like Paul, this subordination was done by making theological arguments based on patriarchal interpretations of the Adam and Eve story.

The evidence from Paul himself, however, suggests that in the first 30 years of the movement women were not restricted in the leadership roles they could assume. They were functioning in a range of offices as apostles or missionaries, prophets, church leaders, deacons, and patrons. Some even knew an interpretation of Genesis 1.27 that allowed them to "equalize" the male hierarchy enough that they had removed their veils. They believed that, in baptism, they had been recreated in God's androgynous image, and this mobilized them to create a church environment in which there was "neither male nor female." Paul converts and finds himself in this environment of male and female co-workers and peers. Paul personally has concerns about the social, cultural, and political implications of women's actions in the church. Although he says nothing to restrict their offices, he appears to have felt that the women had overstepped their social and cultural bounds and disrupted the conventional male hierarchy that underpinned his society. They were acting as licentious women in his society, women whose unveiled bodies would draw men into sexual sin. So he trots out a patriarchal interpretation of Genesis 1.27 which severs the female from ever becoming God's image, and threatens the women with the phalli of the angels, who might rape them for their wantonness.[77]

CHAPTER 5

Is marriage a sin?

The Corinthian women whom Paul knew had begun to transform their lives in such a way that they were living out the early Christian baptismal prayer preserved in Galatians, "In Christ there is neither male nor female." They had mobilized their theology socially, stripping off their veils to show themselves recreated in God's image, which they thought was androgynous, "neither male nor female."

The basis for this baptismal prayer and for the women's interpretation of it was a particular way that some of the early Christians were reading Genesis 1.27. The verse invites the envisioning of the human being as an androgynous or hermaphrodite primal Image of God since the verse can be read to suggest that the singular "him" is composed of the two sexes "them."

> So God created man (Hebrew: *adam*) in his own image, in the image
> of God he created *him*; male and female he created *them*.

In fact, the ancient rabbis, like the early Christians, argued on the basis of this scripture that Adam, before Eve was removed from his side, was androgynous or hermaphrodite.[1] Rabbi Samuel ben Nahman thought that when God created the first human being, he gave him two faces, a male face and a female face, that were connected back to back. The two were sawed down the centerline and separated so they could turn around and face one another.

This type of interpretation of Genesis 1.27 can have profound implications for social behavior. If the ideal that the individuals in your church community are striving to embody is an androgynous or hermaphrodite creature, what does this suggest about males and females in your community? If the original condition of the human being is understood to be a condition that was an amalgamation of male and female, how was sex even possible for the original human being? If sex was not around before the Fall, when and why did it come into existence? And what might all of this mean for matrimony?

Rereading Genesis

The Corinthians to whom Paul wrote had opinions on these subjects, opinions we can reconstruct based on Paul's reaction to them. Paul agrees with the Corinthians that it is better not to touch a woman, but he allows for marriage because "it is no sin!" He also reinterprets Genesis 1.27 in light of the second chapter of Genesis, so that "man" is created in God's image, while the female is created afterwards, not in God's image but for the glory of man. Based on this reaction to the Corinthians, it is plain that the Corinthians themselves were abstaining from sex, were entertaining the possibility that marriage was a sin, and were allowing unveiled women to pray and prophesy in their church. They must have read Genesis 1.27 to mean that the image of God is androgynous.

The Corinthians were fostering an extremely early form of a movement that developed within individual church communities and then swept through the ancient church, a movement known as "encratism." This movement does not represent a specific group or sect of ancient Christians, but a lifestyle that various groups chose to adopt. The word comes from the Greek, *enkrateia*, which means "self-controlled." This was a lifestyle of exaggerated asceticism, beyond what we traditionally might attribute to Catholic and Orthodox monks and nuns. Encratism is a lifestyle where sexual abstinence is not the preferred option, but a requirement. Marriage is not permitted for anyone in the community because it is considered to be sinful. Singlehood and celibacy are its chief characteristics, although abstinence from certain foods and wine was also typical.

Unfortunately, in the past, encratic Christianity was identified with Gnostic Christianity because it was thought that "the" Gnostics were the ones who degraded the world and spurned marriage. This opinion has been discarded now that study of the Nag Hammadi texts has revealed that not all Gnostics spurned marriage. In fact, we will meet pro-marriage Gnostics in the next chapter. Further, more nuanced analysis of the early Christian literature has shown that a number of different Christian communities in different locations engaged in encratic behaviors for different reasons.

The Corinthian community appears to have continued to foster encratism among its members even after Paul's attempt to curb it. At the end of the first century, Clement of Rome admonishes some of the Corinthians to stop bragging about their physical chastity because their ability to be self-controlled (*enkrateia*) is not from their own initiative but is something that God gave to them.[2] He further remarks that discord has spread between husband and wife, and wives needed to be taught subordination again, and this time genuinely mean it![3]

The Corinthians in Greece were not alone. The author of the letter to the Colossians (whether Paul or not) is writing to a group of Christians in Asia Minor in the mid- to late first century. He complains that the Colossians have taken up encratic behaviors, behaviors that he personally condemns. He says that the Colossians promote piety and devotion through a false humbling of the body and severity of discipline, a lifestyle they need to stop.[4] It is fascinating that the author of this letter also commands the Colossian wives to submit to their husbands, making me suspect that the Colossian women may have been viewed as peers to the men within the baptized community.[5]

Not surprisingly, the author of Colossians refers to the baptismal prayer preserved in Galatians, "For as many of you as were baptized into Christ have put on Christ. There is neither Jew nor Greek, there is neither slave nor free, there is neither male nor female. For you are all one in Christ Jesus."[6] But when he refers to this prayer, the author of Colossians leaves out the reference to "neither male nor female." Instead, he writes that everyone in the community should put on the new nature reflecting the image of God, so that there is neither Greek nor Jew, circumcised or uncircumcised, barbarian or Scythian, slave or free, but Christ all in all.[7] The new nature that this author recommends is intentionally devoid of gender so that the renewal of God's image within the Christian community at Colossae cannot be regarded as the recreation of the androgynous ideal where men and women could function as peers who had transformed the traditional social and cultural hierarchy.

In the late first and early second centuries, we can track the establishment and growth of a prominent encratic community in the environs of ancient Edessa, the birthplace of the *Gospel of Thomas*. The community of Christians who wrote and used the *Gospel of Thomas* are typical of Christians in eastern Syria who had developed an understanding of their world based on an interpretation of the Genesis story quite cogent with the one developed in Corinth and Colossae. In this literature, we hear described the primal condition of the human being in terms of androgyny – "neither male nor female" – as we have in the beginning of the *Gospel of Thomas*:

> Jesus saw little babies nursing. He said to his disciples, "These little ones nursing are like those who enter the Kingdom." They said to him, "Will we enter the Kingdom as little babies?" Jesus said to them, "When you make the two one, and when you make the inside like the outside, and the outside like the inside, and the above like the below. And when you make the male and the female into a single being, with the result that the male is not male nor the female female. When you make eyes in place of an eye, and a hand in place of a hand, and a

foot in place of a foot, and an image in place of an image, then you will enter the Kingdom."[8]

Jesus is expressing here the need for the total transformation of the person into the primal image of God, an image that is envisioned to be androgynous and "single" because it has reincorporated the separate genders male and female so that male is no longer male and female is no longer female. Such an imagining of the ideal human being owes much to the widely known myth found in Plato's *Symposium* that the two sexes ought to reunite back into the androgynous progenitor.[9]

The ideal state of the human being for the Thomasine Christians is the recreation of the youth of Adam, an androgyny marked by singlehood and celibacy. They called this state "*monachos*" which means "single unmarried person" or "holy person."[10] In later Christian traditions, it is a word that eventually comes to refer to a consecrated celibate, a "monk" or "virgin" living in a holy community. In the *Gospel of Thomas* it is used for the first time in history to mark singlehood and celibacy as the ideal religious lifestyle, rather than the married.

Curiously, however, the *Gospel of Thomas* contains another saying as its last, a saying that on the surface appears to contradict this androgynous ideal:

> Simon Peter said to them, "Mary should leave us because women do not deserve life." Jesus said, "Look, I myself will guide her in order to make her male, so that she too may become a living spirit – male, resembling you. For every woman who will make herself male will enter the Kingdom of Heaven."[11]

This saying is part of an early Christian tradition that expressed the ideal state of Adam as a state of "*becoming* male."[12] How was the Genesis story being read to yield this metaphor? The Christians noticed that according to Genesis 1.27, the androgynous male-female image that God created was called "man" and identified as "him":

> So God created man (Hebrew: *adam*) in his own image, in the image of God he created *him*; male and female he created *them*.

The Christians also noticed that according to Genesis 2.22, woman was taken out of Adam's side. It did not take them too long to conclude that the female had been concealed inside the male, so that the original creation had been a hermaphrodite that looked like a man, a male entity who concealed the female inside of himself. Gender differentiation occurred when God performed surgery and the two became separate beings. Since all hell broke loose following this surgery, it was further concluded that redemption meant that Eve had to reenter Adam, to rejoin him or "become male."

This interpretation of the Genesis story does not appear to have originated with the Christians alone since the famous early first-century Jew, Philo of Alexandria, says in one sentence that the "heavenly *man*" in Genesis 1.27 was "neither male nor female."[13] He also taught that the soul needed to bring together the original genders that had become divided, not so that the masculine be made "womanish" and "soft," but so that the female be made "manly," guided and impregnated by the male intellect with wisdom, prudence, justice, courage, and virtue.[14]

The expression, "become male," is arresting for its androcentrism, its focus on the power and supremacy of the male. In fact, some contemporary scholars have concluded that this expression cannot be used as evidence of women's "egalitarianism" within early Christianity. While it is true that ancient "egalitarianism" was not egalitarianism by modern standards, such conclusions fail to recognize that the expression "become male" is a product of the ancient worldview of gender, which conceived of the male body as the ideal while the female body was the deviant, the body that had the misfortune to lack a penis. The male was associated with the intellect and spirituality, while the female with emotion and worldliness. The male was active, a mover within the public sphere, while the female was passive, sequestered within the private domain.

The use of the expression "become male" as a reference to the image of God as the ideal hermaphrodite is demonstrative of the cultural and social construct of ancient gender, which is permeated with misogyny. In the ancient world, "femaleness" could not be conceived to be an ideal state because of the contemptuous way in which "femaleness" was defined by the larger community. Thus there is no evidence from the ancient world that the movement from "male" to "female" was ever a positive transformation. Rather the positive movement was always perceived in terms of wiping out the female either by the female "becoming male" when she is subsumed by the male within the primal hermaphrodite, or the female becoming no-female within the androgynous image of the primordial human.[15]

What does this language suggest about the social interactions between genders? Paradoxically, while the expression itself is misogynous, it does not also mean that it necessarily signals an anti-egalitarian attitude. If we judge the expression "become male" against our own modern perceptions of egalitarianism, we might misread the past, making it difficult for us to conceive the "liberating" effect that "becoming male" actually had in ancient Christian circles. For the

Digging in

Box 5.1 A male woman?

In Santa Sabina (Rome), we find a lovely fifth-century mosaic.
The church was founded by Peter of Illyria during the reign of
Pope Celestine (422–432 CE). Occupying the wall space above the
doorway is a mosaic panel with an inscription commemorating
this foundation. The inscription is flanked by two large Roman
matrons dressed in full-length purple draperies against a gold
background. Each matron holds an open book in her left hand.
Her right hand is raised in blessing. Below the feet are inscriptions
that identify the figures with the *Church of the Circumcised* (left)
and the *Church of the Gentiles* (right). For a long time, scholars such
as Robert Milburn have read this mosaic as a representation of the
belief that Christians in Rome understood themselves as a unified
church consisting of Jewish Christians and Gentile Christians.
But I am not so sure this mosaic speaks so positively about the
Jewish–Christian contingency. The *Church of the Circumcised* is
depicted as a *female* in woman's garb. The *Church of the Gentiles*,
however, is not. The Church of the Gentiles is rendered as a *male*
in a woman's robes. Was the artisan trying to capture here the
superiority of the Gentile contingency by portraying the Gentile
church as a male-woman rather than a female?

For deeper digging, read Robert Milburn, *Early Christian Art and
Architecture* (Berkeley: University of California, 1988).

woman to "become male" in the ancient world meant that her stature was supremely elevated within the natural and social order however misogynous the phrase itself is. How powerful the woman Olympias who worked as a deacon in John Chrysostom's church in the fourth century, a young wealthy woman who committed her life and money to the church after her husband died. Even when exhorted by the emperor Theodosius to take another husband, she refused, devoting herself to a life of severe asceticism and almsgiving. John Chrysostom was known to address the famous deaconess of Constantinople as a "man" rather than a "woman" because "she is a man in everything but body."[16]

When we study the ancient literature, we learn about the famous Christian convert, Thecla, who literally performs the male ideal in the literary record of her story.[17] She "becomes male" by cutting off her long hair and donning men's clothing. According to the legend, this action allows her to become a missionary endorsed by Paul. She travels around the ancient world as a Christian teacher, instead of remaining sequestered in a husband's home as a wife.[18] We know that women took Thecla's example seriously and used her story as justification for their own leadership of congregations. Tertullian complains that a woman leader of a local congregation was teaching and performing baptisms using the justification that Thecla, Paul's compatriot, had done likewise. Furious, Tertullian reports that he has found out that the story of Thecla was forged by a presbyter in Asia in order to augment Paul's fame. According to Tertullian, the presbyter had been removed from his office. The only words of Paul are those in his letters that command them to silence and subordination to their husbands.[19] It appears that others in antiquity took a similar stance, even defacing her eyes and hand in an early Christian fresco near the ancient city of Ephesus (see Box 5.2).

Mygdonia, a Christian convert in eastern Syria, acts similarly, chopping short her hair and tearing up her clothing. According to the account in the *Acts of Thomas*, she is found by her husband Charisius who is shocked by her actions and insists she stop her nonsense. She continually refuses to obey the numerous chidings and abuses by her husband, until he eventually allows her to live according to her own will as a celibate woman, apparently separated. She becomes responsible for anointing the bodies of women converts before immersion, while the male apostle Judas (Thomas) anoints the men.[20]

Around 340 CE, soon after the council of Nicaea when the Apostolic Church was consolidating its power, the Council of Gangra took place to condemn Eustathius, the famous bishop of Sebaste in Armenia. In the Synodical letter of the Council of Gangra, we find out that Eustathius and his congregation "abhorred" marriage.

Digging in

Box 5.2 Co-apostles?

In 1906 a cave was discovered cut into the rock above the ruins
of the ancient city Ephesus, in modern day Turkey. Inside the
cave, the archaeologist Karl Herold found images of Paul and
Thecla from the fifth or sixth century. Both figures have their
hands raised in a typical teaching gesture and both are of the
same height. This means that both figures were considered of
equal apostolic authority by the person who commissioned the
fresco. What is disturbing about the fresco is what has happened
to Thecla. Her upraised hand and eyes have been defaced, literally
scratched out and burned off, while Paul remains intact. Crossan
remarks, "An earlier image in which Thecla and Paul were equally
authoritative apostolic figures has been replaced by one in which
the male is apostolic and authoritative and the female is blinded
and silenced. And even the cave-room's present name, St. Paul's
Grotto, continues that elimination of female-male equality once
depicted on its walls" (2004: xii–xiii).

For deeper digging, read John Dominic Crossan and Jonathan
L. Reed, *In Search of Paul: How Jesus's Apostle Opposed Rome's
Empire with God's Kingdom* (San Francisco: Harper, 2004).

They refused to partake in prayer or eucharist services administered by married presbyters or performed in the presence of the married, so they held separate services for the unmarried. They believed that married people had no hope of redemption, and therefore it appears that they did not view them as real members of the church. So it is not at all surprising that we learn that Eustathius taught that it was necessary for men to leave their wives and women to leave their husbands.

It had come to the attention of the larger church that Christian women in Eustathius' church were leaving their husbands and, then, in complete disregard for custom, they were destroying their common dress and were wearing men's clothing. To boot, the women had cropped off their hair. Why? According to Canon 17 of the Synodical letter, the Christians in Eustathius' church – in agreement with the Corinthian women Paul complained about – believed that a woman's long hair was a reminder of her subordination. Cutting it annulled her subjection. The Christians in Eustathius' churches understood membership in the Church to require a severe form of asceticism that erased both gender – as it was traditionally conceived – and the subordination of women.

The result of the Council was a series of 20 Canons, condemning the practices of the Eustathian Christians in order to force the women back into their husbands' beds and make them compliant with the male authorities of the church. Thus the first Canon reads:

> If anyone shall condemn marriage, or loathes and condemns a woman who is a believer and devout, and sleeps with her own husband, claiming she could not enter the Kingdom, let that person be anathema.

Virgins who act arrogantly toward the married are condemned in the tenth Canon. According to Canons 13 and 17, women who wanted to be ascetics were anathematized if they dressed like a man or cut off their hair to try to annul their subordination to men. Anyone who was found in disagreement with these Canons was to be excommunicated as a heretic and separated from the church.

The Council of Gangra and its decision to rein in encratic Christian communities in the eastern part of the Empire was part of the post-Nicene movement by the dominant party to homogenize and gain control of the churches in the east. For its time, Eustathius' form of Christianity was not unusual in the eastern empire. For the first two centuries, churches in eastern Syria demanded permanent celibacy for admission. The Christian literature produced in this part of the world during these formative years privilege the stories of

Christians who were encratic, honoring singlehood *over and against* marriage.

It is in the fourth century that we see a major shift in this position, when the churches in eastern Syria begin to allow married people to be baptized. The Eustathian Christians appear to be resisting this development, but to no avail as Aphraates, the fourth century bishop of Mar Mattai on the eastern shore of the Tigris, reveals in his writings. His homilies, which were written between the years 336 and 345 CE, suggest that the pressure from western orthodoxy was making an impact on the churches in Aphraates' area. The demand for celibacy had been relaxed so that it was now only required of a privileged class of men and women in the Syrian church, an ascetic group known as the "sons and daughters of the covenant." Virginity had become voluntary rather than mandatory.[21] Marriage is conceded for some among "the sheep" as "good," when its single purpose – procreation – is endorsed. But Aphraates is clear that marriage is not the ideal, and in fact, happens to generate conflict between humans and God, having no spiritual value.[22]

Of the ascetic group, the sons and daughters of the covenant, Aphraates raves that they have overcome gender by living as holy and pious solitaries, as single men and women. For them, refusing marriage was an enactment of scripture, a demonstration that there is "neither male nor female" but "all are children of the Most High." By betrothing Christ instead of a human husband, the virgin women no longer belonged to "the daughters of Eve," whom Aphraates considers the "weapons of Satan" responsible for temptation, desire and sin. According to Aphraates, the daughters of Eve birth children in pain as fodder for death and have brought about the cursing of the earth so that it issues forth thorns and tares. But the daughters of the covenant are redeemed because they are "not married to men so as to receive the curses and come into the pains."[23]

Aphraates, however, cautions the solitaries from living together as chaste husbands and wives, because he is concerned about sexual slippage should lust rear up. It would be better for them to marry as a traditional couple, than to commit adultery with one another, he says. So he recommends that the sons and daughters of the covenant live separated into male and female houses, even though the traditional gender categories are no longer operative for them.[24] He understands these privileged people to be like the angels who already live in Paradise, in "that world where there is no female," marriage, or birth. They live in a sacred space where men do not take wives, "nor is male distinguished from female."[25] Given this theology and social construct, it is not surprising that Aphraates discusses the women in scripture whom he considers to have been equal to men, including those who held offices as prophetesses.[26]

The Devil made me do it

Clement of Alexandria, a theologian and teacher at the end of the second century, wrote an entire book about the encratite Christians he knew. In this book, he tells us about the manner in which some of them interpreted the Genesis story.[27] Their interpretation centered on the word "knowledge" in the first four chapters of Genesis. They noticed that the tree of "knowledge" of good and evil was the tree that Adam had been told not to eat from. If he ate from it, he would die.[28] Eve was told by the serpent that, if she ate its fruit, she would "know" good and evil.[29] As the story progressed, the encratite Christians noticed that Adam and Eve "knew" they were naked.[30] Then, after they had been expelled from the garden, Adam "knew" Eve his wife, and she conceived and bore a son.[31]

For these Bible interpreters, this final verse was the key to unlocking the secrets of the creation story. Since the word "knowledge" was used of Adam having sex with Eve, it was obvious to these Bible literalists that when Adam and Eve gained "knowledge" by eating the forbidden fruit, in reality, they had had sex. They concluded that the serpent, the Devil, must have learned about sex through voyeurism, by watching the animals in the garden. The serpent persuaded Adam and Eve to have sex, to taste the forbidden fruit! They had identified the primal sin with sex, and so they reasoned that abstinence would return them to the primordial condition of the human being before sin arose. Their salvation depended on their ability to thwart the Devil and the sexual urge, living as celibates.

One second-century instructor who taught along these lines was Tatian, a man from Syria who had been trained by Justin Martyr in Rome. Clement of Alexandria tells us that when Tatian became a teacher himself, he taught that "marriage is fornication" and "was introduced by the Devil."[32] For Tatian this was proven by Paul's insistence in 1 Corinthians 7 that when intercourse resumed after prayers, it was "because of Satan." Tatian concluded that the couple only serves God if they agree to continence. Otherwise, they serve Satan. They become fornicators, doing the Devil's work. It is within this context that he reminds Christians that no one can serve two masters. He felt that every Christian had to make the choice to serve God by rejecting marriage, a point he highlighted by referring to Paul's teaching that the unmarried care for "the things of the Lord" while the married "how he can please his wife."[33] Tatian thought that Jesus' parable about the man who rejected the invitation to come to the Lord's table, because "I have married a wife and therefore I cannot come," proved his point.[34]

In a treatise mentioned by Clement – *On Perfection According to the Savior* – Tatian taught that the human being had to make a choice between the "old" and the "new." The Jewish Law was the old covenant that governed the old man. The Gospel was the new covenant that governed the new man. Quoting Paul, "we are dead to the Law by the body of Christ, that we should belong to another, to him who was raised from the dead," he argued that the old laws, including marriage and the commandment to increase and multiply," had been overturned by the Christ event. Baptized Christians were dead to the old law, and must embrace the newly revealed pronouncements of the Lord. The new commandments, Tatian argued, included the opinion that marriage was a state only intended for ancient times, having been an invention of Moses.[35] Thus Tatian quoted Jesus' words – "The children of the age to come neither marry nor are given in marriage" – and understood them to be an outright rejection of marriage in the here and now.[36] He understood the reference to "the children of this age" as indicative of the people of the "new" covenant, contrasting with the children of the old.

Tatian went further. He argued that birth was corruption and destined to be abolished. He used scripture to bolster his belief, quoting Isaiah 50.9 – "You all shall wax old like a garment and a moth shall eat you" – to prove that birth ended in death. The Christian should forsake procreation because they ought not to "lay up treasure where moth and rust corrupt."[37] Tatian also used Leviticus 15.18 to his advantage, where it is taught that the body must be washed after the ejaculation of semen because it had been defiled by the emission. By associating ejaculation with conception, he was able to argue that human birth was a defilement. He also argued that Christians only can undergo one washing: baptism. This meant that if they became sexually active after baptism, they had to live in a state of sin and defilement, because there was no way to effectively alleviate it again.

We do not get a sense of Tatian's view of women in the church from his extant writings. But there is a curious citation from the fourth century bishop of Salamis, Epiphanius, a note that is in accord with what we know about other encratic communities. Epiphanius reports about the encratic group that developed Tatian's teachings, particularly his position that marriage is from the Devil. He says that these encratites take so much pride in their continence, that they risk it with questionable behaviors. What is the risky business? The men are found in the company of the women, traveling with them, living with them, and being assisted by them in the performance of their official duties![38]

In defiance of the Creator

By the beginning of the second century, encratism was extremely popular and criticisms of it emerge in the literature written by those Christians associated with the nascent Apostolic churches. For instance, the author of 1 Timothy, writing around 135 CE, condemns those who "forbid marriage and enjoin abstinence from foods which God created to be received with thanksgiving." He characterizes these Christians as godless, having departed from the faith he himself promotes, because they did not think as he did – that nothing should be rejected which God had created.[39]

It may be that the author of 1 Timothy is targeting a specific form of Christianity that was becoming popular especially in the eastern regions of the Roman Empire – in Asia Minor and Syria – during this era. It was so popular by the middle of the second century Justin Martyr and Tertullian complained that it had spread throughout the Roman Empire and rivaled the nascent Apostolic Church they preferred.[40] It was a church founded by Marcion who was a wealthy business man from Sinope, a city on the shore of the Black Sea.[41]

Why did Marcion found a rival church? At the beginning of the second century Marcion traveled to Rome where he devoted himself to Bible theology, scrutinizing the Jewish scripture and trying to understand its relationship to a collection of letters of Paul, which he had in hand and loved. During the course of his rigorous study and criticism of the Jewish scriptures, he noticed that the God of mercy, grace and love proclaimed by Paul was the opposite of the Yahweh God described in the Jewish scripture. Staring out at him from the pages of the Jewish scripture was a god who proclaimed himself to be jealous, wrathful, vengeful, and angry. Marcion viewed this through Paul's claim that Christ brought an end to the Jewish Law and concluded that Christianity needed to sever itself from Judaism and its scriptures, which featured a god who was different from the one proclaimed by Jesus. The Jewish god was the creator of this world, who chose the Israelites to be his people. The Christians were saved from his tyranny by the Unknown God whom Paul spoke about: the god of love, grace and mercy. This god lived beyond our universe and sent his son Jesus to rescue those who believed in him. Jesus appeared on earth as an adult male in a body that only seemed to be human. Because of this teaching, Marcion was accused by his opponents of saying that Jesus was a phantasm.

This new theology met resistance from the Apostolic Church Marcion had been patronizing in Rome. He was, in fact, kicked out when he shared his opinions with the leaders. The church returned his donations, which were sizable. Marcion did not let them go to waste. He immediately became a missionary for his own brand of Christianity, put together the first New Testament scripture, which consisted of the gospel of Luke and the letters of Paul he had. He was extremely successful establishing churches across the empire and his church became as extensive and popular as the Apostolic network. In some instances, Marcionite Christianity represented the indigenous church in some locales, especially in Asia Minor and Syria.

What about marriage and sex? Since both were commanded by the Yahweh creator god whose rule Christians were trying to escape, marriage and sex were not allowed.[42] Marcion would not have Christians breeding children to suffer life under Yahweh's rule. Marriage and sex were sins to be avoided at all costs. Marcion is purported to have taught his followers to center their lives totally around worship of the Unknown good God, and to leave no children behind on earth for Yahweh to abuse. Fasting and strict dietary regulations also were observed as acts of defiance against the creator god.

Clement of Alexandria in his book about marriage in the early church tells us that the Marcionites believed that the soul is the only part of the human being that is divine, having fallen down into this world in order to be purged.[43] This teaching was a common Platonic view of the time, developed in philosophical circles as Plato's treatises, particularly the *Phaedo* and *Phaedrus,* were interpreted by new generations of students. Some ancient philosophers like Philolaus the Pythagorean and Empedocles, and the poets Theognis and Euripides also felt that birth itself is death for the soul. The Marcionites agreed with both of these worldviews. It was their position that birth is evil and that the embodiment of the soul is its purgatory. These common opinions went a long way to bolster the Marcionite's theological position that they were religiously obligated to show defiance to the creator god Yahweh by ceasing procreation and bringing an end to the cycle of birth and death. Only under these circumstances, they argued, could the soul be liberated from the grip of hell.

Because Marcion's writings have not survived history, we do not have firsthand accounts about how Marcion organized his churches or what he thought about the role of women in them. But testimonies from leaders in the Apostolic churches criticize Marcion for allowing women in his churches to hold offices, even administering baptism to catechumens.[44] Marcionite churches were criticized too for having a special office for prophetesses, whom Marcion called "the Holy Sisters."[45] Tertullian of Carthage is enraged by the practices of the Marcionites and others he calls "heretics" for permitting women to teach, debate, perform exorcisms, heal, and baptize.[46] Marcion's successor, Apelles, was accused of leading a company of women in Alexandria, and then, upon his return to Rome, writing down the prophecies of Philumena. She was a reputed virgin and prophetess in Rome known as the "angel of light" for the miracles she performed. So persuaded by her teachings was he, that Apelles' own teachings were reported to have changed so much that he eventually created his own organization based on what he had learned from Philumena.[47]

After considering Marcion's controversial teachings and the resistance in the late second-century Apostolic churches to the official roles that women held in Marcion's churches, if we return to our earlier discussion of 1 Timothy and the other pastoral letters, it is clear why the authors are so adamant that "the *Law* is good" and "in accordance with the glorious *gospel* of the blessed God."[48] The authors of the Pastorals, in criticism of Marcion's doctrine that Yahweh is the God of the Jews, not the Christians, emphasize that only one God exists and only one mediator, "the man" Jesus Christ.[49] They repeatedly remind their communities that they should guard "the truth" and not be persuaded by controversial teachings and myths.[50]

To thwart the authority women enjoyed in Marcionite churches, the authors of the Pastorals epistles rein in the women, forbidding them from teaching or having authority over men. They are told to dress appropriately as is becoming of modest women. Their redemption is said to be dependent on their domestication, particularly on their roles as submissive wives and mothers, a point which the authors try to prove theologically by parading in their misogynist interpretation of the Genesis story. The redemption of women requires their submissiveness because Eve was only formed secondarily and, unlike Adam, was deceived and became a transgressor in the Garden. So they conclude that the salvation of women is dependent on their childbearing and their faithfulness.[51] Older women are commanded to train the younger women in this way, "to love their husbands and children, to be sensible, chaste, domestic, kind, and submissive to their husbands."[52] Encratic behaviors and the rejection of marriage are strictly forbidden, labeled by the authors as "the doctrines of demons" that depart from "*the* faith."[53]

Not surprisingly, the authors demand that the official offices of bishop and deacon be reserved for married men with temperate wives.[54] The only "office" left open to women is that of the "widow" whose job it was to make continual supplications to God day and night in prayer. But even this office is limited by the authors of the pastorals to women over 60 years of age. Younger widows must be returned to the marriage union as quickly as possible, to bear more children and take care of the home. And should a widow have Christian relatives, they are chided to support her so that the church does not have to be burdened with her expenses.[55]

It's the end of the world

By the middle of the second century, it was realized that the end of the world as a cataclysmic event was not going to happen immediately as the original Christians had anticipated. There was not going to be a sudden end to society, either its traditional institutions or its expectations. So as the pastoral letters testify, the nascent Apostolic Church had begun to settle into society. Leaders were advising their congregations to try to fit into the world, rather than resist it and cause trouble with the authorities. Part of this secularization process meant that Christian women had to be brought more in line with the roles afforded them by the larger society, roles that did not include public speaking or jeopardize male authority. Galatians 3.28 and its social mobilization within the early churches had become a liability. Christian women had to be redomesticated.

It is within this environment that the Church of New Prophecy emerged as a protest and reform movement.[56] It was called "Montanism" by its detractors, after the name of one of its leaders, the prophet Montanus. The two other leaders were women prophetesses, Priscilla and Maximilla. Their movement was centered in a village called Pepuza in a province of Asia Minor known as Phrygia. The three prophets knew the Gospel of John and the book of Revelation, and these writings greatly influenced their teachings.

All three leaders claimed to be channels for the Holy Spirit, called in the Gospel of John, the "Paraclete." Montanus thought that he himself was the manifestation of the Paraclete that Jesus had promised to send to the world after his death.[57] He described his indwelling by proclaiming, "I am the Lord God, Almighty, dwelling in a man."[58] The women made similar claims about the indwelling of the spirit. For instance, Maximilla exclaimed in ecstasy, "Hearken not unto me, but hearken unto Christ!"[59]

The aim of Montanus, Priscilla, and Maximilla was to restore Christianity to its original charismatic and "egalitarian" roots, as a religion ruled by the Holy Spirit and the male *and* female prophetic voices that revealed God's truth and predicted the future. We hear from Epiphanius that they claimed to have left the Apostolic Church over the issue of "gifts of grace."[60] Given the stress that they would put on the abolishment of gender within their newly established church and their emphasis on women's prophetic gifts especially, I imagine that they started a new church so that gifted women in the spirit would have a sphere of influence to operate within.

Priscilla and Maximilla reclaimed for women their leadership roles in prophetic offices, serving as models for other prophetesses who emerged within the Church of New Prophecy.[61] In the late third century, Firmilian bishop of Caesarea Mazaca, wrote a letter to Cyprian in which he complains about a prophetess of the Church of New Prophecy who baptized and administered the Eucharist, a fact that appalled him.[62] For their authority, the New Prophecy prophetesses appealed to women prophets in the scriptures like the daughters of Philip, Deborah, Mary the sister of Aaron, Hulda, and Anna the daughter of Panuel.[63] Instead of passing harsh judgment on Eve, the members of the Church of New Prophecy honored her because she was the first to eat from the tree of knowledge, making her especially wise, they said.[64] As support for their ordination of women as clergy – including women bishops and presbyters – they not only pointed to Eve's superiority in matters of wisdom, but highlighted the memory that Moses' sister was a prophetess. But their trump card was the old argument that gender made no difference to church offices at all because, according to Galatians 3.28, "in Christ Jesus there is neither male nor female."[65]

Reports from their Apostolic detractors tell us that Apostolic bishops visited the Church of New Prophecy and tried to exorcise the Devil from Priscilla and Maximilla, but their attempts were prevented by the congregants.[66] Maximilla is known to have spoken in the spirit at that moment, "I am driven away like a wolf from the sheep. I am not a wolf. I am word and spirit and power."[67] The women received tremendous support from their church, which, with reference to Matthew 23.34, began to characterize the Apostolic Christians as "prophet-slayers" because they did not recognize the prophecies of the Church of New Prophecy as authentic.[68]

Using male-inflected language rather than feminine to refer to herself, Maximilla said that she was sent by the Lord to be "a herald," imparting "the knowledge of God."[69] What were their main prophecies? A large part of the knowledge the prophets were imparting was eschatological, that the world would end soon in accord with the visions of John recorded in the book of Revelation and that Christians needed to repent immediately. They should be ready to publicly profess Christianity in face of persecution. Maximilla was under the impression that the age of the world was so advanced that she predicted that after her own death there would not be another prophetess because the end would have arrived by then.[70] Not surprisingly, Maximilla predicted that the immediate future would be marked with wars and revolutions, a common feature of eschatological narratives.[71]

A central teaching focused on a prophecy that was attributed to Priscilla, that the holy Jerusalem would descend upon a hill in

Pepuza.[72] She said that she received this vision from Christ who came to her as *a woman* dressed in a white robe.[73] Clearly, her prophecy is connected to Revelation 21.2, in which we find the expectation that, at the end of time, a new Jerusalem will descend from heaven, prepared as a bride adorned for her husband. It appears that Priscilla understood her vision of Christ as a white-robed woman to be an eschatological sign of Jerusalem's imminent descent as the adorned bride. In fact, Tertullian tells us that the Church of New Prophecy foretold that there would be given a sign of the descent of Jerusalem preceding its eschatological manifestation, and that this sign had been already fulfilled.[74] Did the Church identify this sign with Priscilla's vision?

Montanus renamed Pepuza "Jerusalem" and assembled his congregation there to hold services.[75] It became customary for women and men joining the church to be initiated on this hill in Pepuza, so that they might tarry there with the hope to see Christ as Priscilla had done.[76] The site continued to be the central place of veneration and initiation for the movement, because the Church of New Prophecy continued to teach that the holy Jerusalem would descend there just as the book of Revelation predicted.[77]

Montanus is known to have annulled marriage, forbidding it entirely.[78] Anyone who tried to remarry was expelled from the Church of New Prophecy.[79] In fact, it was said of Priscilla and Maximilla that they left their husbands when the Holy Spirit initially possessed them.[80] Priscilla became known as a "virgin" within the Church of New Prophecy.[81] She connected virginity with the ability to receive visions and auditions. She stated that sexual purity allows the faithful to see visions and hear distinct voices, ecstasies that are both redemptive and secret.[82]

But there seems to have been an eschatological dimension to the rejection of marriage too. Their church services included the procession of seven virgins into the sanctuary to prophesy to the congregation. The virgins carried lamps and were dressed in white.[83] This practice has eschatological overtones, imitative of the wise virgins in Jesus' parable who were prepared to meet the bridegroom when he came, taking their lamps with them and keeping them lit until the bridegroom arrived at the marriage feast. The New Prophecy virgins were performing publicly the parable, reminding the congregation of the immediacy of the end of the world, that they must "watch! For you know neither the day nor the hour."[84] In the performance, the virgins would weep and mourn for humankind, leading the congregation to repentance.[85]

It is likely that the promotion of virginity within the New Prophecy community included the eschatological expectation found in the book of Revelation, that the redeemed consisted of 144,000 virgin martyrs who stood before God's throne.[86] This would explain why the seven virgins were robed in white, like the 144,000 virgin martyrs found in the book of Revelation. Furthermore, according to Tertullian who joined the Church of New Prophecy later in his life, the Paraclete told the women in the movement that they should forsake their marriages and motherhood to die as martyrs: "Seek not to die on bridal beds, nor in miscarriages, nor in soft fevers, but to die the martyr's death, that he may be glorified who has suffered for you."[87] In fact, the Church of New Prophecy was a church that highly regarded martyrs, profoundly influenced by the belief recorded in Revelation that the end of time and Christ's return would be marked by the rise of martyrdom.[88]

A particularly important witness to this liberation from "femaleness" within the Church of New Prophecy comes to us through what may be the only woman's writing to survive from the early Christian period: the diary of Perpetua, a woman who likely converted to New Prophecy Christianity only to die as a martyr shortly thereafter in Carthage at the beginning of the third century.[89] The account contains a first-person memoir believed to have been written by Perpetua while she was jailed awaiting her execution. Her autobiographical account begins with her chilling story about refusing to recant her confession of the Christian faith even at the insistence of her father who is so angry with her that he tries to "pluck out" her eyes. Even his repeated authoritarian interventions are not heeded by her. Neither is she moved by the fact that she has a nursing baby to care for. She rejects her traditional roles as daughter and mother, eventually giving up her baby to her father. She says, "As God willed, the baby had no further desire for the breast, nor did I suffer any inflammation; and so I was relieved of any anxiety for my child and of my discomfort in my breasts."[90] Her transformation from "female" to "male" is completed when she has a final vision before her martyrdom. In the vision, as she is about to enter the amphitheatre, she declares, "My clothes were ripped off, and suddenly I was a man." As a man, she is able to fight the enemy, an Egyptian male. She is victorious, ready to walk toward the Gate of Life. She understands her vision to signal that she will be martyred and ascend triumphant to heaven.

CHAPTER 6

Is marriage salvation?

Due to a certain sympathy in theology, it is true that many Gnostic groups in the second and third centuries forsook marriage and child-bearing for reasons similar to those voiced by Marcion – Yahweh must be defied. One of the defining characteristics of Gnostic thought is a theology with a double feature. It premieres a transcosmic or supramundane holy God who resides in a space *beyond* our universe, while at the same time, débuting a lesser god who creates and rules our universe. The lesser god is an ignorant, and even evil ruler. For these Gnostics, the human body was perceived to be a "prison" for the spirit, formed by the lesser god and his demonic assistants limb by limb to capture the spirit that had fallen into the universe from the transcosmic realm above. Sex is an act instituted by the lesser god to perpetuate the dispersal of the spirit in its human prison. Through birth, the spirit goes into lock up again and again, never tasting the joy of liberation and return to the transcosmic realm from whence it had fallen. To reject marriage and procreation was a conscious act of protest meant to strike the lesser god where it would hurt the most. So many Gnostic groups were encratic.

But renunciation of marriage and procreation was not the only lifestyle embraced by Gnostic groups. The double-feature theology raised serious questions for some Gnostics. How could the spirit be saved if its incarnation were stopped? How could the spirit be returned to the transcomic realm if it was never birthed in a child? If procreation and birth ceased, the spirit would never be exposed to the secret rituals and the holy gnosis that was necessary for its release from the lesser god's dominion.

The Gnostics who asked these sorts of question found themselves in a precarious position, posed on a razor's edge. How could they justify procreation and birthing children so that the spirit could be incarnated and receive instruction when the sex act itself was an act of corruption and trickery instituted by an arrogant god they desired to defy? The answers they provided afforded unusual power to women within their communities and opened them up to attack from their Christian opponents who vied to characterize their behaviors as promiscuous and deviant.

Sacred sex

"Great is the mystery of marriage, because without it the world would not exist!" So writes the author of the *Gospel of Philip*, a text associated with a Gnostic group known as the Valentinians.[1] The Valentinians, referred to themselves as "Christians," in contrast to other believers led by the apostles whom they called "Hebrews."[2] Even though the Valentinians criticized and contrasted themselves with Apostolic Christians, they were closely tied to the Apostolic churches, attending them regularly with hopes to reform them. In addition to participating in the regular Sunday worship services, the Valentinians met as a "secret society" or in esoteric circles whose gatherings were led by famous theologians including Valentinus, Theodotus, Marcus, Heracleon, and Ptolemy.

Because their movement grew out of the Apostolic Church, the rituals they adopted were those of the Apostolic Church – baptism, anointing, eucharist, marriage – although they seem to have developed the performance and meaning of the rituals in unique Gnostic directions. Within their conventicles, they required a second baptism, shared alternative words of institution, and engaged in a unique form of marriage that they called the "marriage of purity." The marriage of purity was a sacralized form of wedded bliss, understood to be a prefiguration of a great marriage that would take place at the end of the world, an event called "the bridal chamber." Since the spirit that needed to be redeemed was harbored in the human soul, trapped in the cycle of birth and death, abstaining from sex was out of the question for the Valentinians. For God to be ultimately restored, children had to be born. This meant that sex had to be limited and sacralized. This was accomplished theologically by taking the concept of androgyny to new heights.

Since God characterized his own image as male and female in Genesis 1.26–27, it was self-evident to the Valentinian Christians that the transcosmic supreme God existed as an androgyne or a *syzygy*. A *syzygy* is similar to a married couple, a male and female "yoked together" in a common union. The *syzygy* relationship is primarily procreative, meant to produce and manifest various aspects of God in his–her fullness. When the process was completed in primordial time, the Godhead consisted of 30 emanations or aeons living in pairs as syzygies. These aeons dwell in the transcosmic divine realm, a place called the Pleroma or Fullness of God. Together they make up the Godhead.

Although there are various versions of the Valentinian myth, they generally agreed that sin resulted when one of the female aspects of God, an emanation named Sophia or Wisdom, desired to "know" the

Father God outside the boundaries of her marriage to the male aeon, Thelêtus or Intention. Her promiscuity disrupted the harmony of the Godhead and, in order to reestablish harmony, she was reunited with Thelêtus, after her promiscuity was separated from her and cast outside the Pleroma. This promiscuous or "whoring" Sophia is called "Achamoth," derived from *hokhmah*, the Hebrew word for "wisdom."

In her loneliness and isolation, Achamoth repents of her promiscuity. This action brings forth a deliverer from the Pleroma, an aeon called "Jesus," who is a child of all the aeons in the Pleroma, since each contributed the best aspect of him–herself when they created Jesus. In other words, the aeon Jesus embodies the entire Godhead. As the embodiment of the Godhead, he descends into the space in which Achamoth sojourns and he begins the process of salvation by giving material form to the substances Achamoth had produced while mourning and repenting. To form these new substances into the universe, Achamoth gives birth to the lesser god, known by the Valentinians as the "Just God" because he is the creator god of the Jews who rules according to the laws recorded in the Jewish scripture. The Just God, however, is ignorant. When he creates the world, he is unknowingly influenced by Achamoth who sows the spiritual substance as "spirits" into the human beings he brings to life. She does this so the spiritual substance will be birthed and given an opportunity to mature, gain "gnosis" and be returned to the Pleroma.

The goal of the human sojourn is for the severed human spirit to rejoin in matrimony its "perfect self," a "male" angel who is awaiting her in heaven. This process of separation and reintegration is connected to the biblical story of creation, when Eve was taken out of Adam's side:

> When Eve was in Adam, death did not exist. When she separated from him, death came into existence. If he enters again, receiving himself, there will be no more death ... If woman had not separated from man, she would not die nor would the man. His separation was the beginning of death. For this reason Christ came – so that the separation which had occurred from the beginning, would be removed by Christ. He would unite the two again. To those who had died as a consequence of the separation, he would give them life and unite them. Woman is united to her husband in the bridal chamber. Whoever has united in the bridal chamber, no longer shall be separated.[3]

So the Valentinians perceive salvation as dependent on Eve, the human spirit, reuniting with Adam, the primordial image of God. This primordial image is envisioned as a male angel in heaven.

This reunion was believed to take place on two levels. The ultimate level is the eschatological, at the end of time, when the Pleroma would become a grandiose bridal chamber and the newly married spirit–angel couples would enter it as sygzgies and live eternally as wedded lovers. But what about the here-and-now? Human marriage is believed to be the shadow and prefiguration of the eschatological. It is called by the Valentinians the "iconic" bridal chamber, by which they meant that marriage is a human imitation of the eagerly anticipated eschatological wedding that would take place in the Pleroma.[4]

But this sacramental understanding of marriage did not apply to all human marriages. For Valentinians, sex could be sinful and corrupting, when engaged inappropriately. So they tightly controlled their marriages, which they patterned after the aeonic syzygies to be monogamous, heterosexual, and procreative, and they ritualized sex. The highest aspiration for the Valentinians was the marriage of purity, a conjugal relationship that was defined by sexual behavior with a spiritual focus. At the moment of intercourse, the thoughts of the aspiring couple were to be elevated in prayer, focused on "the Lord" instead of carnality. The Valentinians defined inappropriate sexual behavior as intercourse elicited through *epithumia*, which is carnal desire or lust, in adulterous liaisons or marriages of "impurity." Impure marriages are those that lack the spiritual focus, so that intercourse is elicited and sustained by lust.

Their concern about whether or not intercourse is governed by a sacred intention or lust has to do with ancient theories about the conception of embryos. In the ancient and medieval worlds, it was a common perception even among physicians that a woman's mentality helped to determine the characteristics of her offspring in both body and soul. The physician Soranus wrote in his book on gynecology:

> What is one to say concerning the fact that various states of the soul also produce certain changes in the mold of the fetus? For instance, some women, seeing monkeys during intercourse have borne children resembling monkeys. The tyrant of the Cyprians who was misshapen compelled his wife to look at beautiful statues during intercourse and became a father of well-shaped children; and horse-breeders during covering, place noble horses in front of the mares. Thus, in order that the offspring may not be rendered misshapen, women must be sober during coitus because in drunkenness the soul becomes the victim of strange fantasies; this furthermore, because the offspring bears some resemblance to the mother as well, not only in body but in soul. Therefore it is good that the offspring be made to resemble the soul when it is stable and not deranged by drunkenness.[5]

We see this idea preserved also by Heliodorus in his *Ethiopian Story*. When a black woman gives birth to a white daughter, she explains to those who question her, "During intercourse with my husband the picture of Andromeda (painted on the bedroom wall) presented her image to my eyes, showing her entirely nude, just as Perseus was taking her down from the rock, and it had thus by ill fortune given to the seed a form similar in appearance to that of the heroine."[6] The physician Galen discourages couples from painting images on their bedroom walls because "a monster ... can be caused by a special action of the imaginative power of a woman having sex. It is possible that when such a figure springs to mind, the fetus will be disposed in accordance with it."[7]

The Valentinians understood conception similarly. So controlling the mental state of the parents during intercourse was a major issue for them. The Valentinians state that the aspiring couple must not be engaged in adulterous relationships. If this were unfortunate enough to happen, the child conceived would resemble the lover rather than the spouse.[8] If the couple were to focus their minds on "the world" during lovemaking, then the child they conceive would resemble "the world."[9] What the couple ought to do is direct their love toward God during the act of intercourse, so that their child will "resemble the Lord."[10] If this is done, God's grace will be drawn down from the heights and shine on the parents and the child they are conceiving. This is "the mystery of intercourse."[11]

Sacral lovemaking, although devoid of lust, was not emptied completely of pleasure by the Valentinians. The Valentinians appear to have made a distinction between sexual pleasure and lust, between lovemaking and hedonism. One Valentinian text, an allegory of the soul and its redemption, states that the soul adorns herself in beauty and "enjoys" her beloved bridegroom. As they "make love," she receives "the life-giving spirit" so that she bears "good children."[12] This suggests to me that the Valentinians, although heavily opposed to carnality, were not rigidly opposed to sexual pleasure, as long as it occurred between married couples and was manifested out of their shared sacred intention.

The Valentinians sacralized sex because they identified sexual intercourse with the moment at which the spirit was generated for the child. The Valentinians believed that there were two grades of spirit or "spiritual seed" that could be incarnated in the embryo: an "elect" grade and a "regular" grade. The elect grade they called "male seed" and it was of the highest quality, ready to be redeemed at once. The regular grade was called "female seed" because it required more work on the part of the child to perfect it – to make it male! – so it could be redeemed.[13] Sex performed while meditating on the Lord guaranteed

Digging in

Box 6.1 Chemistry?

The tradition of sacred marriage and its performance later emerges in Hermeticism and Alchemy, whose practitioners attempted to transmute metals and change them into gold. This woodcut from the seventeenth century (MS Ferguson 210) uses the theme to illustrate the conjunction of opposites as the ultimate goal of the (al)chemical process. In this case, the sun (male figure) and the moon (female figure) unite. The accompanying poem reads: "O Luna, surrounded by me, and sweet one mine. You become fine, strong, and powerful as I am. O Sol, you are recognizable above all others. You need me as the cock needs the hens."

Through their loving and powerful union, they conceive the perfect original child: the hermaphrodite: "Here is born the noble queen rich. The masters say she is like her daughter. She multiples/producing children numberless. They are immortally pure, without nourishment (...) I became a mother, and yet remain a maid. And was in my essence lain with. That my son become my father, as God has decreed in essential way. The Mother who gave birth to me, through me will be born on earth" (*Rosarium philosophorum*, 1550). Was this accompanying poem lyrical language of the first chemists who were trying to describe the chemical reaction, when two different substances are combined to create a third? Or was alchemy a spiritual discipline, hiding Hermetic teachings from the Church? Did the alchemists understand the sacred union of the opposite genders to be the recreation of the original androgyny of Eden? Was it the transmutation into the hermaphrodite that they thought brought about immortality?

For deeper digging, read Florian Ebeling, *The Secret History of Hermes Trismegistus: Hermeticism from Ancient to Modern Times* (Ithaca: Cornell University, 2005); Erik Hornung, *The Secret Lore of Egypt: Its Impact on the West* (Ithaca: Cornell University, 2001).

the conception of a child with the elect grade seed, something that the Valentinians wanted very much. The regular grade spirit was "iffy" because it might not be strong enough to overcome the temptations of the Devil and the world. In that case, the seed would not mature into a redeemable spirit. It would wither and die among the thorns. Lustful thoughts and unacceptable behaviors, therefore, were to be avoided at all costs. So important was this matter that the Valentinians advised non-Valentinians to remain chaste in their marriages and bear the yoke of discipline instead.[14] For non-Valentinians, chastity was better than engaging unwittingly in impure marriages, which would produce children with weak and struggling spiritual seeds that might wither.

Since the Valentinians thought that error originated with the female aeon Sophia, and redemption involves reuniting the female with the male in holy matrimony, it has been long debated whether Valentinian communities afforded leadership roles to women, as the testimonies from Irenaeus and Tertullian suggest. Tertullian tells us – much to his chagrin – that the Valentinians, along with the followers of Marcion, permit women to teach, debate, perform exorcisms, heal, and baptize.[15] Irenaeus reports that the Valentinian leader Marcus ordained women as prophetesses within his community, and that women flocked to his services.[16]

While it is true that sin was the consequence of the behavior of a female aeon, it is also true that, because the female can become male in the Valentinian tradition, the female is empowered in this tradition in ways similar to those who lived as encratites.[17] In the ancient world, this transformation from female to male was "liberating" for women, allowing them to attain a level of worthiness and influence usually only afforded to men. We only have to read the letter that Ptolemy, a Valentinian teacher in Rome, wrote to the Christian woman Flora, to see that women were active learned members within the conventicles. Flora has asked Ptolemy about the identity of the God of the Jewish Law. She is not yet initiated into Ptolemy's conventicle, yet appears to be on the verge of doing so. Ptolemy addresses Flora as "my dear sister" and encourages Flora to study. He insists that she will be counted "worthy" if she decides to go through with her initiation. With reference to the cultivation of her spiritual seed, he tells her that, once initiated, she will be like "good and fair soil which has received fertile seed," allowing "to spring forth the fruit that grows from there."[18]

We have an inscription on a marble gravestone of an initiated Valentinian woman, Flavia Sophe, which tells us that Ptolemy's encouragement of Flora's initiation into the conventicle was not unusual. On this Roman gravestone, Flavia Sophe is addressed by her husband as "my kinswoman, my bedmate, my Sophe." We learn from the inscription that she had been yearning for the Father's light. So she was baptized and anointed in her quest to gaze on the divine faces of the aeons and the Son. Since she has been redeemed, she has gone to the bridal chamber; deathless she has ascended to the bosom of the Father.[19]

Within the Valentinian tradition, initiated women became active partners in the process of redemption. Their traditional roles as wife and mother were endowed with a sacredness and holiness that was all but unique in the ancient world. I know no other religious tradition comparable except the Simonians whom the Valentinians likely were familiar with. Simonianism was a Samaritan Gnostic movement contemporary with the rise of early Christianity and competed with it for religious converts. It was founded by Simon – known in Christian traditions as Simon "the Magician" or Simon "Magus" – a Samaritan who, after studying in Alexandria in the early first century, went home to Samaria to preach his good news.

Simon taught that in the beginning God was androgynous existing as the Father out of whom sprang the Mother, who is his Mind or Thought. She is also called by Simon, "the Holy Spirit," "Ennoia" (Thought) and "Athena." Knowing that the Father wished to create angels, Ennoia descends into the lower regions of space and generated them. In turn, these angels create the world. But all is not well with them. The angels infatuated and frenzied with Ennoia's beauty, turn on one another in war, killing each other. During the slaughter, they capture Ennoia, despoil her, and lock her into a human body to keep her for themselves. Ennoia's mythology represents the mythology of the fallen soul and its perpetual incarnation in the body. Over the years, as Ennoia journeys through the life and death cycle again and again, she is perpetually incarnated into the bodies of different women, including Helen of Troy. During Simon's time, she was residing in the body of a prostitute named Helena who Simon found in Tyre, purchased from the brothel, and then married. He said that he was the Great Power descended to earth to retrieve his wife.

From the testimonies of Simon's opponents (which are scathing) it is clear that Simon's view of sex was favorable. Hippolytus of Rome tells us that among the practices of the Simonians is sexual intercourse, which they call "perfect love." So sacred is sexual intercourse to them that they identify it with the "holy of holies," the innermost and holiest room of God's Temple where only the high priest is allowed entrance. They said that it was in sexual union that they "blessed" each other.[20] Hippolytus characterizes their activity as "promiscuous" and "indiscriminate," an interpretation that may have more to do with political motivation than historical accuracy. Indeed, Simon was perceived to be the arch-heretic by Christian leaders and his religious community was competitive enough with theirs to make him very threatening. When I examine all the evidence, it seems most likely that Simon understood God to be a primal syzygy that had the misfortune of suffering separation. Repair meant reunion in matrimony, the recovery of God's wayward wife. Redemption involved sacred sex within the marital bed, a point that the encratic author of the *Testimony of Truth* is aware of when he criticizes the Simonians for taking wives and begetting children.[21]

So here we have a mythology comparable to the Valentinian, a similarity that did not escape Simon's opponents who said that the Valentinians borrowed their system from him. In the case of the Simonians, we have a good idea about the prominence of women in leadership roles. The reports suggest that both Helena and Simon were active and successful missionaries during the reign of Claudius (41–54 CE). They traveled around together preaching their revelation and teaching those they initiated into their Gnostic community the necessary rituals in order to release all souls from their captivity and redeem them. Helena appears to have been a very popular and renowned teacher. The Roman author Celsus tells us that Helena was so revered among the Simonians that some of them were called "Helenians."[22] So here is direct evidence from the ancient world that a mythological system that honors marriage and sacralizes sex can be empowering for the women within the communities. This evidence, combined with the testimonies of the Valentinian opponents, suggests that the opponents were correct about the Valentinians on this: they allowed women to be leaders in their communities, and women were attracted to their conventicles where they were initiated, becoming "male."

The law is a joke

The Carpocratians are a more complicated group to understand. Their opponents characterize them as sexually "promiscuous" like the Simonians. We are told by their opponents that the Carpocratians believe that it is necessary for the soul to experience all sin in order to be liberated, and so the Carpocratians engage in all sorts of hedonist activities and magical practices for the salvation of the soul. While this is fascinating reading, there is something about these accusations that does not jive with the Carpocratians' teachings about where the soul came from and how Jesus fits into the scheme of things. It appears to me that Irenaeus, our primary resource for information on this group, has misread (intentionally or not) something that the Carpocratians had written, leading to a disjuncture between their ideology and their reported practices.[23]

The Carpocratians, like other Gnostics, taught that the world was an inferior creation. In their opinion, the world was created by a group of angels who were greatly inferior to the unbegotten Father. The mythology recorded assumes the Platonic fall of the soul into matter where it is further and further corrupted by the emotions and passions it endures as a consequence of its sin. In order to save the soul, a power descends from the unbegotten Father and enters the man Jesus because, unlike other men, Jesus had been able to keep his soul steadfast and pure. This acquired power allowed Jesus' soul to destroy the passions that humans suffer as a result of their sins. It also helped his soul become strong enough to escape the creator angels by resisting the Jewish Law. This allowed his soul to ascend all the way back to unbegotten Father.[24]

This is the pattern that the Carpocratians believed was set up for all souls. Like Jesus, every soul had to receive a power from above. This power made them strong enough to work their own redemption, despising and freeing themselves from the dominion of the creator angels and their Law. They do this by despising the world and the Law as Jesus had done. Their doctrine of imitation suggests that they, like Jesus, worked to destroy the passions that their souls suffered as a result of sin.

Irenaeus goes on to report that because of these ideas, the Carpocratians think they have acquired power over everything that is irreligious and impious. This made them arrogant enough to believe that they could become mightier than the apostles and said that they were equal to Jesus.[25] He says that they taught that the soul had to experience everything life has to offer in order to be liberated from it. If this is not accomplished, the soul would be reincarnated into another body at death.[26]

Irenaeus concludes from all of this that they have surrendered their moral compass and lead licentious lives, engaging in all sort sorts of ungodly and forbidden sexual activities. But did they? I'm not so sure. If we separate Irenaeus' reports of their beliefs which appear to be fairly standard Platonic fare, from his own mixed up conclusions about what those beliefs meant "on the ground," I think we can get a fairly good idea about what the Carpocratians actually were doing. They seem to me to have been trying to prove they were as pure and steadfast as Jesus, having overcome their passions as he did. To achieve this, they appear to have put themselves into risky positions. This gave them the opportunities to experience and face everything life has to offer in order to directly and personally endure and overcome all temptation to sin. In this way, they "paid the very last penny" to the inferior creator god who would no longer be able to throw their souls at death back into the bodily prison, because their souls had been purified of all sins.[27] It is a position comparable to what Clement tells us about Nicolaus who taught his followers to "abuse the flesh" by restraining and suppressing passion even for one's wife.[28]

What is fascinating is that we have a text from the Nag Hammadi collection that contains a sermon whose ideology is remarkably similar to this reconstruction of the Carpocratians. The author of the sermon in the *Testimony of Truth* starts by teaching that the Law is defiled, corrupted by the leaven of the Pharisees, which is the errant desire of the angels, the demons, and the stars. This includes marriage and the commandment to procreate. In order to "pay the last penny" to the "archon of darkness," you cannot give in to your passions, to sexual desire. Rather you must overcome evil by struggling against the passions. The only person who can know the true God is the one who has forsaken everything of the world by subduing desire in all ways imaginable. By struggling against the passions, the soul is cleansed of the transgressions it has committed while embodied. This is accomplished with the aid of an eternal power. The supreme example is Jesus who was overtaken by an outflowing power that strengthened his soul and helped him to endure the world and all evil things, and to bear up under them.[29]

Given the remarkable similarities between this sermon and what Irenaeus tells us about the Carpocratian's ideology, I imagine that the *Testimony of Truth* is preserving a teaching consistent with what Carpocrates must have taught. It was a teaching that blended standard Platonic speculation about the suffering of the embodied soul and the need for the control or eradication of the passions with Gnostic teaching that the inferior rulers must be defied by resisting their laws. This led to risky behaviors where the faithful took every opportunity to experience, endure and overcome all sorts of temptations, a practice that made them appear licentious to outsiders and likely led to slippage on their part. I am confident that the Carpocratians were not always successful in their attempts to overcome the tempting situations they put themselves into.

The mobilization of this kind of ideology had other risks, which can be observed in Epiphanes' teaching. Epiphanes is reported to have been Carpocrates' son. He arose as a teacher in his own right who set down his own ideas in a book known to Clement of Alexandria. According to Clement, Epiphanes established his own religious cult and was worshiped as a god in a temple in Same on Cephallenia. His book was entitled *Concerning Righteousness* and Clement quotes from it liberally.

Epiphanes appears to have taken his father's Platonic and Gnostic teachings in new directions. He made a distinction between the laws of the natural world and the Jewish Law, both of which he said came from the creator god. He argues that there is a discrepancy that is laughable between the Jewish laws given by god and the natural order of things, which reflects a higher order of communal equality or "righteousness." Although the quotes from Epiphanes' book do not give us the details, it appears to me that his argument precludes that the creator god has fashioned the natural world after the pattern of the higher world that is all about equity and unity. So Epiphanes points out what a joke it is that the same god who instituted the Jewish laws to bring about transgression and restrain people, created the heaven to embrace the entire earth, the sun to pour its light equally on all, whether rich, poor, male, female, free or slave.

This compelled Epiphanes to conclude that the Jewish Law had to be shunned and a life of liberty based on the natural order established. Since nature showed no limits in procreation, marriage was abandoned, and communal sex enjoined. Since both animal and human were given desire to breed, and only the human was restrained by God's law, it is obvious that the law must be set aside as the joke it is and eroticism fully engaged.[30] So we see in Epiphanes' teaching a reaction to his father's, turning teachings of endurance and restraint into teachings of hedonism.

The opponents of Carpocrates and Epiphanes did not make a distinction between the two communities because they did not recognize a difference between facing eroticism to endure it and overcome it or facing eroticism to fully engage it. All the behaviors appeared licentious, and so two distinct communities and practices were confused. This makes the evidence about women in these communities difficult to assess. What we do know is that the Carpocratians in Rome between 154–165 CE were led by a woman named Marcellina. She styled her group the "Gnostics" and instituted the use of icons of Christ and the philosophers Pythagorus, Plato, and Aristotle in worship.[31] We also know that the ideal Epiphanes' mobilized in his community was communal equality with no distinction between female and male, declaring "righteousness to be fellowship with equality" between males and females. In his community, women could not be given away in marriages as the private property of certain males.[32]

Soul collectors

Some of the most controversial material about Gnostic groups in the ancient world comes from Epiphanius, Bishop of Salamis. In his refutation against groups of "heretical" Christians, he writes two particularly scathing chapters against a number of Gnostic communities.[33] The material is difficult to sort out because Epiphanius employs a number of names to discuss these Gnostics at specific points in his narrative, and appears to confuse different groups with one another.

There is also something personal going on in these chapters. From what I have been able to make out from his narrative, Epiphanius was a proselyte in one of these Gnostic conventicles, considering initiation when he was a young man. The group he knew styled themselves "Gnostics," but they were also members in the Catholic Church in Egypt where Epiphanius met them. The conventicle he was familiar with had several texts which he read as he prepared for his initiation, including the *Gospel of Eve*, the *Greater Questions of Mary*, the *Lesser Questions of Mary,* and the *Birth of Mary*. He tells us that the women in the conventicle had been his "bold" instructors and had the leading role in the initiation rites. He tells us that once he had read their books and received instructions from the women, he decided to ditch the initiation.

I question this rendering of the events. When you read between the lines, it is clear that something happened that embarrassed and upset Epiphanius when his initiation failed. Epiphanius reports that he heard the women who were initiating him joke with each other, "We can't save the kid. We've left him in the hands of the archon to perish!" Following the embarrassing episode, he ran to the bishops of the church and turned in the members of the conventicle. With Epiphanius as informant, the bishops were able to ferret out 80 of the Gnostics "hidden in the church" and expel them from the city. Epiphanius is sure to tell us again and again how he never engaged in any of their practices, but only knew so much about them because he had been deceived as a youth to consider initiation into their conventicle.

It appears to me that Epiphanius' report contains material meant to justify his course of action and convince the authorities that these people were so extreme and corrupted that they had to be immediately removed from the church. In reality, it appears that the Gnostic members could not be distinguished from the Catholic Christians except through an informant. They appear to have been attractive enough to the young Epiphanius that he spent considerable time with the members, read their books, and was on the merge of being fully initiated when something went wrong with the initiation. Over the years since he turned them in, he tried to connect the Gnostic conventicle to some named heretical group and mythology in hopes of trying to understand his own past better and reassure himself that his course of action was indeed justifiable. This has served to jumble up the evidence, so that the Gnostic conventicle he knew becomes confused with the Borborians, Koddians, Stratiotics, Phibionites, Zacchaens, Barbelites, and the Nicolaitans.[34]

How can we sort out fact from fiction, without appearing to

defend or endorse their practices? I suggest we start with the information that Epiphanius gives us about his personal interactions with the Gnostic conventicle and their texts, and allow that to form the basis of our academic analysis, setting aside Epiphanius' attempts to associate the conventicle with other Gnostic groups and his own interpretations of the conventicle's texts and practices.

One of the first things we learn about their mythology from Epiphanius' testimony is that the lesser god who created and rules the world is named Ialdabaoth. He is an opponent of the divine beneficial powers that exist *beyond* the cosmos. Particularly he works in opposition to the main Mother Power, Barbelo. The Gnostics Epiphanius knew taught that the world ruler stole a power from Barbelo the Mother and it was sowed in human beings during sexual intercourse.[35]

This is the same story we have heard again and again, the story of the sowing of the soul into the human body through sexual intercourse when the semen is dispersed into the uterus. It was a common belief in the ancient world that the soul was transmitted in the semen. Tertullian, in fact, taught that the soul of the child was generated from the souls of the parents and was transmitted through the semen. It was also a popular belief that the woman emitted a female seed during intercourse and the competition between the male and female seeds in her womb led to the formation of the child and all its characteristics.

Given this understanding of intercourse and sexual emissions, it is not illogical that we stumble across a conventicle that believed it was necessary to collect sexual emissions in order to save the soul harbored within them.[36] From Epiphanius' matured Catholic perspective, this is disgusting impious behavior. Even other Gnostic groups were wary of the practice and condemned it. For instance, in the Gnostic liturgical handbook, the *Books of Ieu*, the initiates are told not to share their secret ceremonies with those who ingest semen and blood and intone the prayer, "We have known the knowledge of truth, and we pray to the *true* God." Alas, the authors of *Ieu* say, "Their God is wicked."[37] According to the Gnostic author of the book *Pistis Sophia*, the liturgical ingestion of semen and blood is a sin that surpasses every sin possible. Those who do so, this author says, will be cast immediately into the outer darkness with no hope of redemption.[38]

From the perspective of this Gnostic conventicle, however, what they were doing is soul collecting, the most pious thing one can do. This perspective is revealed in one of their books, *The Gospel of Eve*, which contained a vision that Epiphanius quotes. The visionary sees a tall man and a small man while standing on a lofty mountain. The visionary hears the crack of thunder and then the words, "I am you and you are me, and wherever you are, there I am. And I am sown in all things. And from wherever you will, you will gather me, and in gathering me, you gather yourself."[39]

How did the gathering happen? Ritually. It began with a sacred handclasp that only the initiated knew.[40] A sacred celebratory meal was shared, the famous Christian Agape or Love Meal. This festal meal was celebrated within early Christian circles from the earliest times, and it appears to have concluded with the eucharist ritual. Epiphanius' Gnostics had chosen the Agape meal as the moment to collect souls. It was performed between the brothers and sisters of the conventicle. The sisters would sexually arouse the brothers and collect the semen in their hands. They would then stand in a prayer position, with their eyes and hands upraised to the heavens, and they would offer the semen to the supreme Father God, saying, "We offer you this gift, the body of Christ."[41] Similarly, according to Epiphanius, they would collect the female menses and offer it, saying, "This is the blood of the Christ."[42]

Epiphanius tells us that the ritual was completed with the ingestion of the sexual emissions. In support of this claim, he references their book, the *Greater Questions of Mary*, in which Jesus reveals himself to Mary on the mountain to teach her the sacrament. After prayer, like Adam, Jesus takes a woman out of his side. He is sexually aroused by her, collects his semen and ingests it. He says to Mary, "Thus we must do, that we may live."[43]

What is going on here? Quite literally, they were ingesting the sexual fluids in order to collect the soul from within it. They envisioned their bodies as sacred vessels that would be able to transport the suffering soul to heaven. According to Epiphanius, these Gnostics claimed that the "power" they were gathering and eating was the "soul" embedded in the sexual fluids. They claimed that they were showing mercy to the human race by ingesting these substances, saying, "We are doing creatures a favor by gathering the soul from them all and taking it to the heavens with us."[44] I would point out that the Manichaean Gnostics believed something similar. Although they were not involved in semen collection, they did think that it was necessary for the "elect" Gnostics to eat vegetables because they thought the spirit was harbored in watery plants. It was only in the stomachs of the elect Gnostics that the divine substance could be properly purged and made ready for its return to the Kingdom of Light.[45]

Do these controversial soul-gathering practices mean that Epiphanius' Gnostics were sexually promiscuous, involved in adulterous liaisons and whoring as Epiphanius accuses? Certainly this kind of ritual behavior begs such accusations from outsiders. But what was the conventicle's own perspective? According to Epiphanius the members of the conventicle insisted that, while the gathering of sexual emissions is the pinnacle of piety, insemination is filthy and forbidden.

In fact, the conventicle prohibited procreation because Ialdabaoth and his domain must be resisted. Epiphanius quotes from another one of their texts, the *Gospel of the Holy Philip*, as follows: "The Lord has shown me what my soul must say on its ascent to heaven, and how it must answer each of the powers on high. 'I have recognized myself,' it says, 'and gathered myself from every quarter, and have not sown children for the archon. But I have pulled up his roots, and gathered my scattered members, and I know who you are. For I,' it says, 'am of the ones on high.'"[46] Epiphanius is especially upset that they forbid "chaste wedlock and procreation," which is permitted among the catholic laity, while being engaged in erotic practices that hinder procreation.[47]

Certainly this type of ritual practice has its risks, including accidental pregnancy and succumbing to temptation too great to withstand. Yet, the women in the conventicle were treated as "virgins," sacred women who gathered sexual emissions while refusing to be inseminated by the men. These women were the main instructors and mystagogues in the conventicle. They called themselves "elect vessels," believing that they were "saving" others by collecting souls during their sexual performance of their Agape ritual.

This type of behavior put these Gnostics in an unsavory and precarious situation. In order to be soul collectors, they had to engage in sexual activities that traditionally fostered the reign of the chief archon because the activity commonly led to procreation. What were they to do? In order to save souls while also resisting the chief archon, they developed atypical sexual practices and ritualized them within a highly structured communal environment. They refused insemination to stop procreation and resist the chief archon, but gathered the semen as sacred fluid and offered it to Christ. And thus they believed that the soul was returned on high.

CHAPTER 7

Once a woman, always a woman?

In Carthage, North Africa, at the beginning of the third century, Quintus Septimius Florens Tertullian wrote about a "scandalizing" practice ongoing in a local church: the public display of unveiled virgins in the church.[1] The virgins and their supporters had argued that Paul's demand in 1 Corinthians 11.5–16 that women ought to be veiled was a reference to the veiling of *women* and therefore did not pertain to virgins who had transcended their sexuality. They said that Paul actually *intended* virgins to be unveiled because he did not command them to veil as he had done with "women" in his letter.[2] The virgins had sanctified their flesh and their public unveiling signified this sanctification.[3] Virgins constituted a third gender class, a class that had transcended the first two: man and woman respectively.[4] Because of their new sanctified nature, they were recognized as ordained authorities within the church, teaching, baptizing, and performing other "manly functions."[5]

Tertullian's response can be summarized with the quip, *once a woman, always a woman.* He says that the virgin, while abstaining from sexual contact, is still a woman with all her sexual charms and potencies intact. Her sex has not been erased by her virginity. Nothing can sever her from her female nature and its sexual allures and magnetism, not Christian baptism, sexual abstinence, or anything else. In fact, he said that the sexual magnetism of a virgin is more powerful than that of a married and sexually active woman.[6] The virgin, as a woman, invites concupiscence, enough even to entice the angels into her bed.[7] The virgin is not a "third generic class, some monstrosity with a head of its own," Tertullian writes with flourish. She does not govern herself or anyone else, because she is still "woman" and "the man" is still her "head."[8] As a woman, she is not permitted in church to speak, teach, baptize, or be ordained. The virgin is subjected to all the normal laws assigned to "woman": subjugation, humility, and shame.[9] As brides of Christ, even more than wives of human husbands, they must take on the veil.[10] Cover up and build "a rampart for your sex," Tertullian demands, so that the men of the church are not tempted by the blossom of virginity.[11]

The churches of the second and third centuries were fraught with this kind of conflict over gender and sexuality, especially as they related to issues of church leadership and hierarchy. Much of the literature that has come down to us in the form of treatises, homilies, and letters written by leaders in various church communities testify to the presence and authority of women within these communities, if only in the fervor taken up against them by the authors. Time and time again we hear of situations like the one in Carthage, which resulted in the condemnation of the baptismal triumph of women who claimed to have broken the gender boundary, allowing them access to leadership roles in the church.

But the women's story is a sad one. It did not end in triumph for them. Slowly and gradually their power was eroded, limited and denuded by the male leaders. As this happened, their "place" as woman and wife was redefined in ways that even traditional Roman society found excessive. The full weight of sexuality as an evil impulse was laid permanently in their laps. And there was nothing they could do to rid of its stain.

The Church is a household

The public and authoritative activity within the early church of traditionally cloistered and subordinate women was both their rise and their downfall. Traditional Roman society had been built on sensibilities of chastity and shame. The good wife was cloistered in the home and covered and chaperoned when at market. The public woman was a woman on display, a whore or tart. There was very little room for any other conception.[12] So, while Christianity and the church made it possible for unmarried girls to leave traditional household seclusion and wives to leave their husband's beds, it also caused "the greatest dismay in Rome."[13]

The Roman pagans disapproved of the movement of Christian women into public forums and the intimate public associations that Christian men and women enjoyed, criticizing them of gross sexual indecency. In the third century the Roman writer Minucius Felix composed a dialogue called *Octavius*, a conversation between a Christian known as Octavius Januarius and the Roman pagan, Caecilius Natalis. In this dialogue, he says that the Christians "recognize each other by secret signs and marks; they fall in love almost before they are acquainted; everywhere they introduce a kind of religious lust, a promiscuous 'brotherhood' and 'sisterhood'."[14]

Tertullian is very concerned about this Christian public image. In a letter he wrote to his wife, admonishing her to stay unmarried should he die before her, he reasons with her by tapping into her feelings of shame. He postulates a situation in which she might remarry a pagan instead of a Christian. Tertullian demands to know what pagan in his right mind would ever allow his wife to run around in the streets to visit the houses of strangers and enter the poorest hovels in order to help the needy faithful. He wants to know what pagan husband would be willing to have his wife leave him for the evening in order to attend nightly meetings on her own. "Who," he asks, "would tolerate without some anxiety her spending the entire night at the paschal solemnities? Who would have no suspicions about letting her attend the Lord's supper, when it has such a bad reputation? Who would endure her creeping into prison to kiss the chains of the martyrs? Or even to greet any of the brothers with a kiss? Or to wash the feet of the saints. To desire this? Even to think about it?"[15]

Many Christian leaders in the second and third centuries felt that they needed to tame the beast lest the churches experience serious repercussions at Roman hands. The authoritative activity of women, both unmarried and married, within the public sphere of the male was a public image liability some leaders believed they could not afford. We know about a few Christian men who wanted to persuade the Roman pagans that sexual promiscuity with their Christian sisters was not one of their sacred rituals, even though it might look like it from the perspective of the outsider who might so judge their public display of women. Around the year 150 CE, a young Alexandrian man presented the governor of the city a petition, seeking permission to undergo castration for this very reason: to demonstrate to his pagan neighbors that Christians were not indecent.[16] Origen, the head of the Alexandrian theological school in the early third century is rumored to have undergone castration in order to suppress the gossip that he was intimately involved in sexual relationships with the women who were his students.[17]

As interesting as these maneuvers were, they did not contain the damage. The most successful strategy was *not* to convince the Roman pagans that there was nothing indecent about the public display and "manly" authority of women. It was to force the women back into the home and the beds of their husbands – to convince them once and for all that the church was like the home, and the "man" was its "head." As we have already seen in a previous chapter, this strategy of subordination is already at play in the New Testament pastoral letters, 1 and 2 Timothy and Titus. There we find the argument that the church should be run like the traditional Roman household in which the husband rules over the wife. If run as a little household, the church would meet or even exceed the conventional Roman standards of public decency. The women would be veiled and submissive, viewed as perfect wives and congregants. Their public image would be restored.

This line of argument allows leaders like Tertullian to criticize Christian churches with women leaders. He is aware of a church run by a woman teacher and baptizer. As mentioned in an earlier chapter, the church upheld her right to teach and baptize by insisting that Paul himself conferred this authority on Thecla according to the *Acts of Paul*, a popular theological text that circulated in the ancient world. Tertullian will have none of this and forwards a counter-argument anchored in a household analogy, suggesting that the church is like the household in which women should be subordinate and silent. "How could we believe that Paul should give a female authority to teach and baptize, when he did not allow a woman even to learn by her own right?" he asks. "'Let them keep silence, Paul says, and ask their husbands at home'."[18]

Tertullian's solution to the bad press is to urge marriage between young Christians. He pleads "the necessity of a husband to the female sex, as a source of authority and of comfort." Such is the answer to the woman's allure and concupiscence, rendering Christians "safe from evil rumors," he says.[19] To engage women in conventional marriages to Christian men was a practical solution, allowing the couple to function as "brother and sister, fellow servants," without the worry of slanderous gossip arising. Tertullian argued that side by side the married couple attends church and the Lord's supper. Side by side they visit the sick and needy. "They give alms without anxiety, attend the sacrifice without scruple, perform their daily duties unobstructed," Tertullian raves. "They do not have to hide the sign of the cross, or be afraid of greeting their fellow Christians, or give blessings in silence."[20] Because the woman was a good wife, escorted by her husband and under his watchful eye, the Roman pagans could say nothing about scandalous behaviors and sexual promiscuity between them. There was nothing unsavory about their relationship, or about the movement of the woman in the public sphere, as long as her husband was at her side.

Tertullian's contemporary in Alexandria, Clement, had a similar solution. He bade Christians behave as Romans in their marriages, only better. This strategy develops in tandem with other early Christian leaders who wanted to make clear that Christians were not indecent folk or criminals. Christians were morally compatible with the best of Roman society, they said, taking the Roman value of chastity so seriously that sex was only engaged in by married Christians when they were attempting to conceive a child.[21] Clement takes this strategy a step further, a step that began to set Christian marriage apart from the conventional pagan. He argued that Christian marriages ought to exceed the expectations of the Romans. How could they exceed Roman expectations? By making the bedroom the arena of the philosophical contest of the cultivation of reason. The Romans, like the Greeks, placed high value on the reasonable man, the man whose intent rather than his emotions controlled his public actions. Clement moved the reasoned public man into the bedroom, where Clement made his case for the superiority of Christian marriage.[22]

He writes:

> The human ideal of continence which is set forth by Greek philoso-phers teaches that one should fight desire and not be subservient to it...But our ideal is not to experience desire at all. Our aim is not that while a man feels desire he should get the better of it, but that he should be continent even respecting desire itself.[23]

What did this mean for marriage? Because the Christian should "do nothing from desire," a man who marries to beget children "must practice continence so that it is not desire that he feels for his wife." Instead, the procreation of children must be done "with chaste and controlled intent."[24] This type of marriage Clement markets as the "middle" road, something between the encratic and licentious extremes, even though it clearly borders on the encratic and is no middle road. As such he calls it "controlled marriage" and advocates its institution-alization among young Christians.[25] Clement thought that by the time the blossom of youth had faded and procreation ceased, the Christian marriage would be naturally chaste anyway.

The Church literature written by leaders in the east from Cappadocia and Pontus, like Gregory of Nyssa and Gregory of Nazianzus, also try to walk a middle road between the worlds of the household and chastity. They speak of the household as the place that a woman can practice the "philosophical life" while also being wife and mother. They advocate for wives a seclusion within the household, that allows the women the opportunity to combine their active and contemplative lives. While going about their traditional wifely and motherly duties, they can focus on properly ordering their lives so that they give attention to vigils, fasting and prayer, like a virgin would.[26]

Part of the reason that they did not condemn marriage or see sex as an undesirable act, had to do with their perception of Paradise and the image of God in which the human being was formed. Nyssa read Genesis 1.27 as a double reference. "In the image of God, he created him," referred to the creation of the soul and its ontological likeness with God. "Male and female, he created them," was a reference to the capacity for sexual distinction, a capacity that was realized later in the Genesis story. This interpretation meant that the primal human being was "neither male nor female," while the post-Fall human being was sexually differentiated. The singleness of the monk and virgin repre-sents the soul redeemed from the state of the two sexes.[27]

Although sexuality was an additive, it was not a punishment, like the loss of immortality had been. Adam made the mistake of will, wishing to make the physical beauty of the created world his own. This resulted in the transience of this world seeping into his very nature. Sexual differentiation and sex had nothing to do with the Fall. In order to ensure that the human race did not become extinct, however, sex was necessary following the Fall, which had plunged the human being into mortal existence. Sex meant for Nyssa *reproduction*. But it also meant that sex provided fodder for death in the form of progeny.[28] Nyssa understood our lower human nature as transient and tragic. He laments the young husband or baby who dies, as finite relationships of deep loss. How much better it is to look to heavenly things that do not pass away than to commit your heart to transient relationships that will only end tragically.[29] So, in the end, although Christian marriage is an honorable lifestyle, the virgin lifestyle may be the most attractive.

Brides of Christ

It was not only married women who needed to be reined in and controlled. So, too, did the growing number of virgins who were amassing power and glory in the churches, as Tertullian's pen reveals in the opening story of this chapter. As he relates, many Christians he knew believed that the virgin had transcended her sex, and this gave her power and prestige to perform "manly" functions within the churches. They were no longer considered women, but a "third" gender, the so-called "sacred vessels dedicated to the Lord," who were able to teach, baptize and perform other priestly duties.[30]

Not surprisingly, many self-proclaimed and powerful virgins did not bother with the church. Rather they choose to follow the Spirit, leaving their homes and families to take up an independent life in the desert as hermits. Tucked away in caves, they lived out their lives as independent holy women who allowed the austerity of the desert to recreate their physical features in such a way that pilgrims could not distinguish them from men. They starved their bodies until their breasts vanished, menstruation ceased, and they became men to all who came out to the desert to seek their counsel, advice and intercession. As the story cycles of the revered Mary of Egypt relate, Mary's hermitage was frequented by male pilgrims such as the monk Zossimus. She is recognized by him as endowed with the grace of God as a gift of the Spirit. After she reveals to him that she is not male, he begs her as "Mother" to officially "bless" him and intercede for him with her prayers.[31] Other stories about these cross-gender hermits suggest that her sex might not be revealed to pilgrims until after her death when her clothing was removed and she was discovered to be female.[32]

Some independent virgins took their maleness so literally that they adopted the habit of dressing in men's clothing and cropping off their hair, virgins such as Pelagia, who also changed her name to its male form, Pelagius, and received at her cell on the Mount of Olives visitors seeking spiritual intercession.[33] Castissima tonsured her hair, gave up women's clothing, took on the name Emerald, and passed herself off as a eunuch monk in order to live in a monastery rather than a nunnery. She fasted to the point that she was mistaken as a man by her own father when he visited the monastery where she had cloistered herself.[34] The stories of these independent virgins are usually stories of adult women, who had decided for one reason or another to leave behind their former lives and embrace asceticism and celibacy.

We also hear stories of the recently widowed wealthy adopting the hermitic or ascetic life. Because of their connection to the ruling aristocracy, these rich women took over the role of patron, funding everything from pilgrimages to the holy land to the establishment of new monasteries and nunneries. Although their power as widows in the fourth century did not lead to their ordination as it may have before the office of widows began to be restricted in the second and third centuries, these wealthy widows gained some personal independence, disposing of their possessions at will and traveling on whim.[35]

It is well known that Jerome developed close spiritual relationships with female virgins such as Marcella in Rome, many of them widows from aristocratic families whom he had convinced not to remarry.[36] Although these women were versed in Greek and Hebrew along with scriptural exegesis, he never suggests that their intellectual achievements annulled Paul's prohibition against women teachers.[37] In fact, he says that they must learn with modesty and restraint, concealing their learnedness.[38] He delights in the fact that such women are acting *against their nature*. He writes to the aristocratic Demetrias, a woman who has chosen the life of the virgin, "You must act against nature or rather above nature if you are to forswear your natural functions, to cut off your own root, to cull no fruit but that of virginity, to abjure the marriage bed, to shun intercourse with men and, while in the body, to live as though out of it."[39]

But these powerful "female men" as some were called, did not come to make up the majority of the virgin population in early Christianity.[40] The majority lived their lives as dependent virgins within Christian households. These were young girls whose family dedicated them to the Church as virgins, often to avoid paying out dowries or to dispose of unwanted baby girls or to discard the weak or ill.[41] The Christian families transferred the well-known intercessory powers of the virgin to their households, believing that her presence within their home and her constant prayers secured the salvation of the entire household from invaders and raiders.[42] So every Christian household was encouraged to foster one.[43]

In 403 CE, Jerome wrote to Laeta, a mother who wished to dedicate her infant girl to the church. In his letter, he spells out all the details of fostering a virgin whose body would become the temple of God. The girl child must be kept in total seclusion and her servants must be carefully vetted so that they do not do or say anything that might teach her about the world and its lewd ways. She should be taught such shame of her female body that after puberty she should never bathe again, being humiliated by the mere thought of seeing herself naked. She should learn to mortify her body, to subjugate it and live in deliberate squalor to spoil her natural sexiness. Whenever she is taken into public or to church, she must be accompanied by her mother. She can never receive a greeting or compliment from a young man. Neither can she be allowed to associate with people of the world. Her austere chaperoned life is to be organized around learning to read scriptures and the writings of certain prescribed church leaders, to recite prayers and hymns at particular hours of the night and day, to fast regularly, and to spin wool.

The main reason for this upbringing was to erase the virgin's independence before it could even bloom. As Jerome explains, "Leave

Digging in

Box 7.1 What woman?

> *Thrust back by hands from the sanctuary door*
> *Mary of Egypt, that hot whore,*
> *Fell on the threshold. Priests, candles, acolytes,*
> *Shivered in flame upon her failing sight ...*
> *And when at last she died,*
> *With burning tender eyes, hair like dark flame,*
> *The golden lion came*
> *And gave that dry burnt corpse to the earth's womb.*
>   John Heath-Stubbs, "Maria Aegyptica." In *The Swarming of the Bees*
>   (London, 1950: 15).

On the fifth Sunday of Lent, the western liturgy celebrates Mary of Egypt as a model of repentance. Her story is the story of a young Alexandrian woman living indulgently. She joins a pilgrimage to Jerusalem, but does not give up her reckless sexual seductions until she visits the Church of the Holy Sepulchre and is overwhelmed by a sense of conviction. She leaves Jerusalem, crosses the Jordan, and goes out into the desert to live as a repentant hermit. Forty-seven years later, by accident, the priest Zossima discovers her living naked in her cave. He thinks she is a man until she tells him otherwise. He offers her his cloak, listens to her story and gives her communion. Later, when he returns, he finds her dead, so he buries her with the help of a lion. In other versions, a group of anchorites visit her and find her dead, only to discover to their surprise that she was no man, but a naked woman who had covered herself with her hair. So Mary of Egypt is typically depicted in ancient art as a naked or poorly clad figure with long hair. But is she a woman? Her dressed representations depict a flat-chested body, so we might imagine an emaciated woman under her garments. But when her body is naked, it is clear that this is not the case. As is shown in this eighteenth-century Russian icon, Mary's body has no breasts at all. She is the female-become-male *par excellence*.

For deeper digging, read Benedicta Ward, *Harlots of the Dester: A Study of Repentance in Early Monastic Sources* (Kalamazoo: Cisterian Publications, 1987).

her no power or capacity of living without you, and let her feel frightened when she is left to herself."[44] Dependent, afraid, and humiliated, the virgin was circumscribed in the meanest of ways so that her position was emptied of power. Whether intentional or not, the development of the dependent household virgin circumscribed the power of the virgin, taming and redomesticating this class of women. The young dedicated virgin had no life outside her parent's household. She had to live in the interior rooms of the home, leaving only to attend church where she sang in choirs of dedicated virgins and received instruction from the male clergy.

This type of program meant that these sheltered women lived within a very restricted network of people: their families, church officials, and other virgins and ascetics. So it is not hard to imagine why intimate friendships developed between dedicated virgins. It was not unusual for close-knit groups of virgins to dwell together in one family's home or on the property of a woman patron who herself had adopted virginity, often later in life. The well-known Melania the Younger, who, after a life-threatening pregnancy, convinced her husband at a young age to adopt a chaste marriage, became a significant patron for other ascetics in the late fourth century and early fifth century. Later in her life, she took up residence in a cell on the Mount of Olives and became acquainted with a number of ascetics dwelling there as well. After 15 years of living in this loose hermitage, she decided to build a monastery for herself and 90 virgins so that they might live and worship together as a community.[45]

Clever bishops, like Maximin, recognized the power of the virgins and tried to harness it to their own advantage by erecting steeply built thrones, canopied pulpits, and surrounding themselves with singing of crowds of virgins.[46] The church historian Eusebius tells us about Paul of Samosata, the Bishop of Antioch from the years 260–269 CE, who built himself a lofty throne as his seat in the middle of his church. In order to impress his congregation and increase his popularity, he surrounded his throne with a choir of women whom he had trained to sing hymns of praise. Apparently, he also formed intimate relationships with some of them, living with a couple of these virgins, female companions the Antiocheans called "call-in girls."[47]

It is not hard to imagine why intimate friendships developed between the virgins and male clergy and monks, such as those which had developed between Paul of Samosata and some of the virgins of his church. Many of the teachers and leaders of the Church gave spiritual counsel and theological instruction to circles of virgins, initiating strong bonds of companionship between the men and the women. In addition, some of the male ascetics and virgin women found it practical to live together under one roof, forming households of spiritual couples. This situation caused alarms to reverberate within the Church, since the women were becoming ensconced in permanent intimate relationships with men who were not their fathers, brothers or husbands. They were living together under one roof, even sharing the same bed, while remaining continent.[48]

These relationships began to be restricted and even forbidden on the basis of the sexual dangers of women, especially the sexual dangers of women who were continent. Even though the virgin had refused marriage, sexuality was her nature and it would allure and trap the friends into the very deed they had renounced. Indeed, John Chrysostom was worried that sexual desire would be intensified in these permanently abstinent relationships because it was never satisfied. The couple would be living in a constant state of sexual arousal, the man committing adultery a thousand times a day by lusting after the woman.[49] It is for this reason that John characterizes them as enticing harlots and Jerome calls them "one-man whores."[50] In the middle of the fourth century Basil wrote *On the Preservation of Virginity*, in order to stop these sorts of living arrangements. He argued that even though the virgins had given up marriage, they were still women. They were still sexual creatures. Because of this, the only relationship there could be between men and women, even virgins, was a sexually charged one. His solution was to separate the virgins from the men, to segregate them.

How were these virgins ultimately contained? The church leaders built around them the powerful myth of sacred marriage, a myth that sanctified their subordination within the Church. By making them "brides of Christ," the virgins were subordinated in furtive and even inhumane ways. They were bound into a non-human relationship, a permanent marriage to Christ, which made them no-man's wife (ever!) yet subject to the authority of a divine husband whose physical representatives were the male clergy of the Church. In this way, the virgins' subordination to the Church and its male clergy was sacralized, at the very time their sexuality was restrained. The dedicated virgin was desexualized, not by turning her into an independent female man, but by raising the girl in such a manner that, on her own volition, she would shun and starve her body, to limit its "natural" propensity to tempt and tart. She would be driven into a living paradox, wedded to a god who could be no husband, and subordinated to the clergy as Christ's bride.

The Devil's gateway

The story of women in the early Church is a story of their increasing marginalization and limitation, a process that was fully engaged in the fourth and fifth centuries. One of our primary witnesses of this process is the Bishop of Salamis, Epiphanius. He takes great effort to demonstrate that women have never baptized, been apostles, or been bishops. He paints a portrait of a Church that has condensed and flattened originally separate and powerful offices of women – deacon, widow, and elder – into the same office – that of the deacon. And her activities as deacon are circumscribed as narrowly as possible. She assists with the baptism of women, and she only administers the Eucharist once it has already been consecrated.[51]

This marginalization and restriction is seen across the board from the writings of the church leaders to the liturgical handbooks and canons published by church synods. Widows are admonished not to be ordained.[52] Female elders are said never to have been called "elders" or "priestesses."[53] Those elderesses who had been acting as leaders of their congregations are told that they may not be installed in the Church.[54] Female deacons are to be counted among the laity, their ordination severely restricted or discontinued.[55] Women priests are not allowed to be appointed by a church.[56] They must stop officiating at the sacred altars and taking on manly appointments within the Church.[57] Women are to be excluded from the chancel area entirely.[58]

Throughout the early Christian literature, we discover that those Christians who favored the ordination of women referred to Exodus 15.20 where Miriam is referred to as a "prophetess, the sister of Aaron," and Galatians 3.20 where baptism is said to erase gender distinctions for those in the church, a consequence that had its roots in a hermaphroditic reading of Genesis 1.27. Those who opposed the ordination of women did so through a misogynist appeal to Genesis 3.16 where God punishes Eve by prescribing patriarchy, 1 Corinthians 11.8 where Paul says that woman is created from and for man as a glorious image of him rather than of God, and 1 Timothy 2.12–15 where women are denied authority over men because woman was the original sinner.

Along these lines, Epiphanius claims that those who favor the ordination of women are women. And what are women but "unstable, prone to error, and mean spirited."[59] They are crazy and suffer the malady of the deluded Eve.[60] The source of the desire for women's ordination is women's pride and female madness, which tempt the rest of the human race to their cause.[61] Such women should not be heeded, since it is evident from Proverbs that a man must rise above the evil counsel of women who are out to snare men's precious souls.[62] Eve should never be obeyed lest she convince her children to eat of the tree. Adam must desist obeying her. She is the cause of Adam's death and all her children's because she has overthrown creation by transgressing God's commandment. Death entered the world through a woman's action. As a consequence, she cannot be trusted or obeyed.[63]

Epiphanius' misogynist interpretation is not original. It can be traced back to some of our earliest Christian sources, perhaps most punctuated in Tertullian's terse prose, "Do you not know that you are an Eve? The sentence of God on this sex of yours lives in this age. The guilt must of necessity live too. *You* are the Devil's gateway. *You* are the unsealer of that forbidden tree. You are the first deserter of the divine Law. *You* are she who persuaded him whom the Devil was not valiant enough to attack. *You* destroyed so easily God's image man. On account of *your* desert, that is death, even the Son of God had to die. And do you think about adorning yourself over and above your tunics of skin?"[64]

This portrait not only made woman the sinner, but her body became the instrument of sin, the source of desire and lust that perpetually brings down even the best of men. Her natural female body was connected with sin in such a way that, uncontrolled, woman was nothing more than (potential) whore in the opinion of many of the male leaders of the churches. Her natural propensity to tart had to be controlled through a negation or denial of her female nature.

This resulted in an obsession in the church literature with the abasement of the female image, the blotting out of her sexiness through the concealment of dress and veils, and the voluntary neglect and mutilation of her physical appearance.[65] Tertullian says that a woman's "natural" beauty must be obliterated by covering and neglecting it. This curtails the commission of sin lest a man see a woman's natural beauty and be brought into hell because of it. The beauty of the woman's body is the "sword that destroys him." Although the woman might be free of the actual commitment of the crime, she is never free from the disgrace of being the cause of the man's downfall.[66] Tertullian suggests that women go about garbed with "meanness of appearance" as a penitent does, because she ought to be repenting Eve's sin anyway.[67]

This obsession created among Christian men and women a kind of schizophrenia, as reflected in Augustine's words, "A good Christian is found in one and the same woman: to love the creature of God whom he desires to be transformed and renewed, but to hate in her the corruptible and mortal conjugal connection, sexual intercourse and all that pertains to her as a wife."[68] How should a Christian husband love his wife? Augustine compares it to Jesus' commandment to "love our enemies."[69] Augustine understands this "love" relationship to operate in such a way that the wife's body, as tart, must be defused. Sex itself is not the culprit. But sexual desire is, brought on as an irrational response to the visual stimulation of her body. According to Augustine, the "hideous" unwilled erection of his penis was the conse-quence of sin and woman was its source.

But this was not always so. In Paradise, before the Fall, Adam and Eve engaged in sexual intercourse for procreative purposes, but the act was devoid of desire, intentionally willed like a "handshake" according to Augustine. It was a simple act of will, and had Eve conceived and bore a child from that union, she would have done so with no birth pain. This kind of intentional sex is no longer possible. One of the filthy consequences of the disobedience of the first couple, who forfeited their power not to sin, was carnal desire. This was evident to Augustine in the uncontrollability of his penis and its unwilled erection at the sight of woman.

What are humans to do in the face of this kind of tragic predicament? Earlier, Jerome had taken up the call to asceticism, arguing fiercely that even first marriages are regrettable, and second marriages were little more than prostitution.[70] He writes to the widow Furis, "Confess the shameful truth. No woman marries to avoid cohabiting with a husband. At least if passion is not your motive, [your desire to remarry] is mere madness to play the harlot just to increase your wealth."[71] Jerome points out that the command to "increase and multiply" in Genesis 1.28 was not actually enacted until *after* Adam and Eve sinned. "Eve was a virgin in Paradise," he writes. "After the garments of skins, her married life began."[72] Consequently, virginity and seclusion became Jerome's gold standards. "Virginity is natural," he says to Eustochium, "while marriage only follows guilt."[73] Although sexual desire would still torment the virgin, it would have little opportunity to be engaged in Jerome's world. It would be controlled by rigid conduct and avoidance of sexual contact.[74]

Jerome's extreme position was not well received, especially among the wealthy laity in Rome. Romans much preferred the reasoning of Jerome's opponent, Jovinian, who argued that marriage and virginity were both acceptable lifestyles in the Christian Church.[75] Jovinian thought that *once baptized*, married women, virgins, and widows were all of the same merit, as long as they were not sinning otherwise. He admonishes virgins not to be prideful in their virginity. "You belong to the same Church as married women," he says.[76] Jovinian expresses concern over the elevated status of the virgin in the Church as the "bride of Christ." He reminds the ascetics that Paul's words from 2 Corinthians 11.2 – "I betrothed you to Christ to present you as a pure bride to her one husband" – was not spoken to virgins alone, but to "the whole Church of believers." All women who were baptized – the married, remarried, widows, and virgins – were equally betrothed to Christ.[77]

Other voices added to the fervor. An unknown author whom we call Ambrosiaster wrote in Rome during the episcopate of Damasus (fourth century CE). He was opposed to Jerome's support of virginity and his degradation of marriage, a position he argued as heretical, akin to the fashion of the Gnostic Manichaeans whose leaders were vowed encratites.[78] He opens his work *On the Sin of Adam and Eve* with the call, "Hear now, O Catholic, while the gospel testifies that the birth of a human being is something good."[79] He argued against the position laid out by Jerome, instead reading God's commandment to "increase and multiple" as a blessing bestowed on Adam and Eve at the beginning of creation *before* the Fall. Sex was not symptomatic of original sin. It did not cause original sin nor was it altered as a penalty for that sin. The crime was disobedience and death was the punishment.[80] This did not mean that men and women were on equal footing, however. Ambrosiaster understood Eve's subordination to her husband following the Fall to be a *return* to the original order of creation. He says, "Because it is through the woman that the man was made subject, and because, without doubt, he was formerly in a superior position ... God's order was restored by the sentence."[81] For Ambrosiaster, Adam's original God-endowed supremacy was renewed after the Fall. Woman would never again have a position of authority to bring down man as Eve had done with Adam.

In the beginning of the fifth century, Julian of Eclanum wrote a treatise *To Florus*.[82] Like Jovinian and Ambrosiaster, Julian was writing against the severe asceticism that some Christian leaders were endorsing during this period. As a follower of Pelagius, Julian was particularly engaged in a debate with Augustine's position over human free will and the nature of humanity. Augustine's identification of sexual desire and the uncontrollability of the penis – the loss of the power not to sin – with the consequences of original sin led him into dangerous territory. Since all humanity shares the consequences of original sin – an uncontrollable desire for sex, sexual shame, excruciating pain in childbirth, and death – human nature itself must have been affected by the original sin. Augustine thought that the damage had to be passed on from parents to the child through the sex act itself. He identified the semen as the culprit. Everyone at birth is already damaged by sin, enslaved to it from the moment of conception.

Julian would have none of this because it devalued marriage and procreation in a way that reminded him of Manichaeism, the powerful Gnostic movement that arose in the third century and spread throughout the Mediterranean world. The Manichaeans preached the evil nature of the human condition and their leaders practiced a vowed celibacy and asceticism. Marriage for the laity was allowed, but only as a "forgiven" sin. Augustine had been a Manichaean layman before he converted to Christianity. So, in Julian's opinion, Augustine was a leopard who had not changed his spots. Why? Because Julian understood Augustine to say that a permanent element of evil exists in human nature and that this evil element has damned us through the sex act, a position strikingly similar to that taught by the Manichaeans.

Julian's picture of humanity was utterly different. He believed that creation was essentially good. He understood that every human being, like Adam and Eve, had to make their own choices not to sin. Human beings are responsible and capable of doing good. The power not to sin has been part of human nature since creation and continues to be. Adam's sin did not destroy this. Adam's sin did not injure the entire human race, passed on through the sex act as Augustine imagined. Adam's sin injured only Adam. All babies are born in the same state that Adam was before the Fall, and each is faced with the responsibility to choose to live without sin.[83]

Although Julian talks about Adam's sin, he did not go so far as to exonerate Eve. Julian thought that the first woman was the one who originated sin, but that Adam was the more powerful and had greater authority than she did. Because of this, Adam's sin, although not the first, was more likely to be imitated by later generations than Eve's. This is how he explains Paul's language in Romans 5 where sin is said to come into the world by one man.[84]

Julian argued fiercely that Augustine's association of original sin with sexual desire was disproven by our natural experiences. He felt that the sexual libido and pleasure were part of human nature, given to us by God at creation before original sin. Procreation, commanded by God, necessitates them.[85] He insists that our modesty to cover our sexual organs is not universal, but differs with persons, locations, and customs.[86] Pain in childbirth is a natural experience of females generally, including non-human females in the animal world. Although a woman's pain in childbirth might increase because of sin, it is not a punishment for original sin.[87]

Julian has a very practical reason for ferociously engaging Augustine and setting forth the arguments he does. Julian is concerned about the implications, whether intentional or not, that Augustine's teaching had on real marriages. Julian suggests that Augustine's view might lead Christians to condemn marriage and posit that children born in wedlock were the work of the Devil.[88]

Augustine, however, does not yield to these implications. He tries to walk the razor's edge between Jerome's glorification of asceticism and Julian's positivist view of marriage, offering up what Augustine imagined to be a middle road by promoting marriage as second best to virginity.[89] Since paradisial handshake sex was no longer a possibility, marital sex was risky. Sexual pleasure was an involuntary side-effect of the procreative act. It was the expression of sin's penalty. It could easily cause the couple to slip into whoredom. As such, it was particularly debasing to women whose bodies were both its cause and its satisfaction.[90]

So Augustine circumscribed sex to marriage and procreation. He severed the sex act from sexual pleasure. He prescribed it as a passive and submissive act on the part of the woman. The wife's sole intent during the sex act should be on impregnation, since procreation was the only purpose for the existence of her sex apart from the male body. She must allow her husband to use her body for the sowing of his seed like a farmer who sows his seed in the furrow of the field.[91] If she submits her body to her husband's plow in an intentional but dispassionate embrace, she will be forgiven the involuntary pleasure of sex. As long as she despises sexual desire and intends to be impregnated, pardon is possible, although the sex act, even performed in this manner, will never be restored to the conditions of Paradise before the original sin.[92] It will always be associated with sin, and the woman's body along with it.

The result? The woman had to surrender her body to the male, forfeiting pleasure or suffering guilt in her obedience to her husband, her "head," even to the point of her own disfigurement and abuse.[93] Not only was her body to be used sexually for seed sowing by her husband, but also as a masturbatory object. Since Paul had conceded "it is better to marry than to burn," Augustine promoted marriage as the cure for concupiscence and illicit fornication.[94] He also suggested that marriage was a "symbol of unity."[95] His vague formulation of this as a reflection of the abstract concept of God's unity with the soul or Christ with the Church had nothing to do with the personal relationship between the husband and wife as more contemporary Catholic writers would like to suggest.[96]

What did Augustine's view mean to women in his world? The case of Ecdicia is telling.[97] Augustine's letter to her is a response to her own letter to him, asking his advice on the subject of her husband and her marriage. From what Augustine states, Ecdicia vowed to take up the continent life while still married and without her husband's consent. Eventually, her husband comes around to her position and agrees to take the vow himself. In the meantime, Ecdicia begins to dress as a widow, rather than a married woman. This dismays her husband. She does not heed his request for her to continue to dress by the normal standards of married women. In the midst of this angst, she gives most of her money and possessions away to two wandering monks who promise to give it, in turn, to the poor. When her husband finds out what has happened, he is furious, despising her for her foolish actions and the monks for robbing his house. Angry, he gets involved sexually with another woman, leaving Ecidica in a torrid state, especially in terms of her son whom she wants to keep away from him.

Augustine has words for Ecdicia. He considers her a woman who thinks too highly of herself, wrongly assuming that her chastity has erased her traditional role as her husband's subordinate. Augustine opens his letter by blaming Ecdicia for her husband's adultery, telling her that she ought to have been mindful of her husband's sexual needs and her sexual duty as his wife. He scolds her for vowing continence before her husband was willing to commit to this vow as well. He tells her that her first duty as a wife is the debt of her body that she owes her husband. This duty surpasses her desire for marital chastity. He argues that "it is a sin to refuse the debt of your body to your husband." Ecdicia ought to have been submissive to her husband and obeyed his will with regard to sex. He might not have been carried off by the diabolical temptation to commit adultery if Ecdicia had given her body to him as she should have. Her desire to live in continence has resulted in her husband's destruction and her own sin.

Augustine then says that she is absolved of this particular sin because her husband eventually did consent to live in continence with Ecdicia. He reminds her of Paul's words in 1 Corinthians 7.4. The decision for continence cannot be her decision, but must be her husband's since *a wife does not have authority over her own body, but her husband does*. Since her husband agreed, even late in the game, Ecdicia is absolved of his crime.

However, even as vowed virgins, this does not mean that her marriage ceased to exist or that she ceased to be a subordinate wife. The fact that she altered her dress against her husband's wishes and that she disposed of her property without consulting her husband first is sin *par excellence*.

Augustine suggests a remedy to undo the damage that she personally has wrought on her husband. Since she remains married to her husband, she has no grounds to deny her husband access to their child. Augustine tells her to straighten out her marriage because her son needs unity between his parents. To do so, she needs to humble herself before her husband. Pray for him. Weep for him. Write him a letter of apology asking pardon for having sinned against him because she disposed of her property without his advice or consent. If he returns to the continence he abandoned, promise to obey him in all things as is proper of a Christian wife.

CHAPTER 8

How do we solve a problem like Maria?

Mary of Magdala. Who was she, memorialized for us in the Bible as the woman who stood at Jesus' cross and visited his tomb, the woman who saw Jesus shortly after his resurrection? From the pulpit, we might hear of her as the sinner woman who anointed Jesus' feet with her tears and wiped them away with her hair, the repentant prostitute and exemplar of the reformed sinner. Feminist voices today laud her as a prophet and visionary, a woman leader among equals, a beloved disciple, the Apostle to the Apostles.[1] Her pop image has been cultivated as the outspoken demon-possessed whore. Who can forget that provocative scene of the Magdalene from Cecil D. DeMille's famous film, *King of Kings*, when Jesus stares at her haughty figure and the seven deadly sins emerge from her body as ghostly apparitions? Or Martin Scoresse's tattooed temptress, naked behind the gauzy veil, hurling insults at Jesus for his voyeurism? Then there is the Magdalene as wife of Jesus and mother of his dynasty, most recently popularized by Dan Brown in his bestseller, *The Da Vinci Code*.

What is difficult to distinguish among all these faces of Mary is the historical from the rest, especially when we are operating in the realm of pop culture where references in ancient manuscripts are so easily mistaken to be historical facts about Mary. Just because an ancient text identifies her as a visionary or Jesus' lover, does not mean that she was so. In fact, we know that the old literature that mentions Mary was produced by ancient Christians with their own special interests. They used the Magdalene's image in much the same way as pastors, priests, and pop writers like Dan Brown do today – to support and forward their own convictions, platforms, and agendas.

In the case of Mary Magdalene, we have multiple, even contrasting, memories of her in the early Christian literature – what I call "counter" or "alternative" memories. Is she a repentant whore? The Apostle to the Apostles? The wife of Jesus? Groups create counter-memories by remodeling earlier traditions they know, focusing on less prominent features of these earlier traditions, and reframing them in new contexts. This is done so that the new way of remembering Mary will be considered "old" and "legitimate" instead of "new" and "suspect."

Over time, a master narrative emerges that reflects the stance of the dominant group and marginalizes and erases the competing memories of the minority groups. Groups in power tend to use their commonly held memories to support and maintain their own dominance, often at the expense of other groups and their alternative memories.[2] We certainly find this to be the case with the Magdalene who emerges after Nicaea from the counter-memory battle with the face of a repentant whore rather than an apostle equal in stature to Peter or Paul.

So the real historical situation is very complicated and difficult to reconstruct. Various Christian churches in the second century inherited cycles of oral and written stories from the Christian communities in the late first century. I call these inherited stories the foundational memories. It is quite likely that many of the foundational stories that were known to the second-century Christians were not preserved for future generations. It is also true that the foundational memories that were written in the New Testament gospels were not written down until at least 40 years after the historical events. So even these canonical foundational narratives are adaptations of older received oral and written stories.

It is quite clear that Mary Magdalene was remembered as a prominent and significant woman in Jesus' mission. The foundational stories agree that she was present at Jesus' crucifixion and empty tomb.[3] There is a strong independent tradition preserved in Matthew and John that Jesus appeared first to Mary and even commissioned her to teach the other disciples about what she had witnessed and learned from Jesus. The synoptic gospels – Mark, Matthew, and Luke – name her as one of the women who functioned as a deacon in the Jesus movement, a role that appears to have involved substantial patronage. Although she does not turn up on the canonical lists of the 12 male disciples of Jesus, she is remembered in the foundational stories as the prominent female "follower" who traveled with Jesus from Galilee along with a number of other women, both named and unnamed.

Luke reports that Mary Magdalene suffered from an illness that was healed by Jesus when the demons that were causing the sickness were exorcised by him. We hear no mention of a husband or any other familial attachment as we do for the other named women in the movement who are usually identified as the wives or mothers of specific men. Mary is presented to us in the foundational narratives as a woman without a husband or a child, a woman alone and identified only by the place of her birth, Magdala.

Over time, these foundational stories are developed by the early Christians and many faces of the Magdalene emerge across the literature. In some texts, she is remembered as Jesus' lover and wife. In other second-century texts, she steps forth as a bold disciple and teacher, a great leader of the church. And then there is our dominant memory of her today as a repentant whore, a memory with a long history dating back to the second-century literature and the conflict over women and their roles in the early church.

Mary caught in the crossfire

The foundational gospel stories of Mary Magdalene are written in the period immediately following Paul's letters. It is likely that these narratives are based on oral stories about Mary Magdalene that had been circulating in the early Christian communities. The foundational written stories, however, are not unadulterated preservations of history. When the stories are written down 40 years after the events they record, they already have enjoyed a long life passed by mouth from person to person. When they finally are cast in ink by the gospel authors, the contents are recast in light of the author's own time and circumstances and concerns. Given the fact that, during Paul's time, women still had access to the leadership roles afforded Christians, but concerns were being levied regarding their social and cultural status in respect to the males, we should not be surprised to see Mary's story similarly adjusted at this time so that she appears prominent yet subservient to her male associates.

We see in the gospel sources a demarcation of 12, and only 12, male "disciples" (sg. *mathêtês*; pl. *mathêtai*) of Jesus. *Mathêtês* is not used by the gospel writers to identify his women disciples. Instead, they are referred to as Jesus' "followers" (from *akoloutheô*). *Akoloutheô* is a verb meaning "to follow" or "be a disciple." It is not restricted to the women disciples in the gospels, but is used broadly by the evangelists to indicate any person who was one of Jesus' disciples, including the Twelve themselves. In fact, the call narratives of the 12 disciples include the command, "Follow (*akoloutheô*) me," as do Jesus' stories about discipleship.[4]

As for *mathêtês*, the evidence suggests that it, too, once had a broad application, used to identify a large number of Jesus' intimate pupils, including Joseph of Arimathea.[5] In fact, Luke says that Jesus chose the Twelve *from* "his disciples (*mathêtai*)," clearly knowing that *mathêtês* was broadly construed in the earliest traditions.[6] Originally, the word was not even restricted to the male followers of Jesus. In two early Christian texts, it describes women followers such as Mary Magdalene and Tabitha ("the Gazelle") who are each identified by independent authors as a *mathêtria* or female disciples of Jesus.[7] The New Testament gospels, however, bear witness to a recent restricting of the word *mathêtai*, "the disciples," since the authors of the gospels begin applying it in a more limited sense, as an alternative form for the Twelve male pupils who were called by them "the Disciples."

The story cycles about Mary Magdalene in the New Testament

gospels preserve an earlier tradition in which Mary was remembered as a prominent female disciple of Jesus, who was the primary witness to Jesus' resurrection and the first to worship him. This tradition can be located in a post-resurrection story preserved in the gospel of Matthew:

> So they (Mary Magdalene and the other Mary) departed quickly from the tomb with fear and great joy, and ran to tell his disciples. And behold, Jesus met them and said, 'Hail!' And they came up and took hold of his feet and worshiped him. Then Jesus said to them, 'Do not be afraid. Go and command my brothers to go to Galilee, and they will see me there.'[8]

According to this passage, Mary Magdalene was commissioned by Jesus to teach the "brothers" what she had seen and learned from Jesus.[9] This earlier, likely oral, tradition is contextualized in the gospel of Matthew in such a way that it begins to diminish her identity as a sister disciple.[10] Throughout Matthew's gospel, she is not numbered among the Twelve, neither is she remembered as a *mathêtria*. Her story in this particular post-resurrection passage is recast by the author of Matthew so that she appears to be separate from "the disciples" of Jesus rather than among them. To achieve this, Matthew contextualizes the oral tradition he inherited – that she was commanded by Jesus to tell the "brothers" to go to Galilee – by framing her prominent commission with the statement that she "ran to tell *his disciples*" rather than the "brothers." Whereas Jesus' commission assumes her to be a sister in the movement, a female among his disciples, Matthew's recasting of her story excludes her from the party. The author of Matthew further minimizes her prominence when, a few verses later, he closes his gospel with Jesus' commission to the eleven male disciples – and only the 11 male disciples – to preach to and baptize all the nations.[11]

Mary has a similar prominence in the gospel of John, and similarly her old story has been reconfigured in such a way that her prominence is dampened. Her old story begins in John 20.1. She comes to the tomb and sees that the stone has been taken away. What happens next? According to the other versions of the empty tomb story in Mark, Matthew and Luke, she looks into the tomb and has a vision of angel(s) with whom she converses. In Matthew, she next sees Jesus who commands her to tell the disciples to go to Galilee. Then she runs to tell the male disciples what she has seen.

Now, the author of the gospel of John knows this same storyline, in this same order, but he does not preserve it. Instead, he inserts into her narrative an interloping story about the disciple whom Jesus loved and Peter.[12] When he does this, the storyline shifts so that Mary comes to the tomb, sees the stone gone, and runs back to get the men. The men have a race back to the tomb, and it is the beloved disciple who arrives first and peers into the tomb, becoming the first witness to the empty tomb. When Peter gets there, he is the second witness, going into the tomb to inspect it with the beloved disciple by his side. The beloved disciple is declared as the first to "believe" and understand that Jesus had to rise from the dead according to the scripture.

At this point in the story, we return to the original plot line.[13] Mary is crying at the empty tomb and she stoops to look into it. When she does so, she sees two white angels sitting where Jesus had lain. They converse. Then she turns around and sees Jesus standing there, although she mistakes him for a gardener at first. After she recognizes him, Jesus tells her that he will be ascending to the Father. Mary goes back to the men and tells them, "I have seen the Lord," and reports what Jesus had said to her.

So the Johannine author breaks open her narrative and adds the remarks about the men's footrace to the tomb. In so doing, he erases Mary's prominence as the primary witness to the empty tomb and the resurrection of Jesus. In his revised account, her witness appears secondary to the men's witness and supportive of it. Her once powerful story is reduced to a woman's confirmation of the male leaders of the church and what they had to say about Jesus.

The author of the gospel of Luke preserves a version of Mary's story that has been modified even further so that Mary Magdalene is recalled as one among a number of women who collectively were the first witnesses to the empty tomb, but not to the resurrected Jesus.[14] In fact, when they go to tell the 11 disciples about the empty tomb and the two dazzling "men" to whom they spoke inside the tomb, the "apostles" did not believe them because they thought the women were "talking nonsense."[15] Later in Luke's narrative, we learn that some of the apostles went back to the tomb to confirm what the women had seen.[16]

Instead of Mary's witness to the resurrection and commission, we find preserved two differing accounts by Luke.[17] The first account involves a pair of apostles, one named Cleopas and the other unnamed. They meet Jesus on the road to Emmaus, converse with him, and recognize him after participating in a eucharist celebration with him. They are taught by Jesus that the Messiah was supposed to suffer and be glorified. They return to Jerusalem and tell "the 11 and those who were with them" what had happened. Their story becomes anti-climactic when the collective of apostles responds, "The Lord has risen indeed and has appeared to Simon!" So Simon Peter gets the credit as the first to see the resurrected Jesus in Luke's gospel. Mary's witness and commission are completely wiped out of his retelling of the story.

Whenever I ponder Luke's decision to erase Mary's eminence as a witness so thoroughly, and his mention that the women's story was considered nonsense by some, needing male witnesses to confirm their story, I am reminded of the words of Celsus, a Roman critic of Christianity who wrote in the late second century. One of the main reasons he finds Christianity to be a ridiculous religion is the fact that its foundational doctrine, the resurrection of Jesus, was witnessed by a "hysterical" woman. To this end he writes:

> We must examine this question – whether anyone who actually died ever rose again with the same body? ... Who saw this? A hysterical female, as you say, and perhaps some other one of those who were deluded by the same sorcery, who either dreamed in a certain state of mind and through wishful thinking had a hallucination due to some mistaken notion (an experience which has happened to thousands of people), or, which is more likely, wanted to impress others by telling this fantastic tale, and so by this cock-and-bull story to provide a chance for other beggars.[18]

Since women could not be witnesses according to Roman Law, and were believed by many people who lived at that time to be easily swept away by religious frenzy and hysteria, what good was Mary's witness to the promulgation of the Christian message among Romans? Her old story was a liability as Celsus' criticism points out, and Luke seems to know this and cover it up the best he could. But in doing so, Mary's witness is erased from the tradition. Were it not for other sources of her story, Mary's witness would have been completely forgotten and impossible to recover from Luke alone.

When a comparative analysis among the New Testament gospels is done, it is clear that even the foundational stories of Mary Magdalene in the gospels represent a remodeling of an older story about her. This older story knew that Mary, a prominent disciple of Jesus, had been the primary witness of his resurrection and had been commissioned by him to teach the other disciples about what she had experienced and learned from Jesus. By reframing certain elements of her old story and inserting new elements within it, her prominence is marginalized or replaced by the male heroes and leaders of the movement when the gospels were written. This remodeling of Mary's traditional story occurred at a time when women's roles in some of the churches were being called into question because of the social and cultural implications of their leadership. Although women were still permitted in leadership positions within the churches, their power and prominence were already beginning to wane as the dominant male social and cultural hierarchy was threatened, aroused, and asserted in the mid- to late first century.

The male Mary

Encratic communities harbored their own memories of Mary Magdalene. Most prominently they present her as Jesus' "male" woman disciple. She appears to have played a particularly prominent role in early Syrian Christianity, at a time when baptism into the Church meant that the convert had vowed to forsake the matrimonial bed.

The most famous reference to Mary found in the encratic texts is one we already discussed in some detail. It is the final saying found in the *Gospel of Thomas* where Jesus asserts that he will make Mary "male" so that she will become "a living spirit." He promises that every woman who will "make herself male will enter the Kingdom of Heaven."[19] Mary Magdalene is presented here as the role model for Christian women, as the woman whom Jesus made "male" and thus "a living spirit." This was the state of "man" before he sinned, when Adam was created in God's image with the female, Eve, concealed inside of him. This recreation of the primal Adam reflected a paradisiacal time when the first "man" was "a living spirit" as is stated in the then popular Greek translation of Genesis 2.7.[20]

So Mary is being is honored in the *Gospel of Thomas* as the woman who was transfigured into the primordial hermaphrodite. Since the "male" woman was the woman who rejected her traditional female roles and took on celibacy and singlehood as her custom, Mary becomes the iconic representation of this custom according to the *Gospel of Thomas*.

This "egalitarian" understanding of celibate single women was not universally accepted among Christians. As we saw earlier in this book, many Apostolic churches were shutting women out of leadership roles while also insisting that women marry. They justified this course of action by pointing to their reading of the Genesis story where they saw woman as a secondary creation responsible for sin. Her only salvation is acceptance of her perpetual punishment – to submit to the totalitarian rule of her husband and to painful childbearing. In no case should she be permitted to teach men. This is the line of reasoning that Simon Peter represents in the *Gospel of Thomas* when he insists that Mary should leave the company of the male disciples, the male leadership, because women are not worthy of salvation. This Genesis-inspired teaching appears to have been a well-known appeal by authorities in various churches wanting to discredit and invalidate women's leadership roles.

The encratic community in Syria wholeheartedly disagreed with this interpretation of Genesis, understanding it to be an abuse of the text. So in the *Gospel of Thomas*, the encratic author cleverly brings

Digging in

Box 8.1 Teaching the Apostles?

This painting from the St Albans Psalter (1123–1135 CE) depicts Mary Magdalene standing in her own isolated rectangle of color. She is emerging from the green garden onto the road. Her right hand is raised in a gesture of teaching and authority. The 11 disciples are crowded into the right-hand space, gesturing with raised hands and clutched books. The scene is a depiction of John 20:18 where Mary tells the disciples that she has seen Jesus outside of his tomb and relates to them all that Jesus told her. She is portrayed in her role as the Apostle to the Apostles. The painting graces the cover of Graham Brock's book on the Apostle Mary. This scene, however, is not popular in ancient or medieval western art. When it is found, it is sometimes accompanied by speech scrolls in which the disciples ask, "*Dic nobis, Maria, quid vidisti in via?*: Tell us, Maria, what did you see on the road?" These words were composed in the eleventh century and, in the twelfth century, became part of the liturgical Easter pageant, *Quem quaeritis* (Young 1933:149). Their presence in the artwork is another example of how the tradition of her powerful apostleship is deflected. With the disciples' question posed, Mary no longer is the one who initiates the teaching to the apostles following Jesus' command to her. The apostles take front and center as the authorities who demand to know *from her* what she saw.

Reprinted as public domain image.

For deeper digging, read Ann Graham Brock, *Mary Magdalene, The First Apostle: The Struggle for Authority* (Cambridge: Harvard University Press, 2003); Karl Young, *The Drama of the Medieval Church* (Oxford: Clarendon Press, 1933).

forward his own appeal to Genesis, a saying of the "living" Jesus to counter the sexist position voiced by Peter. According to the encratic position, women are worthy of life. Women too can become "living spirits" like the original Adam. How? To become the primordial Adam, the first man, they believed that women had to reject "femaleness," which they understood to be marriage and procreation, just as they thought Mary had been able to do as Jesus' "male" disciple.

The 'memorial' Magdalene in the encratic texts is the celibate disciple Mary, a student Jesus favors for her chastity. She stands up in encratic texts to combat widespread teachings that were being used by some church leaders to subordinate and silence women by reducing them to temptresses, tricksters, and transgressors. This combat over the worth of women is nowhere more visible than in the *Dialogue of the Savior*, an encratic Syrian Christian text from the early second century. The text quotes a saying, which it attributes to Jesus: "Pray where there is no woman."[21] This saying is in line with the words of Peter in the *Gospel of Thomas*, "Mary should leave us because women do not deserve life," and the words of the author of 1 Timothy, "I permit no woman to teach or to have authority over men. She is to keep silent." The Christians who were touting this saying must have been using it as leverage to deny women access to their traditional roles as Christian leaders in their churches.

The authenticity of this saying in the eyes of the author of the *Dialogue of the Savior* appears to have been undisputed since he assumes its veracity. He knows the saying as one that has been bandied about as Jesus' own, but he does not like how other churches are using it to subjugate women. So to defuse its abuse, he addresses the meaning of the saying. Immediately he offers his own interpretation of it. "Pray where there is no woman," he says, means that we must "destroy the works of femaleness," that is, women "should stop [giving birth]."[22] The author is saying that the erasure of "woman" should not be understood as the rejection of women from the church's body of clergy. Rather, he says, it refers only to the cessation of female activity. The saying is rekeyed to promote encratic ideals rather than the removal of women from church offices. A troublesome teaching about women's widespread subjugation in some churches, becomes a commandment from Jesus to stop having sex and children in the encratic churches.

In this context, Mary asks Jesus if procreation will ever be destroyed. Jesus tells her that she knows that this will be so. His statement assumes that Mary herself is an exemplar of the celibate woman.[23] Her responsibilities do not include traditional marriage, procreation, and childrearing. In her capacity as the woman who has put off the "female," Mary is the ideal disciple who says to Jesus, "I want to understand everything [as] it is." Jesus responds by telling her to seek "life" rather than the wealth of the world.[24]

She is granted a vision of the future along with the male disciples Matthew and Judas (Thomas) who was the apostolic hero of Syrian Christianity.[25] She is described by the encratic author as the "woman who understood everything," and, consequently is confident to teach Jesus' words to others.[26] So, in the course of the dialogue between Jesus and his inner circle of disciples, it is the disciple Mary who speaks three sayings of Jesus: "'The wickedness of each day.' And 'laborers deserve their food.' And 'the disciple resembles the teacher.'"[27] When she speaks, she does so with the authority of a teacher, and Jesus responds by telling her that her remarks show "the greatness of the revealer."[28]

What inspired encratic communities to form this particular "memorial" Magdalene? They appear to have linked their knowledge of Mary from the old oral memories of her as a disciple and leader with their interpretation of the written foundational stories about her preserved in the canonical gospels. The written narratives present her as a woman alone, far away from her home in Magdala. In these stories, she is the woman without a husband or children. Unlike Joanna, the wife of Herod's steward Chuza, or Mary the mother of James and Joseph who appear beside her, Mary's name does not connect her to a husband, or suggest any other familial associations.[29] The encratic Christian may have wondered whether it was her willingness to renounce her traditional female roles that earned her Jesus' favor. Had she given up her home in order to become Jesus' favored student?[30]

Such an understanding of the foundational written stories about Mary would easily result in memorializing this woman as the encratic Magdalene who had renounced her traditional roles as wife and mother to attend to the teachings of Jesus, and carry them on after his death as an apostle herself. Mary's "maleness" derived, in fact, from her refusal to marry and take on the traditional roles of the female, including procreation. This is a subversive memory, undermining the conventional picture of women in the ancient world. Because the women have become "men," however, it is a powerful argument that allowed women in some ancient churches to continue to operate as public Christian leaders.

The sexual Mary

The Gnostic Christians in the second century held diverse opinions about their world and their place in it. The scope of this book has revealed Gnostic groups with tantalizing (and even scandalizing) views of the sex act and its association with the fallen spirit. The scandalizing practices of Epiphanius' Gnostic conventicle also provided women the opportunity to perform important liturgical functions. They were regarded as virgin soul collectors responsible for gathering the soul from seminal emissions. Mary Magdalene is their cipher. She is the one who receives the ritual from Jesus himself in their book the *Greater Questions of Mary*. It is clear that the community traces the authority of the Agape ritual back to Mary's revelation and understands her to be the incipient of their primary liturgical tradition. The true meaning of the Agape feast is given to Mary Magdalene by Jesus in the *Greater Questions of Mary*. Given Mary's extraordinary authority, it is not surprising that this community possessed several books that rely on her testimony including the *Lesser Questions of Mary*, the *Greater Questions of Mary*, and the *Birth of Mary*.[31]

In a post-resurrection vision in the *Greater Questions of Mary*, Jesus reveals to Mary how collection of semen is to be ritually performed and says to her, "Thus we must do, that we may live."[32] In this vision, Jesus draws a woman from his side, re-enacting the primal moment at which Eve was drawn from Adam's side. But instead of procreating with her, he collects his semen for ingestion, demonstrating that redemption involves rejecting procreation while ritually gathering the soul from the sexual fluids and returning it to God. It is Mary who is privy to this.

In the case of the Valentinian Christians, it was believed that the spirit of the child was created or drawn into the child at the moment of conception. In order to attract the purest spirit for their offspring, the Valentinians engaged in a sacralized form of marriage which they believed imitated the divine sygyzy, the male–female yoking of God's own androgynous self. This was a monogamous heterosexual form of marriage whose eroticism was imbued with prayer and sacred intention. Even the divine aeon Jesus was yoked with the female aeon he had saved. Achamoth became his bride at the end of time when they led the saved angelic couples into the Pleromic bridal chamber and were enraptured with each other as newlyweds.

In Valentinian tradition, during historical time, the divine aeon Jesus descends and resides in the human being Jesus of Nazareth. Since marriage is the paradigm for salvation, it should not surprise us that Jesus of Nazareth is not perceived as a single man in the Valentinian literature. He is partnered with Mary Magdalene who is perceived to be his spouse. She is memorialized in the *Gospel of Philip* in just this way: "And the partner of the [Savior] is Mary Magdalene. The [Savior loved] her more than all of the disciples, and often he kissed her on her [mouth]. The other [disciples...] said to him, 'Why do you love her more than all of us?' The Savior answered and said to them, 'Why do I not love you all like her?'"[33] The English translation, "partner," for the noun *koinonos* is a bit deceptive, since its verbal form, *koinoô*, can mean, "to have intercourse with." In this sort of context, the noun *koinonos* can refer to "spousal partner." Their spousal partnership is quite clearly indicated in another passage from the Gospel of Philip, which reflects on three women in his life: "There were three walking with the Lord all the time. Mary his mother and her sister and Magdalene, the woman who was called his partner. For 'Mary' was his sister and his mother and his partner."[34]

The Magdalene memorialized in the Valentinian Gnostic literature is quite different from the Magdalene found in the encratic literature. You might even say that the memories developed by the Valentinians rendered her into her doppelgänger. But she was not only remembered by the Valentinians as Jesus' wife. Mary was also his favorite disciple who carried on Jesus' esoteric teaching after his death as a leader among the apostles. This iconic portrayal of her is very prominent in the *Gospel of Mary*, a gospel that appears to be a Valentinian midrash on John 20.18: "Mary Magdalene went and announced to the disciples, 'I have seen the Lord.'[35] And she told them that he had said these things to her." In the Gospel of Mary, she delivers to the male disciples esoteric teaching, a teaching that the Valentinians believed Mary had received earlier from Jesus in the Garden. What did the Valentinians think this esoteric teaching was? It was a Valentinian homily on the significance of the eucharist to the ascent of the soul.

To set up her delivery of this homily, the gospel opens with a discussion between Jesus and the disciples about the nature of sin. Mary is present as one of his disciples. Jesus explains that sin has arisen because the soul has become embedded in matter. When the soul descended into the material body, it descended into a condition of disturbance and temptation. This disturbed condition of the soul leads us to commit sins like adultery. The only way that this situation can be resolved, he says, is with the descent of the Savior, when he unites with our souls. So Jesus exclaims: "Watch out that no one leads you astray, saying, 'Lo here!' or 'Lo there!' For the Son of Man is within you. Follow him!"[36] When he finishes speaking, Jesus leaves the disciples, who then begin to grieve.

Mary steps forward and consoles them, reminding them that Jesus' "grace" is with them. She tells the other disciples not to despair, but to "praise his greatness, for he has made us ready. He has made us men."[37] And with this, she turns the hearts of the disciples to God. This language resonates liturgy. The word normally translated as "praise" in Coptic is *cmou*, which means "to give thanks." In many cases, it can mean "to take" or "give a sacrament." The "thanksgiving" sacrament is the eucharist, and this is what is referred to here. Mary is leading the disciples in a eucharist ceremony, beginning by lifting their hearts to God, just as is done in modern day Catholic Mass. What does the ceremony do according to the Gospel of Mary? It is a ritual that brings about the descent of the Son of Man within the person, or as Levi says at the end of the gospel, it enables the person to "put on the Perfected Man and have him for ourselves."[38]

This is technical language. Like many other Valentinian texts, "putting on the Perfected Man" refers to receiving the body of Christ by participating in the eucharist ceremony.[39] According to the Valentinians, Jesus the Perfected Man is the reflection of the primordial Man, who is the androgynous Man before Adam's sin. It is this body that we acquire in the eucharist sacrament. They believed that, when the faithful ate the divine Man Jesus, his body would work internally like medicine, healing our brokenness. By eating and drinking the Perfected Man, our fallen bodies are rebuilt or resurrected into glorious bodies. This is not a reference to a new fleshly body, but to a spiritual or angelic one that will be able to ascend through the spheres of heavens undetected by the vicious celestial guardians, a topic that Mary preaches about throughout the rest of the extant Gospel of Mary.[40] So redemption by participation in the eucharist is characterized as the recovery and transformation of the woman Eve into the primordial Man Adam. As Mary says to the male disciples in the *Gospel of Mary*, that, in this way, Jesus "made us into men."

But that is not all. In Valentinian traditions, the transformation into the primordial Man is also connected to marriage. Twice referencing Eve's movement back into Adam, the author of the *Gospel of Philip* teaches that the return to the prelapsarian unity is the joining of husband and wife in marriage.[41] So what we have in the Valentinian Gnostic community is the argument that through marriage, women are able to achieve the primal androgyny of the first "man," thus becoming "male." This "male" conversion allowed the women Gnostics to stand up as church leaders alongside the men, giving sacraments and delivering homilies like the "male" Mary Magdalene in the *Gospel of Mary*.

Given this interpretation of the Genesis story, it should not be surprising that, in the *Gospel of Mary*, Mary's leadership role is threatening to Peter and Andrew, who represent the opinion of the Apostolic Church. Mary is in direct conflict with Peter and Andrew who challenge her opinions as "some other ideas."[42] They question whether Jesus taught esoteric things to a woman, while leaving themselves, the male disciples, out of the conversation. Didn't he speak openly to us? Does he want us to listen to her? Did he prefer her to us? These are all social questions that have arisen as a result of the gender debate that gripped early Christianity.

Mary responds by asking whether Peter thinks that she is lying. Levi, an advocate for the Gnostic position, jumps in and tells Peter to be quiet. "If the Savior made her worthy, who are you to cast her out?," Levi says. "Certainly the Savior knows her very well. This is why he loved her more than us. Let us be ashamed, put on the Perfected Man, and have him for ourselves as he commanded us. Let us preach the gospel, and stop laying down rules that are beyond what the Savior said."[43] These words are telling, revealing a social situation in which the Valentinians, like the Syrian encratites, are arguing that some of the Apostolic churches are institutionalizing rules that exclude women from pulpit activities when Jesus never meant or said any such thing. Instead, the Valentinians argue that women, like Mary Magdalene, do have a route to "maleness." It is achieved sacramentally, mainly through their participation in the eucharist and marriage.

Why did the Valentinians choose Mary Magdalene as Jesus' *koinonos*? Like the encratic Christians, the Valentinians based their own memories of the Magdalene on universal givens about Mary, elements such as her discipleship and leadership that transcended the written narratives but were generally accepted by Christians as genuine. They also appear to be very familiar with the canonical narratives, favoring the version of Mary's story found in the Gospel of John because of the intimacy featured between Jesus and Mary. From these narratives, the Valentinians also seem to have recognized her as a single woman. This, however, did not mean that she had renounced marriage and procreation as the encratic Christians claimed. This meant that she was available for marriage. Jesus is single. Mary Magdalene is single. What could be more convenient than their marriage?

The memories of the Valentinians are not so much subversive as they are adaptive. Socially, the Valentinians considered themselves to be members of the Apostolic Church until the early to mid-third century. So they accepted the Apostolic pro-marriage argument, but they refocused it. They agreed with the other Apostolic Christians that the marriage of the female to the male is salvific, but they disagreed about what type of relationship it should be. They argued that it is not a relationship of subordination, but one of harmonious cooperation between partners mirroring the Aeonic syzygies. Marriage is a unification of the divided primal androgyny, before Eve became separated from Adam. This primal Adam, the androgynous "male," was their redemptive goal, and had to be achieved sacramentally through the eucharist and marriage. Because women could recreate this primal androgyny by participating in the eucharist and marrying, they could return to the Garden as the prelapsarian Man. They could become "men" as Mary Magdalene did. On this basis, they concluded, women should be allowed to stay in the clergy.

The Apostolic Mary

The Apostolic or Catholic tradition emerged as the orthodox tradition by the fourth century, and when this happened women definitively were locked out of the clergy. Mary's memory as a powerful leader could not survive within the Catholic environment. In order to control her memory, two different master narratives about Mary Magdalene arose in the western and eastern Apostolic churches.

Western theologians realigned her with the stories of Mary of Bethany and the prostitute from Luke's gospel who wept on Jesus' feet and wiped them with her hair. This new counter-narrative transformed the foundational stories of Mary by confusing them with stories of other Maries and women, casting Mary as a prostitute.[44] This counter-memory appears to have been fairly well known already in the mid-second century, since the pagan philosopher Celsus refers to it when he insinuates that Jesus and his disciples were supported by certain women whom Jesus healed, and that this support was garnered through "a disgraceful and importunate way."[45] Tertullian calls Mary Magdalene "the woman who was a sinner," a clear reference to her conflation with the sinner woman in Luke.[46] In a sermon once attributed to Hippolytus, Mary and Martha, Lazarus' sisters, seek Christ in the Garden. Martha's sister is confused with Mary Magdalene. Hippolytus considers her a second "Eve" whose obedience to Jesus compensates for the sin of the first Eve.[47]

Mary as the repentant whore becomes the official master narrative of the Roman church by the sixth century. In a sermon delivered on September 14, 591, Pope Gregory the Great seals her fate. He definitively transposed the story of the Magdalene into the stories of Mary of Bethany and Luke's sinful woman who used her flesh "in forbidden acts."[48] In so doing, Gregory was able to successfully suppress the earlier contrasting memories of Mary as a powerful woman leader, memories that had the potential to continue to threaten the hegemony of the patriarchal order. What is most disturbing about this recreation was that Gregory did not just lock women out of the clergy. He cemented a memorial bridge that would connect all women with Mary the repentant whore. As the redeemed whore, she became the character model for women, a manageable and controllable woman, whose "new" story would be used as propaganda to subjugate women on divine writ for hundreds of years.

Interestingly, the Apostolic churches in the west were silent when it came to memories of Mary's discipleship and her leadership. When the western Apostolic churches created their counter-memories of Mary the prostitute, they did not invoke either memories of her discipleship or her leadership. They neither disputed them nor agreed with them. Their silence is telling. If these two memories were universally accepted givens about Mary, to deny them would sabotage the new prostitute memory that the Apostolic community was producing because the prostitute scenario would be openly defying accepted knowledge about Mary. So to subdue these threatening but accepted memories of Mary, the western Apostolic churches overwhelmed them by confusing Mary Magdalene's story with the story of other women found in the gospels. Furthermore, they focused on her singleness at the expense of all other memories of her. In the ancient world, in which unmarried public women were stereotyped as prostitutes, Mary's public singleness was her greatest liability and the western Apostolic churches used it against her. Once her name was linked with the image of the Lukan prostitute, her good reputation was irrevocably damaged. Mary Magdalene was brought to her knees along with all women leaders in the west who emulated her.

In the eastern Apostolic tradition, a different memory shift takes place. By the fourth century the hierarchies in the Syrian churches had become male dominated and, under pressure from Rome, the Syrian churches were accommodating married members into its congregations. When this happened, the memory of the "male" Magdalene became less and less necessary. Memories of Mary in the fourth-century Syrian literature become eclectic and confused. Her image erodes when she is superimposed with other characters, oftentimes male, but most prominently the Virgin Mary. This further exaggerated the suppression of women's leadership, because women were faced with a paradox, a woman model who was both a virgin and a mother, a Mary they could never emulate. The result of this shift in communal memory is a Syrian tradition that the resurrected Jesus appeared to Mary his mother first, not the Magdalene as scripture relates. Other than her name "Mary," the memory of the Magdalene all but disappeared from the garden.[49]

In other eastern traditions, she is neither confused with the Virgin Mary nor amalgamated to Luke's prostitute or Mary of Bethany as she is in the west. Rather, in later eastern Orthodoxy she remains her own woman. She is depicted in late legends as so chaste that the Devil sends seven demons into her because he mistakes her for the Virgin Mary and wants to hinder the incarnation. She is given the honorable title "Apostle to the Apostles" and is considered an "Equal to the Apostles." Although this might seem like an acknowledgment of her old apostolic prominence, it does not work that way in the eastern Orthodox tradition itself. The title "Equal to the Apostles" is given to Mary because she was the first messenger commissioned by Jesus to announce his resurrection.[50] "Apostle to the Apostles" is her title because she proclaimed the resurrection to the apostles, who then proclaimed his resurrection to the whole world.[51]

What happened to Mary when this master narrative formed in eastern Orthodoxy? The later eastern traditions may be aware of Mary's prominent reputation in the early church as a single woman who was commissioned by Jesus as an apostle. Yet in their official master narrative there is a reliance on the canonical gospels to restate her narrative as it is told by the evangelists, where earlier memories of her prominence are recontextualized in a hermeneutic that subordinates her to the male apostles whom she entrusts with her vision and its dissemination. The male apostles are reconfirmed as the official bearers of the Christian traditions in the east, and Apostle Mary is effectively silenced as were all the women who wished to emulate her.

CHAPTER 9

Because the Bible tells us so?

The story of women and the early church is far from easy to understand since the ancient sources obstruct our view of this story more often than they assist it. It is an understatement to say that the women's story is *complex*, given that it has been so marginalized, overwritten, and in some cases deliberately erased by the authors of the surviving texts that the presence and activities of women has dimmed or dropped out of sight. The story of women recorded in ancient sources simply cannot be understood at face value since the texts were written by male leaders in emerging churches who had their own interests to front and authority to assert and maintain. So it must be reconstructed and reimagined carefully from what the ancient sources tell us *and* from what they don't.

It is dismaying to realize that, although women were present and active historically, their authentic story has been forgotten. It is nowhere to be found in the Church's main narrative. Even more dismaying is the evidence that the authentic memories of women in the early church were intentionally replaced with misogynist narratives that grew out of misogynist interpretations of events and select scriptures. But most dismaying is the fact that the misogynist narrative was made *sacred* or *holy*, so that *it* rather than the authentic narrative, became Christianity's *truth*. A bogus, yet sacralized, representation of our past has been used to control and subject half of the Christian population to the other half, affecting the real lives of men and women at the altar and in the bedroom for 2,000 years.

My reflections in this book have led me to conclude that this tragic situation is not so much the consequence of the interpretation of scriptures, the growth of theology, or the existence of social structures as I had previously thought and other scholars have argued.[1] Although these things play their part, I have come to see that the crux of the matter is the female body itself. Misogynist hermeneutics, theology, and social structures are the torrid by-products of conceptions of the female body that made *it* a *naturally* deficient body, even subhuman.

The male body was the standard body in the ancient world.[2] It was taken for granted that the woman's body was a pitiful body, an undesirable body caught between the station of man and beast.[3] In fact, it was a popular axiom in the ancient world to be grateful that you were born human and not beast, man and not woman, Greek and not barbarian.[4] This axiom made its way into ancient Jewish prayer practices, where it was attributed to Rabbi Judah:

> Three blessings one must say daily. Blessed (are you) who did not make me a gentile. Blessed (are you) who did not make me a woman. Blessed (are you) who did not make me a boor.[5]

On the female body was heaped male contempt, scorn, and hatred. Since the male body was the norm, the woman's body was substandard, deviant. In fact, ancient scientists used anatomical differences such as menstruation, breasts, womb, and lack of body hair to define females as naturally inferior to the male.[6] The female body is, according to Aristotle, "a deformed male."[7] Because it also lacked the penis, it was constructed by the ancient mind as the "imperfect male."[8] Upon it was projected everything ancient men detested or feared: weakness, deception, death, disease, slavery, meanness, sluggishness, emotion, desire, sexuality, sin, and unmanliness.[9] The female body was depersonalized, imagined as the passive earth, the field in which the male sowed his spirit-filled seed, the furrow to be plowed by his penis.[10] Reincarnation into a woman's body was believed to be the ultimate punishment for men who sinned in their current lives.[11]

The dehumanization of the female body meant that there could be no equality between men and women in the ancient world. This was an oxymoron. The early Christians who argued that baptism in Christ allowed women access to church offices, did not appear to believe that *females* had access to church offices. The women who had authority in their communities were the women who had either transformed themselves into *males*, or wiped out their femaleness in favor of *androgyny* or *hermaphroditism,* which some framed as a "third" gender that was *neither male nor female.* They were making the argument that baptized women were no longer females, but had transcended their sex. The women who went to the desert, emaciated and punished their bodies out of shame and penitence as Eve's daughters. They physically became men through a voluntary starvation program that forced the loss of their breasts and ceased menstruation. The dedicated virgins were taught from their birth to loath and neglect their bodies, to purge their bodies of a sexuality that would always stain them. Women who married were expected to suffer frigid intercourse at their husbands' command, as receptacles for the seed that her body would incubate. While her husband orgasmed to ejaculate his seed, she was expected to submit to pleasureless penetration, an act that ought to lead to painful childbirth, which was her just desert.

In an environment that so devalued the female, how could the female Spirit of God remain? This is especially a question once the doctrine of the Trinity began to form around the idea of three *consubstantial* aspects: Father, Son and Spirit. The female Spirit could never be framed as equivalent to the Father and Son. Those groups that did retain the female Spirit did so within an androgynous mythos, not a Trinitarian one, and laid upon her the cause of sin and death. There is little glory for the mother Spirit here in either scenario.

The real serpent in the Garden is misogyny. The story of women in the early church is the story of the creation of a religious institution to foster and perpetuate misogyny and patriarchy in the cruelest of ways, by making divine writ the subordination of the female *at her own hand.* The Genesis story came to be read by the leaders of the churches as the downfall of man, caused by woman. Foremost, woman is held responsible for the distortion of human sexuality. This distortion includes her own subordination as punishment for her sin. Her actions result in the mortal condition of humanity and the yoke of male domination. Her natural body becomes the Devil's gateway. Blame for her inferiority and subjugation is laid at her feet.

One of the most horrifying aspects of this situation is its longevity. Because this version of the story became the backbone of conventional religious tradition and theology for 2,000 years, it continues to collide with the lives of modern men and women. The Roman Catholic Church refuses ordination of women priests on the basis that original sin has changed the way in which man and woman live with each other. In 2004 Pope John Paul II issued a letter to the bishops of the Catholic Church on gender relationships. He stated that, as a result of original sin, the relationship between the sexes has been distorted and damaged. Woman is told by God that this new relationship will be one of subordination: "your desire shall be for your husband, and he shall rule over you." The equality, respect and love that God intended for man and woman have been lost. The best that can happen is "collaboration" between the genders, whose functions in the church are qualitatively different.[12]

The contemporary leaders of the Roman Catholic Church also stand firm on the position that only male bodies can represent Christ at the altar, because only the male body can act as Christ's image. They base their justification on a tradition from Thomas Aquinas, who thought that the signs of the sacraments represent by natural resemblance whatever they are signifying.[13] Aquinas was under the impression that the female body was a deficient or "failed" male.[14] She was *naturally* a subordinate creature, created according to man's image (not God's) and out of Adam. She was further subjected and limited as the result of original sin, "for to the woman it was said after sin: 'You shall be under the man's power.'"[15] It is not possible for the female body "to signify eminence of degree," Aquinas reasoned, "since a woman is in the state of subjection." He concluded from this that the female body – a deformed male and subjected sinner – cannot represent Christ. Thus women cannot be ordained priests, although they can serve as subordinate workers.[16]

This is the reasoning that the contemporary leaders of the Catholic Church continue to use to deny women access to ordination as priests. In face of fierce criticism and with reference to Galatians 3.28, they have admitted that Christ re-established the unity of men and women with no gender distinctions. But they continue to insist that Christ incarnated *as a man* in order to fulfill God's plan of salvation. While the incarnation *as a man* should not imply man's natural superiority over woman, they say, it is in line with "the economy of salvation."[17] In other words, we are back to Aquinas who argued that, as a result of original sin, woman is in a state of subjugation to man. Because of this, her body is not equivalent to the male body and can never stand in for it.

This degrading mentality is not limited to modern Roman Catholic leaders. While it is true that about half of Protestant traditions today ordain women, it is also true that the U.S. Federal Labor statistics indicated that, as of 2005, only 15.5 percent of all clergy in the U.S. was female.[18] This gain appears to have more to do with the secular women's movement than with any radical shifts in Christian theology. While the churches that ordain women welcome alternative interpretations of scriptures and inclusive language translations of the Bible, the snake of the Eden story still lurks in the shadows, waiting to strike again. These are not words of idle fantasy or empty rhetoric. In 1995 the snake slithered out of the shadows and struck one of the major Protestant denominations in the United States. That year at the Southern Baptist Convention, the conservative leadership took over the convention and *revoked* women's right to ordained positions within affiliate churches. The resolution was passed and became part of the official literature: "While both men and women are gifted for service in the church, the office of pastor is limited to men as qualified by Scripture."[19]

This had an immediate and cataclysmic affect on seminaries and churches associated with the Southern Baptist tradition, which had previously supported the ordination of women. For instance, the Southern Baptist Theological Seminary in Louisville, Kentucky, fired its women scholars and theologians, and refused to allow women students access to ministerial degrees with the same programming as men. In support of their actions, the leaders quoted the standard texts from the New Testament that have been used for centuries to deny women access to church leadership positions, including 1 Timothy 2.11–14.[20] While male students at the seminary take "pastoral ministry" coursework, female students must substitute a class in the "practice of ministry for women." The seminary offers certificates for female students through its "Wives' Institute" where women are taught the essentials for being a minister's wife and its "Women's Ministry Institute" where women learn how their ministry differs from the ministry of the men of the church.

This reversal of the practice of women's ordination within the Southern Baptist tradition did not occur suddenly. It developed over two decades as a conservative response to the secular women's movement. In the early 1970s the leaders of the Southern Baptist Convention framed the women's liberation movements as "a great attack" on the scriptural laws regarding "women's place in society." They reaffirmed that man is the head of the woman, that woman is the glory of man and made for him, and that she would not have existed without him.[21] The female body was declared to be derivative of the male, created by God as a subordinate body. In 1980 the convention resolved not to endorse the Equal Rights Amendment because the Bible stresses that the role of women is not the same as that of men.[22] The next year, the convention asserted that Christian women should "follow the pattern of Jesus and the teaching of the Scripture" when determining their priorities and responsibilities, beginning with the home.[23]

This type of argument led to a bolder resolution in 1984, which laid out the select scriptures the convention leaders were using to deny women access to full ministry. While the leaders of the convention openly acknowledge the equality of baptized men and women according to Galatians 3.28, they interpret this to be an equality of "dignity" not function. While they recognize that the Holy Spirit at Pentecost was poured out on men and women alike, and that early Christian women were active in the churches, they choose to emphasize that this does not alter God's "delegated order of authority" where man is the head of woman. Women are excluded from pastoral leadership in 1 Timothy 2.12 in order to preserve "a submission God requires because the man was first in creation and the woman was first in the Edenic fall." This leads them to conclude that women and men are gifted "for distinctive areas of evangelical engagement."[24]

The contemporary gender positions that have developed in the Roman Catholic Church and the Southern Baptist tradition are reminiscent of the "separate but equal" argument that allowed Jim Crow laws to be used by white supremacists to justify and continue the segregation of races following the Civil War. The laws were justified by the reasoning that separate services, facilities, and public accommodations can exist for different races, on the condition that the quality of each group's services, facilities and accommodations are equal.

The "separate but equal" situation that women face in the religious traditions such as the contemporary Roman Catholic Church and the Southern Baptist tradition is severe, since the "separate but equal" justification is flaunted as a divine prescription – God's word – resulting from the woman's own fall from grace. Unlike the legal system of the United States of America, which can be questioned and modified to reflect contemporary views about human and civil rights, the Bible cannot because it is sacred scripture whose interpretation is controlled by churches with longstanding vested interests in the maintenance of male supremacy.

It is not surprising that the women who first began the fight against the subordination of women were the women who fought for the right to vote. They realized almost immediately that they faced a situation similar to those who wanted to abolish slavery at the time. The biggest obstacle to both groups was the Bible and its invocation by their opponents who wanted to maintain slavery and women's subordination as divine prescriptions – because God allowed or commanded them. In order to challenge the scriptural subordination of women, Elizabeth Cady Stanton set out to revise the traditionally male interpretations of the scripture. She employed the few women during her time who were educated to read the primary languages and had learned the history to write commentaries on all the passages from Genesis through Revelation that concerned women. She says that some of the invited women refused to participate in the project because they feared "they might compromise their evangelical faith by affiliating with those of more liberal views, who do not regard the Bible as the 'Word of God' but, like any other book, to be judged by its own merits."[25]

The preface to her book, *The Woman's Bible*, was written in 1895. She opens her book by identifying the problem with the traditional way in which the Genesis story has been interpreted by men who use it to demonstrate that woman is a sinner and inferior being:

> From the inauguration of the movement for woman's emancipation, the Bible has been used to hold her in the "divinely ordained sphere," prescribed in the Old and New Testaments. The canon and civil law; church and state; priests and legislators; all political parties and religious denominations have alike taught that woman was made after man, of man, and for man, an inferior being, subject to man. Creeds, codes, Scriptures and statutes are all based on this idea ... The Bible teaches that woman brought sin and death into the world,

that she precipitated the fall of the race, that she was arraigned before the judgment seat of Heaven, tried, condemned and sentenced ... Here is the Bible position of woman briefly summed up.[26]

Towards the end of her introduction, she writes very openly about her own view of religion. She argues that religions and holy books like the Bible are human products, reflecting the patriarchal culture of the ancient people who created them. The prescriptions in the holy books that subordinate women must not be accepted as originating from the Spirit of God, which works for the good of all people:

The only points in which I differ from all ecclesiastical teaching is that I do not believe that any man ever saw or talked to God, I do not believe that God inspired the Mosaic code, or told the historians what they say he did about woman, for all the religions on the face of the earth degrade her, and so long as woman accepts the position that they assign her, her emancipation is impossible ... There are some general principles in the holy books of all religions that teach love, charity, liberty, justice and equality for all the human family, there are many grand and beautiful passages, the golden rule has been echoed and re-echoed around the world. There are lofty examples of good and true men and women, all worthy of our acceptance and imitation whose lustre cannot be dimmed by the false sentiments and vicious character bound up in the same volume. The Bible cannot be accepted or rejected as a whole, its teachings are varied and its lessons differ widely from each other ... [in their discrimination of women] the canon law, the Scriptures, the creeds and codes and church discipline of the leading religions bear the impress of fallible man, and not of our ideal great first cause, "the Spirit of all Good," that set the universe of matter and mind in motion, and by immutable law holds the land, the sea, the planets, revolving round the great centre of light and heat, each its own elliptic, with millions of stars in harmony all singing together, the glory of creation forever and ever.[27]

The fight for women's equality in the churches is a formidable fight because it can never be won on the turf of the traditional churches, which continue their program of discrimination each time they recycle and reframe the ancient traditions that dehumanize the female body. As long as the Bible's devaluation of the female body as part of the natural order of creation is viewed as sacred, as holy misogyny, no reasonable argument can dislodge it. As long as the Bible's story of the subjugation of woman is viewed as God's deserved decree laid upon all women for all time, there can be no liberation. How much longer must women suffer the dreadful and damning consequences of the ancient male imagination, which valorized the male body while it vulgarized the female, because the Bible tells us so?

Further reading

Adam, Betty Conrad. 2006. *The Magdalene Mystique: Living the Spirituality of Mary Today.* Harrisburg: Morehouse.

Baer, Richard A. 1970. *Philo's Use of the Categories Male and Female.* Leiden: Brill.

BeDuhn, Jason David. 2000. *The Manichaean Body in Discipline and Ritual.* Baltimore: Johns Hopkins University.

Benko, Stephen. 1967. The Libertine Gnostic Sect of the Phibionites according to Epiphanius, *Vigiliae Christianae* 21: 103–119.

Boer, Esther De. 1996. *Mary Magdalene: Beyond the Myth.* London: SCM Press.

Boer, Esther De. 2004. *The Gospel of Mary: Listening to the Beloved Disciple.* London: T&T Clark.

Boer, Esther De. 2006. *The Mary Magdalene Cover-Up: The Sources Behind the Myth.* London: T&T Clark.

Bonnet, Maximilianus. 1972. *Acta Apostolorum Apocrypha.* Vol. 2.2. New York: Hildesheim.

Brock, Ann Graham. 2003. *Mary Magdalene, The First Apostle: The Struggle for Authority.* Harvard Theological Studies 51. Cambridge: Harvard University Press.

Brock, Sebastian. 1979. *The Holy Spirit in the Syrian Baptismal Tradition.* Syrian Churches Series 9. Oxford: Oxford University Press.

Brock, Sebastian. 1990. The Holy Spirit as Feminine in Early Syriac Literature in Janet Martin Soskice (ed.) *After Eve: Women, Theology and the Christian Tradition.* London: Collins: 73–88.

Brown, Peter. 1988. *The Body and Society: Men, Women and Sexual Renunciation in Early Christianity.* New York: Columbia University Press.

Buckley, Jorunn Jacobsen. 1986. *Female Fault and Fulfillment in Gnosticism.* Chapel Hill: University of North Carolina Press.

Buckley, Jorunn Jacobsen. 1994. Libertines or Not: Fruit, Bread, Semen and Other Body Fluids in Gnosticism, *Journal of Early Christian Studies* 2: 15–31.

Bynum, Caroline Walker. 1982. *Jesus as Mother: Studies in the Spirituality of the High Middle Ages.* Berkeley: University of California Press.

Charlesworth, James H. 1969. The Odes of Solomon – Not Gnostic, *Catholic Biblical Quarterly* 31: 357–369.

Charlesworth, James H. (ed.). 1985. *The Old Testament Pseudepigrapha .* Volume 2. Garden City: Doubleday.

Clark, Elizabeth A. 1986. *Ascetic Piety and Women's Faith: Essays on Late*

Ancient Christianity. Studies in Women and Religion 20. Lewiston: Edwin Mellon.

Clark, Elizabeth A. 1990. Julian of Eclanum, To Florus (in Augustine, *The Unfinished Work Against Julian*) in V.L. Wimbush (ed.) *Ascetic Behavior in Greco-Roman Antiquity: A Sourcebook.* Minneapolis: Fortress: 156–168.

Clark, Elizabeth A. 1994. Ideology, History, and the Construction of "Woman" in Late Ancient Christianity, *Journal of Early Christian Studies* 2:2: 155–184.

Cloke, Gillian. 1995. *This Female Man of God: Women and Spiritual Power in the Patristic Age, AD 350–450.* New York: Routledge.

Collins, Raymond F. 2000. *Sexual Ethics and the New Testament: Behavior and Belief.* New York: Crossroad.

Corwin, V. 1960. *St. Ignatius and Christianity in Antioch.* Yale Publications in Religion 1. New Haven: Yale University Press.

Davies, Stephen J. 2001. *The Cult of St. Thecla: A Tradition of Women's Piety in Late Antiquity.* Oxford: Oxford University Press.

Dean-Jones, Lesley. 1991. The Cultural Construct of the Female Body in Classical Greek Science in Sarah B. Pomeroy (ed.) *Women's History and Ancient History.* Chapel Hill: University of North Carolina Press: 111–137.

DeConick, April D. 2005. *Recovering the Original Gospel of Thomas: A History of the Gospel and its Growth.* London: T&T Clark.

DeConick, April D. 2006. *The Original Gospel of Thomas in Translation, with a Commentary and New English Translation of the Complete Gospel.* London: T&T Clark.

Deming, Will. 1995. *Paul on Marriage and Celibacy: The Hellenistic Background of 1 Corinthians 7.* Cambridge: Cambridge University Press.

Dever, William G. 2008. *Did God Have a Wife? Archaeology and Folk Religion in Ancient Israel.* Grand Rapids: Eerdmans Publishing Company.

Drijvers, H.J.W. 1966. *Bardaisan of Edessa.* Assen: Van Gorcum & Co.

DuBois, Page. 1988. *Sowing the Body: Psychoanalysis and Ancient Representations of Women.* Chicago: University of Chicago Press.

Ehrman, Bart D. 2006. *Peter, Paul, and Mary Magdalene: The Followers of Jesus in History and Legend.* Oxford: Oxford University Press.

Eisen, Ute E. 2000. *Women Officeholders in Early Christianity: Epigraphical and Literary Studies.* Collegeville: Liturgical Press.

Fiorenza, Elisabeth Schüssler. 1983, 1994. *In Memory of Her: A Feminist Theological Reconstruction of Christian Origins.* New York: Crossroad.

Freedman, David Noel. 1987. Yahweh of Samaria and His Asherah, *BA* 50: 241–249.

Grant, R.M. 1944. The Odes of Solomon and the Church of Antioch, *Journal of Biblical Literature* 63: 363–397.

Griffith-Jones, Robin. 2008. *Beloved Disciple: The Misunderstood Legacy of Mary Magdalene, the Woman Closest to Jesus.* San Francisco: Harper One.

Gryson, Roger. 1980. *The Ministry of Women in the Early Church.* Collegeville: Liturgical Press.

Harris, Rendel and A. Mingana (eds). 1920. *The Odes and Psalms of Solomon*. Vol. 2. Manchester: Manchester University Press.

Harvey, Susan Ashbrook. 1993. Feminine Imagery for the Divine: The Holy Spirit, the Odes of Solomon, and Early Syriac Tradition, *St. Vladimir's Theology Quarterly* 37: 111–139.

Haskins, Susan. 1993. *Mary Magdalen: Myth and Metaphor*. New York: Harcourt Brace.

Hearon, Holly E. 2004. *The Mary Magdalene Tradition: Witness and Counter-Witness in Early Christian Communities*. Collegeville: Liturgical Press.

Horsley, G.H.R. (ed.). 1987. *New Documents Illustrating Early Christianity: A Review of the Greek Inscriptions and Papyri Published in 1979*. North Hyde, NSW: The Ancient History Documentary Research Centre, Macquarie University Press.

Hunter, David G. 1992. *Marriage in the Early Church*. Minneapolis: Fortress Press.

Hunter, David G. 2007. *Marriage, Celibacy, and Heresy in Ancient Christianity: The Jovinianist Controversy*. Oxford: Oxford University Press.

King, Karen L. 2003. *The Gospel of Mary of Magdala: Jesus and the First Woman Apostle*. Santa Rosa: Polebridge.

Kitchen, Robert A. and Martien F.G. Parmentier (eds). 2004. *The Book of Steps: The Syriac Liber Graduum*. Kalamazoo: Cisterian Publications.

Klijn, A.F.J. (2003). *The Acts of Thomas*. Supplements to Novum Testamentum 5. Leiden: Brill.

Lambertsen, Isaac E. (trans.). 1999. *Holy Myrrh-Bearer Mary Magdalene: Equal of the Apostles: Life, Liturgical Service, & Akathist Hymn*. Liberty: Saint John of Kronstadt Press.

Lang, Bernhard. 1986. *Wisdom and the Book of Proverbs: An Israelite Goddess Redefined*. New York: Pilgrim.

Lemay, H. 1992. *Woman's Secrets: A Translation of Pseudo-Albertus Magnus's De Secretis Mulierum with Commentaries*. Albany: State University of New York Press.

Lewis, Agnes Smith. 1984. The Life of Euphrosyne of Alexandria, *Vox Benedictina*, July: 140–156.

Loader, William. 2005. *Sexuality and the Jesus Tradition*. Grand Rapids: Eerdmans Publishing Company.

Marjanen, Antii. 1996. *The Woman Jesus Loved: Mary Magdalene in the Nag Hammadi Library*. Nag Hammadi and Manichaean Studies 40. Leiden: Brill

Marjanen, Antti. 2005. Montanism: Egalitarian Ecstatic "New Prophecy" in Antti Marjanen and Petri Luomanen (eds) *A Companion to Second-Century Christian "Heretics"*. Supplements to Vigiliae Christianae 76. Leiden: Brill: 185–212.

Martin, Dale B. 1995. *The Corinthian Body*. New Haven: Yale University Press.

McCambley, Casimir. (ed.). 1987. *Saint Gregory of Nyssa Commentary on the Song of Songs*. Brookline: Hellenic College Press.

Meeks, Wayne A. 1974. The Image of the Androgyne: Some Uses of a Symbol in Earliest Christianity, *History of Religions* 13:3: 165–208.

Metzger, Bruce M. 1975. *A Textual Commentary on the Greek New Testament* 3rd rev. edn. New York: United Bible Societies.

Murray, Robert. 1975. *Symbols of the Church and Kingdom: A Study in Early Syriac Tradition*. Cambridge: Cambridge University Press.

Olyan, Saul M. 1998. *Asherah and the Cult of Yahweh in Israel*. Society of Biblical Literature Monograph Series 34. Atlanta: Scholars Press.

Pagels, Elaine. 1988. *Adam, Eve, and the Serpent*. New York: Random House.

Patai, Raphael. 1990. *The Hebrew Goddess* 3rd enld edn. Detroit: Wayne State University Press.

Räisänen, Heikki. 2005. Marcion in Antti Marjanen and Petri Luomanen (eds) *A Companion to Second-Century Christian "Heretics"*. Supplements to Vigiliae Christianae 76. Leiden: Brill: 100–124.

Rudolph, Kurt. 1977. *Gnosis: The Nature and History of Gnosticism*. San Francisco: Harper, 1977.

Ruether, Rosemary Radford. 1974. Misogynism and Virginal Feminism in the Fathers of the Church in Rosemary Radford Ruether (ed.) *Religion and Sexism: Images of Woman in the Jewish and Christian Traditions*. New York: Simon & Schuster: 150–183.

Salisbury, Joyce E. 1991. *Church Fathers, Independent Virgins*. New York: Verso.

Salisbury, Joyce E. 1997. *Perpetua's Passion: The Death and Memory of a Young Roman Woman*. New York: Routledge.

Satlow, Michael L. 2001. *Jewish Marriage in Antiquity*. Princeton: Princeton University Press.

Schaberg, Jane. 2004. *The Resurrection of Mary Magdalene: Legends, Apocrypha, and the Christian Testament*. New York: Continuum.

Scholem, Gershom. 1991. *On the Mystical Shape of the Godhead: Basic Concepts in the Kabbalah*. New York: Schocken Books.

Schwartz, Barry. 1993. Memory as a Cultural System. Abraham Lincoln in World War I, *International Journal of Sociology and Social Policy* 17:6: 22–58.

Stanton, Elizabeth Cady. 1895. *The Woman's Bible*. Vol. 1. New York: European Publishing Company.

Tabbernee, William. 2007. *Fake Prophecy and Polluted Sacraments: Ecclesiastical and Imperial Reactions to Montanism*. Supplements to Vigiliae Christianae 84. Leiden: Brill.

Tishby, Isaiah. 1949, 1961, 1989. *The Wisdom of the Zohar: An Anthology of Texts*. Vol. 1. Oxford: Littman.

Torjesen, Karen Jo. 1993. *When Women Were Priests: Women's Leadership in the Early Church and the Scandal of their Subordination in the Rise of Christianity*. San Francisco: HarperCollins.

Tuckett, Christopher. 2007. *The Gospel of Mary*. Oxford: Oxford University Press.

Vogt, K. 1995. "Becoming Male": A Gnostic and Early Christian Metaphor in K.E. Børresen (ed.) *The Image of God: Gender Models in Judaeo-Christian Tradition*. Minneapolis: Fortress Press: 170–186.

Ward, Benedicta. (ed.) 1973. *The Prayers and Meditations of Saint Anselm*. London: Penguin.

Ward, Benedicta. 1987. *Harlots of the Desert: A Study of Repentance in Early Monastic Sources*. Kalamazoo: Cistercian Publications.

Warner, Marina. 1983. *Alone of All Her Sex: The Myth and the Cult of the Virgin Mary*. New York: Vintage Books.

Wolfson, Elliott. 2005. *Language, Eros, Being: Kabbalistic Hermeneutics and Poetic Imagination*. New York: Fordham University Press.

Notes

Notes to Introduction

1 Genesis 1.27.
2 Previous studies have highlighted the social, cultural and political dimensions of the gender dynamic in ancient Christianity: Brown 1988; Fiorenza 1983, 1994; Pagels 1988; Torjesen 1993.
3 1 Corinthians 11.7.

Notes to Chapter 1

1 Genesis 6.17; 7.15, 22; Isaiah 42.5.
2 Ezekiel 37.5.
3 Eccl. 12.7; Ps. 104.29.
4 Genesis 1.1–2; Ezekiel 37.9–10.
5 Genesis 2.7; Job 33.4.
6 Isaiah 30.28; Job 4.9.
7 Isaiah 63.10.
8 Isaiah 4.3–5.
9 Isaiah 32.14–18.
10 Psalm 143.10.
11 Isaiah 61.1.
12 Nehemiah 9.20.
13 Isaiah 59.21; 2 Samuel 23.2.
14 Zechariah 7.12.
15 Matthew 10.20; Luke 12.12.
16 Genesis 41.38; 1 Kings 22.24; 2 Samuel 23.2; Ezekiel 11.5; 2 Chronicles 18.23; 24.20; Numbers 24.2–3.
17 Numbers 22.35.
18 Numbers 24.2–9.
19 Philo, *The Life of Moses* 1.274, 1.277.
20 Josephus, *The Antiquities of the Jews* 4.108. 118–119.
21 Ezekiel 8.3.
22 Ezekiel 11.24.
23 Joel 2.28–29.
24 Exodus 19.18.
25 Acts 2.1–21.
26 *Wisdom of Solomon* 7.7.
27 *Wisdom of Solomon* 7.22–29.
28 *Wisdom of Solomon* 7.27.
29 *Wisdom of Solomon* 9.17–18.
30 Luke 7.35; Matthew 11.19 reads "deeds" instead of "children."
31 *Sirach* 1.10. 15.

32 *Wisdom of Solomon* 10.1–11.1.
33 *Wisdom of Solomon* 10.18–19.
34 *Baruch* 4.1.
35 Cf. Lang 1986.
36 Proverbs 8.22–30.
37 Proverbs 8.23, 27–30; *Wisdom of Solomon* 9.9; *Sirach* 1.4, 9.
38 Sirach 24.3.
39 *Sirach* 24.9.
40 *Wisdom of Solomon* 7.21.
41 *Wisdom of Solomon* 9.1–2.
42 *Baruch* 3.9–30.
43 *1 Enoch* 42.1–2.
44 *Sirach* 24.4; *Wisdom of Solomon* 9.4, 9.10.
45 *Sirach* 24.1–2.
46 *Wisdom of Solomon* 8.4.
47 *Wisdom of Solomon* 8.3.
48 Philo, *On the Cherubim* 49.
49 Isaiah 43.10–11; 45.5–4, 18, 22; 46.9; 47.8, 10; cf. Deuteronomy 32.39; Hosea 13.4; Joel 2.27.
50 Deuteronomy 5.8–9; Exodus 20.4–5.
51 Genesis 1.26.
52 Genesis 1.27.
53 Jeremiah 7.18; 44.15–19.
54 1 Kings 14.23; 15.13; 16.33; 2 Kings 17.10, 16; 21.3–7; 2 Chronicles 15.16; 33.3–7,15, 19; Isaiah 27.9.
55 Cf. Olyan 1998; Dever 2008.
56 There is a dispute among scholars whether these inscriptions should read, "Yahweh and his asherah" or "Yahweh and his Asherah." For more information, see Freedman 1987. 241–249.
57 Patai 1990: 34–53.
58 2 Kings 23.5.
59 Jeremiah 44.15–19.
60 Ezekiel 8.3.
61 Ezekiel 16.38–42.
62 Aboth diRabbi Nathan, ed. Schechter: 102.
63 Lam. Rab. Introduction: 25.
64 Elliott Wolfson's scholarship has pointed out that the Shekhina is not always female. She is also male, and she is androgynous in the Kabbalistic traditions. See Wolfson 2005: 63–77.
65 Patai 1990: 155–160; Scholem 1991: 140–196.
66 Patai 1990: 155–201; Tishby 1949, 1961, 1989: 371–422.

Notes to Chapter 2

1 Mark 1.10.
2 Mark 1.11–12.
3 Jerome, *de viris illustribus* 3.
4 Jerome, *Adversus Pelagianos* 3.2.

5   Eusebius, *History of the Church* 4.22.
6   Eusebius, *History of the Church* 3.39.
7   Quoted by Jerome, *Commentary on Isaiah* 4.
8   Mark 1.12–13; Matthew 4.1–11; Luke 4.1–13.
9   Quoted by Origen, *Commentary on John* 2.12.87.
10   *Gospel of Thomas* 101; for this particular reconstruction of the saying, see DeConick 2006: 277–278.
11   *Gospel of Philip* 56.9, 63.21–25.
12   *Gospel of Philip* 55.23–36.
13   Mark 9.2–8; Matthew 17.1–8; Luke 9.28–36. The mountain's name is known as Mt. Tabor by Origen of Alexandria (*Comm. in Ps.* 88.13), Cyril of Jerusalem (Catech., 2,16), and Jerome (Ep. 44, ad Marcel.; Ep. 8, ad Paulin.; Ep. 108, ad Eust.).
14   Mark 1.11; Matthew 3.17; Luke 3.21.
15   Genesis 3.7–12.
16   Genesis 3.21.
17   I have argued that the *Gospel of Thomas* contains an old kernel gospel from Jerusalem that was carried to Edessa in the mid-first century by some of the first missionaries from Jerusalem. On this, see DeConick 2005.
18   Aphraates, *Demonstrations* 18.
19   Macarius, *Homily* 28.4.
20   *Acts of Thomas* 27, as it reads in the Greek recension. See Bonnet 1972:142–143.
21   *Acts of Thomas* 50, as it reads in the Greek recension. Bonnet 1972: 166.
22   *Acts of Thomas* 133, as it reads in the Greek recension. Bonnet 1972: 240.
23   *Acts of Thomas* 7 and 39, as they read in the Greek recension. Bonnet 1972: 110, 157.
24   Quran 5.116.
25   *Acts of Thomas* 108–113.
26   Aphraates, *Demonstrations* 6.292.24–293.5.
27   Ephrem, *Epiphany Hymn* 6.1.
28   English translation in Brock 1979: 4.
29   Brock 1979: 4.
30   Romans 6.3–4.
31   Ephrem, *Hymns on the Crucifixion* 3.7.4.
32   Brock 1979: 84.
33   Brock 1979: 84.
34   Brock 1979: 84.
35   Brock 1979: 4.
36   Corwin 1960: 71–80; Grant 1944: 363–397.
37   Drijvers 1966: 209.
38   On this, see Charlesworth 1969: 357–369.
39   *Ode* 7.22–26; trans. from Charlesworth 1985: 741.
40   *Ode* 24.1; trans. from Charlesworth 1985: 757.
41   *Ode* 19.1–5; trans. from Charlesworth 1985: 752.
42   Psalm 22.9–10; Isaiah 42.14; 49.15; 66.13.
43   Harris-Mingana 1920: 304–305.
44   Harvey 1993: 126.

45 1 Corinthians 3.2.
46 1 Peter 1.3; 2.2–3.
47 1 Peter 1.12–14.
48 *Epistle of Barnabas* 6.
49 Tertullian, *Against Marcion* 1.14.
50 Hippolytus, *Refutation of All Heresies* 5.8.30.
51 Hippolytus, *Apostolic Tradition* 27–37.
52 Clement of Alexandria, *Instructor* 1.6.
53 Marius Victornius.
54 Irenaeus, *Demonstrations* 5.10.
55 Theophilus, *Theophilus to Autolycus* 2.15; cf. 1.7; 2.18.
56 Irenaeus, *Against Heresies* 3.24.1.
57 Irenaeus, *Against Heresies* 5.20.2.
58 Irenaeus, *Against Heresies* 4.38.1–2.
59 Clement of Alexandria, *The Instructor* 1.6.
60 Clement of Alexandria, *Who is the Rich Man That Shall be Saved?* 37.
61 Augustine, *Homilies on 1 John* 3.1.
62 Augustine, *Confessions* 7.18.4.
63 Augustine, *Confessions* 4.1.1.
64 *Odes of Solomon* 8 and 19.
65 Ephrem, *Nativity Hymns* 3.6, 4.150, 13.7, 21.7, 27.15, 27.19; *Hymns on the Resurrection* 1.7; *Hymns on the Church* 25.18.
66 *Liber Graduum* 12.2. English translation in Kitchen-Parmentier 2004, 121.
67 Brock 1990: 74–75; Harvey 1993: 118.
68 Klijn 1962: 1–17.
69 Gregory of Nazianzus, *Fifth Theological Oration* 7.
70 McCambley 1987: 145.
71 Jerome, *In Isa.* 11; *CC* 73.1, p. 459.75–86.
72 Bynum 1982: 110–169. Cf. Anselm, prayer 10 to Saint Paul, *Opera omnia* 3.33, 39–41; Bernard of Clairvaux, *Letter* 322, PL 182: col. 527; Aelred of Rievaulx, *De Jesu puero duodenni*, sect. 3, par. 31.
73 Ward 1973: 141–156.
74 Aelred of Rievaulx, *De Jesu puero duodenni*, sect. 3, par. 30.
75 Warner 1983.
76 Warner 1983: 197–198.

Notes to Chapter 3

1 Genesis 1.28.
2 Exodus 20.14, 17.
3 Genesis 1.28.
4 T. Asher. 1.2–9.
5 T. Ben. 8.1–3.
6 T. Issac. 4.4.
7 Sirach 9.8; cf. Sirach 26.21; 41.20–21.
8 T. Asher 2.8–10.
9 1QS III.17–IV.13.
10 T. Reuben 2.

11 b Sanh. 76b; m. Abot 5.21; b. Qid. 29b–30a.
12 b. Qid. 29b–30a.
13 b. Qid. 29b–30a.
14 m. Yed. 10.8; m. Nid. 5.4.
15 For references in Tannaitic sources, see Satlow 2001: 307–308, note 33.
16 m. Ketub. 5.6.
17 m. Ta`an 1.6; t. Ta`an 1.5.
18 Philo, Vita Mos. 2.68–69; b. Yebam. 62a; b. Shabb. 87a; b. Pesah. 87b; `Abot R. Nat. 9.2; Tg. Num. 12.1–2; Sifre Num. 99; Deut. Rab. 11.10; Exod. Rab. 46.3; Cant. Rab. 4.4.
19 Philo, Cont. Life 64.
20 Midr. Ps. 146.4; cf. b. Ber. 17a.
21 On sex and the Jesus traditions, see Collins 2000; Loader 2005.
22 Matthew 5.27–30.
23 Mark 10.1–12.
24 Git. 9.10; Yer. Sotah 1.1.16b.
25 Git. 9.10.
26 Git. 9.10.
27 Philo, Spec. Laws 3.30–31; Josephus, Ant. 4.8.23.
28 1 Cor 7.10–11.
29 Matthew 19.9.
30 Luke 8.1–3.
31 Mark 15.40–41; Matt 27.55–56.
32 Luke 10.38–42.
33 Fiorenza 1983: 1994.
34 Mark 5.24–34.
35 Lev 15.19–31.
36 Lev. 18.19; 20.18.
37 Matthew 21.28–31.
38 Mark 12.40.
39 Mark 12.41–44.
40 Josephus, *Antiquities of the Jews* 4.254–256.
41 Mark 12.18–27; Matt 22.23–33; Luke 20.27–40.
42 Luke 23.29; Gos. Thom. 79; Mark 13.17–19; Matt 24.19–21; Luke 21.20–24.
43 Mark 7.24–30; Matt 15.21–28.
44 John 4.4–42.
45 John 4.9, 27.
46 John 4.1–39.

Notes to Chapter 4

1 1 Corinthians 14.33b–36.
2 Deming 1995 provides Greco-Roman background to this discussion.
3 See especially 1 Cor 7.36.
4 1 Corinthians 7.1.
5 1 Corinthians 9.4.
6 For a different understanding, see Fiorenza 1983, 1994: 172.

7   1 Corinthians 7.8.
8   1 Corinthians 7.2–7.
9   James 1.14–15, 27.
10 James 3.23, 4.1; 1 Peter 2.11.
11 1 Peter 4.1–2; 2 Peter 1.4–6.
12 2 Peter 2.10.
13 *Didache* 3.
14 1 Corinthians 7.9.
15 1 Corinthians 7.36.
16 1 Corinthians 7.6–9.
17 1 Corinthians 7.38.
18 1 Corinthians 7.28–35.
19 1 Corinthians 7.25–26.
20 1 Corinthians 7.29, 31.
21 1 Corinthians 9.5.
22 Matthew 19.10–12.
23 Matthew 19.12.
24 Compare Luke 18.29 with Mark 10.29–30 and Matthew 19.29; compare Luke 14.25–27 with Matthew 10.37–38 and Gos. Thom. 55 and 101.
25 1 Corinthians 7.10–11.
26 1 Corinthians 7.11.
27 1 Corinthians 7.12–15.
28 1 Corinthians 7.39–40.
29 1 Corinthians 25–35.
30 Philo, Special Laws 3.56.
31 1 Corinthians 11.5–6.
32 Philo, Special Laws 3.52–63; Josephus, Antiquities of the Jews 3.7.6.
33 Martin 1995, 234.
34 Tertullian, Virgins 1.15.
35 Tertullian, Virgins 1.3.
36 Tertullian, Virgins 1.16.
37 1 Corinthians 11.10.
38 *Gospel of Philip* 65.1–24.
39 1 Corinthians 11.3.
40 1 Corinthians 11.8–9.
41 1 Corinthians 11.7.
42 Genesis 1.27.
43 Galatians 3.27.
44 Cf. Romans 8.1–13;12.2–2; 1 Corinthians 1.10–17; etc.
45 1 Clement 1.3.
46 1 Clement 6.3, 38.2, 21.6–7.
47 Philippians 4.2–3.
48 Romans 16.12.
49 1 Corinthians 16.19; Romans 16.3–5; Acts 18.2–3, 18–19, 26; 2 Timothy 4.19.
50 Romans 16.7.
51 Ehrman 2006: 252.
52 For more information on this subject, see Eisen 2000:47–62.
53 Romans 1.1; 1 Corinthians 1.1; 9.1; etc.

54 1 Corinthians 12.28.
55 1 Thessalonians 5.12.
56 1 Timothy 5.17.
57 Mss. F G.
58 1 Corinthians 1.11.
59 Colossians 4.15.
60 Acts 12.12; 16.14–16.
61 Romans 16.1–2.
62 See Eisen 2000: 158–198.
63 Pliny, Letters 10.96.8.
64 Horsley 1987: 239.
65 Horsley 1987: 109.
66 Mark 15.40–41; Matthew 27.55–56.
67 Acts 17.4; 17.12.
68 1 Corinthians 11.4–5.
69 1 Corinthians 12.27.
70 Acts 21.9.
71 Acts 21.10–11.
72 Acts 11.27–18.
73 Acts 13.1.
74 Acts 2.17–21.
75 1 Corinthians 14.1–5.
76 Metzger 1975: 565.
77 Martin 1995.

Notes to Chapter 5

1 Bereshit Rabbah 8.1.
2 1 Clement 38.2.
3 1 Clement 21.6–7.
4 Colossians 2.18, 20–23.
5 Colossians 3.18.
6 Galations 3.27–28.
7 Colossians 3.10–11.
8 *Gospel of Thomas* 22.
9 Plato, *Symposium* 189D–190.
10 Cf. *Gospel of Thomas* 4, 16, 22, 23, 49, 75.
11 *Gospel of Thomas* 114.
12 Cf. Clement of Alexandria, *Stromata* 6.12.100; Shepherd of Hermas, *Vision* 3.8.4; *Acts of Paul and Thecla* 40; *Acts of Philip* 44.
13 Philo, *Opif. mundi* 134.
14 Philo, *Quaest. in Gen.* 2.49.
15 DeConick 2005: 187–188. Cf. Vogt 1995: 170–186. For androgyny language, see *Gos. Thom.* 22; *2 Clem.* 12.2; *Gos. Egy.* according to Clem. Alex., *Strom.* 3.13.92. For "male" language, see Clem. Alex., *Strom.* 6.12.100; Hermas, *Vis.* 3.8.4; *Acts of Paul and Thecla* 40; *Acts of Philip* 44.
16 Palladius, *Dialogue concerning the Life of Chrysostom* 56.
17 On Thecla, see Davies 2001.

18 *Acts of Paul and Thecla* 40.
19 Tertullian, *On Baptism* 17.
20 *Acts of Thomas* 157.
21 Aphraates, *Homily* 18.12.
22 Aphraates, *Homily* 18.8.
23 Aphraates, *Homily* 6.6.
24 Aphraates, *Homily* 6.4.
25 Aphraates, *Homily* 22.12–13.
26 Aphraates, *Homily* 14.11 and 14.33.
27 Clem Alex, *Stromata* 3.17.102.
28 Genesis 2.17.
29 Genesis 3.5.
30 Genesis 3.7.
31 Genesis 4.1.
32 Clement of Alexandria, *Stromata* 3.6.49; 3.12.80–81.
33 1 Corinthians 7.32–33. Clement of Alexandria, *Stromata* 3.12.88.
34 Luke 14.20. Clement of Alexandria, *Stromata* 3.12.90.
35 Clement of Alexandria, *Stromata* 3.12.82–83.
36 Luke 20.35.
37 Matthew 6.19.
38 Epiphanius, *Panarion* 47.3.1.
39 1 Tim 4.1–5.
40 Justin Martyr, *1 Apology* 26; Tertullian, *Against Marcion* 5.19.
41 On Marcion, see Räisänen 2005.
42 Tertullian, *Against Marcion* 1.29.
43 Clement of Alexandria, *Stromata* 3.3.12.
44 Epiphanius, *Panarion* 42.4.5.
45 Tertullian, *Against Marcion* 5.8.
46 Tertullian, *On Prescription Against Heretics* 41.
47 Tertullian, *On Prescription Against Heretics* 6, 30; *On the Flesh of Christ* 6; *A Treatise on the Soul* 36; *Against Marcion* 3.11. Pseudo-Tertullian, *Against All Heresies* 6.
48 1 Timothy 1.8, 11.
49 1 Timothy 2.5.
50 1 Timothy 3–7; 4.1–11; 6.2–6; 2 Timothy 1.14; 2.23; 4.3–5; Titus 1.9–2.1; 3.9–10.
51 1 Timothy 2.9–15.
52 Titus 2.3–5.
53 1 Timothy 4.1–5.
54 1 Timothy 3.1–13; Titus 1.5–9.
55 1 Timothy 5.3–16.
56 On Montanism, see Marjanen 2005; Tabbernee 2007.
57 John 16.13; Epiphanius, *Pan.* 48.11.5–8.
58 Epiphanius, *Pan.* 48.11.1.
59 Epiphanius, *Pan.* 48.12.4.
60 Epiphanius, *Pan.* 48.12.1.
61 Two other prophetesses are mentioned in the literature: Tertullian, *An.* 9; Cyprian, *Ep.* 75.10; cf. Eusebius, *Hist. eccl.* 5.18.7–11.

62 Cyprian, *Ep.* 75.10.
63 Epiphanius, *Pan.* 49.2
64 Epiphanius, *Pan.* 49.2.2.
65 Epiphanius, *Pan.* 49.2.2.
66 Eusebius, *Hist. eccl.* 5.16.17; 5.19.3.
67 Eusebius, *Hist. eccl.* 5.16.17.
68 Eusebius, *Hist. eccl.* 5.16.12.
69 Epiphanius, *Pan.* 48.13.1.
70 Epiphanius, *Pan.* 48.2.4.
71 Eusebius, *Hist. eccl.* 5.16.18.
72 Epiphanius, *Pan.* 48.14.1. Epiphanius remarks that this vision may have been Quintilla's, but he is the only source to mention her.
73 Epiphanius, *Pan.* 49.1.3.
74 Tertullian, *Against Marcion* 3.25.
75 Eusebius, *Hist. eccl.* 5.18.2.
76 Epiphanius, *Pan.* 49.1.4.
77 Epiphanius, *Pan.* 48.14.1–2.
78 Epiphanius, *Pan.* 48.9.7; Eusebius, *Hist. eccl.* 5.18.2.
79 Epiphanius, *Pan.* 48.9.7.
80 Eusebius, *Hist. eccl.* 5.18.3.
81 Eusebius, *Hist. eccl.* 5.18.3.
82 Tertullian, *On Exhortation to Chastity* 10.
83 Epiphanius, *Pan.* 48.2.3–4.
84 Matthew 25.1–13. This performance also alludes to Isaiah 11.2 which mentions seven spirits, a passage that was associated with female prophecy in early Christianity. Cf. *1 Apoc. James* NHC V,3 40.25–26.
85 Epiphanius, *Pan.* 48.2.4.
86 Revelation 7.4–17; 14.1–5.
87 Tertullian, *De fuga in persecutione* 9; cf. Tertullian, *An.* 55.5.
88 Eusebius, *Hist. eccl.* 5.16.20.
89 *Martyrdom of Perpetua and Felicitas.* On Perpetua, see Salisbury 1997.
90 *Martyrdom of Perpetua and Felicitas* 6.8.

Notes to Chapter 6

1 *Gospel of Philip* 64.31–33.
2 *Gospel of Philip* 51.29–31; 52.22–25; 55.28–30.
3 *Gospel of Philip* 68.24–26, 70.10–21; trans. DeConick.
4 *Gospel of Philip* 65.13–14.
5 Soranus, *Gynecology* 1.39.
6 Heliodorus, *Ethiopian Story* 4.8.
7 Pseudo-Albert's citation of Galen in Lemay 1992: 116.
8 *Gospel of Philip* 78.14.
9 *Gospel of Philip* 78.20–25.
10 *Gospel of Philip* 78.20–25.
11 Irenaeus, *Against Heresies* 1.6.4.
12 *Exegesis on the Soul* 133.31–134.5.
13 Clement of Alexandria, *Excerpts of Theodotus* 1.21.1–3.

14 Irenaeus, *Against Heresies* 1.6.4.
15 Tertullian, *On Prescription Against Heretics* 41.
16 Irenaeus, *Against Heresies* 1.13.3.
17 On the complex problem of "female fault and fulfillment" in these types of Gnostic community, see Buckley 1986.
18 Epiphanius, *Panarion* 33.7.10
19 *CIG* 4.9595a. For an English translation, see Rudolph 1977: 212.
20 Hippolytus, *Refutation* 6.19.5.
21 *Testimony of Truth* 58.2–4.
22 As reported by Origen, *Contra Celsum* 5.62.
23 Irenaeus, *Against Heresies* 1.25.5.
24 Irenaeus, *Against Heresies* 1.25.1–2.
25 Irenaeus, *Against Heresies* 1.25.2.
26 Irenaeus, *Against Heresies* 1.25.4.
27 Irenaeus, *Against Heresies* 1.25.4.
28 Clement of Alexandria, *Stromata* 3.4.26.
29 *Testimony of Truth* 29.6–44.30.
30 Clement of Alexandria, *Stromata* 3.5–10.
31 Irenaeus, *Against Heresies* 1.25.6.
32 Clement of Alexandria, *Stromata* 3.5–10.
33 Epiphanius, *Panarion* 25 and 26.
34 Cf. Benko 1967.
35 Epiphanius, *Panarion* 26.1.9.
36 Cf. Buckley 1994.
37 *Books of Ieu*, 100.18–22.
38 *Pistis Sophia*, 381.6–20.
39 Epiphanius, *Panarion* 26.3.1.
40 Epiphanius, *Panarion* 26.4.2.
41 Epiphanius, *Panarion* 26.4.3–7.
42 Epiphanius, *Panarion* 26.4.8.
43 Epiphanius, *Panarion* 26.8.2.
44 Epiphanius, *Panarion* 26.9.3–5.
45 Augustine, *De haer.* 46.114–132; cf. BeDuhn 2000.
46 Epiphanius, *Panarion* 26.13.2–3.
47 Epiphanius, *Panarion* 26.16.4.

Notes to Chapter 7

1 Tertullian, *On the Veiling of Virgins* 3.
2 Tertullian, *On the Veiling of Virgins* 4.
3 Tertullian, *On the Veiling of Virgins* 9.
4 Tertullian, *On the Veiling of Virgins* 7.
5 Tertullian, *On the Veiling of Virgins* 9.
6 Tertullian, *On the Veiling of Virgins* 8.
7 Tertullian, *On the Veiling of Virgins* 11.
8 Tertullian, *On the Veiling of Virgins* 7.
9 Tertullian, *On the Veiling of Virgins* 9.
10 Tertullian, *On the Veiling of Virgins* 16.

11 Tertullian, *On the Veiling of Virgins* 11.
12 Torjesen 1993.
13 *Acts of Peter* 34.2.
14 Minucius Felix, *Octavius* 9. Cf. Brown 1988: 140–141.
15 Tertullian, *To His Wife* 4.
16 Justin, *Apology* 1.29.2. Cf. Brown 1988: 140.
17 Eusebius, *HE* 6.8.2.
18 Tertullian, *On Baptism* 17.
19 Tertullian, *To His Wife* 4.
20 Tertullian, *To His Wife* 4.
21 Justin Marytr, *1 Apology* 15, 29; Aristrides, *Apology* 15; Athenagoras, *Plea* 33. Cf. Hunter 1992: 7–9.
22 Cf. Brown 1988: 133; Hunter 1992: 14–15.
23 Clement of Alexandria, *Miscellanies* 3.7.57.
24 Clement of Alexandria, *Miscellanies* 3.7.58.
25 Clement of Alexandria, Miscellanies 3.12.81.
26 Ruether 1974, 177. Gregory of Nyssa, *De Virg.* 8; *Dial de Anima et Resurrect.*, to Marcrina; Gregory of Nazianzus, *Orat. 8*, on Gorgonia; *Orat. 7*, on Caesarius; *Orat. 43*, on Basil.
27 Ruether 1974, 153–154. Gregory of Nyssa, *De Opif. Hom.* 16.
28 Brown 1988: 294–296.
29 Ruether 1974: 176–177. Gregory of Nyssa, *De Virg.* 2.
30 Tertullian, *On the Veiling of Virgins* 9; cf. Eusebius of Emesa, *Homily* 6.18.
31 *Life of St. Mary of Egypt* 10.
32 See the stories of Mary of Egypt translated in Ward 1987: 26–56.
33 Eustochius, *Life of Saint Pelagia the Harlot.* English translation available in Ward 1987: 66–75.
34 *The Life of St. Castissima*, Escorial Ms. a II 9, fol. 113, as discussed in Salisbury 1991: 104–110. The same story is told of a woman called Euphrosyne. See Lewis 1984: 140–156.
35 Eisen 2000: 143–157.
36 Brown 1993: 259–286; Clark 1986.
37 Jerome, *Eps.* 127, to Marcella; 39, on Blesilla.
38 Jerome, *Ep.* 127.7.
39 Jerome, *Ep.* 130.10.
40 Cf. Cloke 1995: 214.
41 Brown 1998: 260–261.
42 *Canons of Athanasius* 98: 62–63; Palladius, *Historia Lausiaca* 31.1; cf. Eusebius of Emesa, *Homily* 7.24. 191.
43 Brown 1988: 263–264.
44 Jerome, *Letter* 107.
45 Salisbury 1991: 89–96.
46 Augustine, *Letter* 23.3.
47 Eusebius, *HE* 7.30.9–15. Cf. Brown 1988: 259–260, 267.
48 John Chrysostom, *Quod regulares feminae* 3. Cf. Brown 1988: 266–267.
49 John Chrysostom, *Adv. eos* 1, 3; *Hom. 17 Matt.*, 2.
50 Jerome, *Ep.* 22.14.

51 Epiphanius, *Panarion* 79; cf. Apostolic Constitutions 8.28.6.
52 *Ecclesiastical Canons of the Apostles*, Canon 9.
53 Epiphanius, *Panarion* 79.
54 Canon 11 of the Synod of Laodicea.
55 Canon 19 of Nicaea; Canon 15 of Chalcedon.
56 Canon 11 of the Synod of Laodicea.
57 Gelasius I, *Ep.* 14.26.
58 Canon 44 of the Synod of Laodicea.
59 Epiphanius, *Panarion* 79.1.6.
60 Epiphanius, *Panarion* 79.2.1.
61 Epiphanius, *Panarion* 79.4.2.
62 Epiphanius, *Panarion* 79.8.2–3; cf. Proverbs 6.26.
63 Epiphanius, *Panarion* 79.8.4–9.1.
64 Tertullian, *De Cultu Fem* 1,1.
65 Ruether 1974: 161.
66 Tertullian, *De Cultu Fem* 2,2.
67 Tertullian, *De Cultu Fem* 1,1.
68 Augustine, *De Sermone Dom. in Monte*, 41. Cf. Ruether 1974: 161.
69 Augustine, *De Sermone Dom. in Monte*, 41.
70 Jerome, *Adv. Jov.* 1.13, 15.
71 Jerome, *Ep.* 54.4.
72 Jerome, *Ep.* 22.19.
73 Jerome, *Ep.* 22.19.
74 Ruether 1974: 169–176.
75 Hunter 2007.
76 *Jov.* 1.5.
77 Jerome, *Adv. Jov.* 1.37.
78 Hunter 2007, 159–170.
79 Ambrosiaster, *Quaest.* 127.19.
80 Ambrosiaster, *Quaest.* 127.23–24.
81 Ambrosiaster, *Quaest.* 127.29.
82 Clark 1990: 156–168.
83 Augustine, *Unfinished Work Against Julian* 2.56. A English translation of selections of this work can be found in Clark 1990: 158–168.
84 Augustine, *Unfinished Work Against Julian* 2.56.
85 Augustine, *Unfinished Work Against Julian* 1.71, 2.59, 3.142, 4.40, 4.120, 5.46.
86 Augustine, *Unfinished Work Against Julian* 4.44.
87 Augustine, *Unfinished Work Against Julian* 6.26.
88 Augustine, *Unfinished Work Against Julian* 1.62, 2.24, 2.39.
89 Ruether 1974: 156–166.
90 Augustine, *De Bono Conj.* 3, 15; *De Bono Viduit.* 8, and 1.
91 Augustine, *De Civitate Dei* 14, 26; *Contra Julian* 3, 13, 27; *De Grat. Chr. et de Pecc. Orig.* 2, 40.
92 Augustine, *De Grat. Chr. et de Pecc. Orig.* 2, 38, 42; *De Nupt. et Concup.* I, 8–9, 19, 25–26; *De Bono Conj.* 10; *Duas Epist. Pelag.* I, 27, 30.
93 See Ruether 1974: 163–164, where she refers to Augustine's narrative about his mother as a wife to a violent man. Augustine, *Confessions* 9.9.19; *De Conj. Adult.* 2, 15.

94 Ruether 1974: 166. Augustine, *De Grat. Chr. et de Pecc. Orig.* 2, 39; *De Nupt. et Concup.* 1, 19; *De Bono Conj.* 17; *De Genesi ad Lit.* 9, 7.
95 Ruether 1974: 166. Augustine, *De Grat. Chr. et de Pecc. Orig.* 2, 39; *De Nupt. et Concup.* 1, 19; *De Bono Conj.* 17; *De Genesi ad Lit.* 9, 7.
96 Ruether 1974: 166.
97 Augustine, *Ep.* 262.

Notes to Chapter 8

1 For a variety of interpretations of Mary Magdalene, see Adam 2006; Boer 1996, 2006; Brock 2003; Griffith-Jones 2008; Haskins 1993; Schaberg 2004.
2 Schwartz 1993.
3 Mark 15.40–41; 16.1; Matt 27.56, 61; Luke 24.10; John 19.25; 20.1.
4 Cf. Mark 2.14 and parallels; Matt 8.19.
5 Matt 27.57.
6 Luke 6.13.
7 *Gospel of Peter* 21.50; Acts 9.36.
8 Matthew 28.9–10.
9 Matthew 28.9–10; John 20.18.
10 Cf. Hearon 2004.
11 28.16–20.
12 John 20.2–10.
13 John 20.11–18.
14 Luke 24.1–11.
15 Luke 24.1–12.
16 Luke 24.24.
17 Luke 24.13–35.
18 Origen, *Contra Celsum* 2.55, 3.55.
19 *Gospel of Thomas* 114.
20 Genesis LXX 2.7.
21 *Dialogue of the Savior* 144.15–16; trans. DeConick.
22 *Dialogue of the Savior* 144.19–21; trans. DeConick.
23 *Dialogue of the Savior* 144.22–145.2.
24 *Dialogue of the Savior* 141.12–19; trans. DeConick.
25 *Dialogue of the Savior* 134.24–137.3.
26 *Dialogue of the Savior* 139.8–13; trans. DeConick.
27 *Dialogue of the Savior* 139.8–13; trans. DeConick; cp. Matthew 6.34; 10.10; 10.35; Luke 10.7; 1 Tim 5.18.
28 *Dialogue of the Savior* 140.17–19; trans. DeConick.
29 Luke 8.3; Matthew 27.56.
30 John 20.18.
31 Marjanen 1996: 189–202.
32 Epiphanius, *Panarion* 26.8.2.
33 *Gospel of Philip* 63.30–64.6; trans. DeConick.
34 *Gospel of Philip* 59.6–11; trans. DeConick.
35 For alternative interpretations of the *Gospel of Mary*, see Adam 2006; Boer 2004; King 2003; Marjanen 1996;Tuckett 2007.

36 *Gospel of Mary* 8.15–20; trans. DeConick.
37 *Gospel of Mary* 9.19–20; trans. DeConick.
38 *Gospel of Mary* 18.15–18; trans. DeConick.
39 *Gospel of Philip* 55.11–14; 73.27.
40 Cf. *Gospel of Philip* 76.23–30; 86.6–11.
41 *Gospel of Philip* 70.10–22; 68.23–26; cf. *Interpretation of Knowledge* 10.24–36.
42 *Gospel of Mary* 17.15; trans. DeConick.
43 *Gospel of Mary* 18. 10–21; trans. DeConick.
44 For a good overview of this process, see Haskins 1993: 3–97; Schaberg 2004: 65–120.
45 Origen, *c. Cels.* 1.65.
46 Tert., *Against Marcion*, 4.18.9, 16–17.
47 Hipp., *Comm Cant.* 8.2; 24.60.
48 Gregory the Great, *Hom.* 33.
49 Brock 2003: 123–142; Murray 1975: 144–150, 329–335.
50 Lambertsen 1999: 14.
51 Lambertsen 1999: 15.

Notes to Chapter 9

1 Cf. Fiorenza 1983: 1994; Pagels 1988; Torjesen 1993.
2 Cf. Meeks 1974: 167–168, 176–180.
3 Plato, *Timaeus* 90E.
4 Diogenes Laertius 1.33 (attributed to Thales); Lactantius, *Divinae institutiones 3.19 (attributed to Plato)*.
5 Tosefta, *Berakot* 7.8.
6 Dean-Jones 1991: 111–137.
7 Aristotle, *Generation of Animals* 737a25.
8 Philo, *Quaestiones et Solutiones in Exodum* 1.7.
9 Baer 1970: 42; Clark 1994: 166–184.
10 DuBois 1988: 39–85.
11 Plato, *Timaeus* 90–91.
12 John Paul II, May 31, 2004; *Letter to the Bishops of the Catholic Church on the Collaboration of Men and Women in the Church and the World* 7.
13 *Inter Insigniores,* October 1976: 25–28.
14 Thomas Aquinas, *Summa Theologica* 1, qu. 92, art 1, ad 1.
15 Thomas Aquinas, *Summa Theologica* 1, qu. 92, art. 1, ad 2; 1, qu. 93, art. 4, ad 1.
16 Thomas Aquinas, *Summa Theologica Suppl.* Qu. 39, art. 1.
17 *Inter Insigniores,* October 1976: 25–28.
18 Http://www.bls.gov/cps/wlf-databook2006.htm.
19 *Baptist Faith and Message*, revised 2000, *Article 6. The Church*: http://www.sbc.net/bfm/bfm2000.asp.
20 The takeover of the Southern Baptist Theological Seminary in Louisville, Kentucky, is documented by film producer Steven Lipscomb in *Battle for the Minds.*
21 *Resolution On the Place of Women in Christian Service*, June 1973: http://www.sbc.net/resolutions/amResolution.asp?ID=1090.

22 *Resolution On Women*, June 1980: http://www.sbc.net/resolutions/amResolution.asp?ID=1091.
23 *Resolution on the Role of Women*, June 1981: http://www.sbc.net/resolutions/amResolution.asp?ID=1092.
24 *Resolution on Ordination and the Role of Women in Ministry*, June 1984: http://www.sbc.net/resolutions/amResolution.asp?ID=1088.
25 Stanton 1895: 9.
26 Stanton 1895: 7.
27 Stanton 1895: 12–13.

Index